COLLECTIBLE LIONEL CLASSICS

Roger Carp

KALMBACH BOOKS
WAUKESHA, WI

Kalmbach Books
21027 Crossroads Circle
Waukesha, Wisconsin 53186
www.KalmbachHobbyStore.com

Published in 2017
21 20 19 18 17 1 2 3 4 5

Manufactured in China

ISBN: 978-1-62700-415-2
EISBN: 978-1-62700-416-9

Editor: Randy Rehberg
Book Design: Tom Ford

Opposite page: Lionel Consumer Catalog for 1946. All catalog images used with permission of Lionel Corporation.

Library of Congress Control Number: 2016943721

LIONEL has everything—*Plus*

Smoke — Clean, white, odorless puffs, that spiral upward. Shown first time in the world by LIONEL.

Electronic Control — A revolutionary development exclusive with LIONEL. Full selective control of locomotives and operating cars anywhere on the track.

Built-In Whistle — Operates by remote control whether loco is standing still or moving in forward or reverse. Standard whistle signals can be sounded.

Twenty-Wheel Steam Turbine Penn R. R. locomotive — Exclusive with LIONEL. Beautifully scale detailed. A magnificent giant of the rails.

Solid Steel Wheels — Plus scale detailed die cast trucks — and heavy steel axles.

Real R. R. Knuckle Couplers — Electro magnetic remote control operation.

Double Worm Drive Motor — Featured in LIONEL locos for 1946 — most realistic locomotive performance ever revealed.

Realistic Accessories — Marvelous assortment of new operating cars and model R. R. accessories.

Compare — Comparison proves the superiority of LIONEL locomotives, cars, and equipment. For the best in model railroading insist on LIONEL.

THE LIONEL CORPORATION • 15 EAST 26th STREET • NEW YORK 10, N. Y.

Contents

Introduction

The moment has arrived when you have the desire *and* the resources to collect Lionel trains and accessories from the post-World War II era (1945-1969). Or the bug has already nipped and you're now seeking ways to direct your feverish wish to acquire a lot more while adding character and quality to the stacks of vintage models in your home.

Answers and insights fill this new book. Here, you'll discover valuable information about the O gauge locomotives, rolling stock, and accessories that can help form a unique and gratifying collection. Let it be your guide to assembling a group of trains reflecting your personality, knowledge, and love of some of the best toys ever made.

A central purpose of this book is to recommend meaningful and affordable Lionel trains. The expensive jewels some hobbyists claim are essential to a collection with distinction will not be found here. Instead, as has been true with the Collectible Classics feature I write for *Classic Toy Trains* magazine, the focus is on noteworthy engines, cars, loaders, and more that remain plentiful and reasonable.

Anyone can put together a terrific and impressive collection without going broke!

What will you find in the pages to follow? A representative sampling of the outstanding, attractive, and iconic models Lionel developed and marketed during a significant period in its long history. Be aware that more of them made their debut during the first half of the era than in the second, when innovation reluctantly gave way to a wish to survive. That's when fancy overwhelmed realism in toy trains.

Several years ago, I devised a system for evaluating toy trains. As explained in my book *101 Classic Toy Trains: Best of the Postwar Years*, every item can be judged by six criteria. Start with its appearance and then go to how it runs. Next, consider its acclaim when first shown to consumers and move on to how experts view it now. Evaluate fifth how much of an innovation it was when designed and produced. Now finish with the story it tells and insights it offers about the business producing it.

These half-dozen categories still work and expand my understanding of electric trains. Only here, I concentrate on models that fell in the middle of Lionel's line.

The Lionel Corporation released catalogs in the autumn of the year to show consumers the outfits and individual trains and accessories available. Magnificent artwork graced the covers in 1947 (left) and 1951 (above) to build demand from children and families.

They stand out despite not being luxury pieces then or scarcities now.

Included as well are overviews of what Lionel engineers and executives sought to develop and market in regard to locomotives, motorized units, freight cars, and operating accessories between 1945 and 1969. These short essays provide big views and should help you understand where the individual models described in detail fit in and how those pieces reflect notable trends at Lionel during its glory days.

The newly written overviews and 100 one-page articles promise to deepen your appreciation of the superbly operating, beautiful, and ingenious trains put on the market by Lionel. You'll find everything here, except passenger cars. Those models can be appreciated only as entire sets and not individually, as is the intent here.

Prepare to jump ahead and savor the locomotives, cars, and accessories Lionel made available more than half a century ago. Congratulate yourself if you already own pristine examples of some of these classics. Then start chasing at train shows and on Internet websites the ones missing from your display shelves or layout.

By all means, please think about which engines and cars will stand the test of time with you. Contemplate why you want to own them. Hunt for what you'll prize as the finest and most important pieces to show guests and run on your layout.

How much will you have to pay for these trains? Updated reference guides will inform you about their different values. To provide perspective for each item, I have included its retail price when it debuted and show that price adjusted for inflation (in the More Information box). You can then gauge how much an engine or flatcar really cost.

Taken together, the essays arranged in chronological order aim to broaden your comprehension of what Lionel achieved during postwar days. This should prove true regardless of whether you read them to obtain more knowledge or rely on them to inform your collecting. Either way, I hope you will, after reading page after page, be able to view these trains with the respect and satisfaction their creators did. If you do this, there's no way you'll regret bringing them home to share with others.

The Postwar Era at Lionel

A quarter-century of toy train production overflowing with excitement and nervousness, innovation and tradition, boldness and hesitation, legendary leadership and shortsighted guidance. There you have it—the post-World War II era at the Lionel Corporation summarized rather generally in just a single sentence.

Of course, collectors of Lionel trains and accessories demand a more detailed and careful explanation of what happened at the toy train giant between 1945 and 1969. Not content to acquire examples of different locomotives, cars, and so forth, they want to understand how Lionel put together great lines of toys year after year and then how those items were marketed.

For what is plain to hobbyists is that the postwar era stands out as a noteworthy period in the development of electric trains. These toys became symbols of the wonder and delight children felt at the time, feelings collectors and operators from that generation still feel decades after the end of their childhood. Such emotions motivate many of these individuals to buy and cherish individual Lionel pieces.

New era begins

To understand the meaning and significance of Lionel electric trains requires first considering the boundaries of the quarter-century known as the postwar era. The period began, according to toy train historians, late in 1945, a few months after the surrender of Japan ended World War II. The release by frantic executives at Lionel of a new O gauge train outfit for the holiday season launched what many hobbyists proclaim was the most significant era in the history of American toys.

Frankly, identifying the opening of the postwar period with events taking place immediately after the conclusion of global hostilities makes sense. After all, a federal mandate enacted in the spring of 1942 had curtailed the production of various consumer items, including electric trains, that depended on "strategic materials."

Lionel could not have defied that order, lifted only as the end of the war came into sight. The toy firm had been unable to manufacture its signature products for three years. Only when federal authorities relented could Lionel again make trains.

The moment when Lionel enthusiasts contend the era concluded had nothing to do with international relations or domestic events. They focus, instead, on a shift in the electric train industry occurring in 1969. Namely, the release of the final cataloged line marketed by the Lionel Corporation. During that year, General Mills leased the rights to make and sell Lionel toy trains. That well-known producer of consumer items soon announced its first line in 1970.

Definitely a tidy chronological package with neat boundaries. Too bad that, when analyzed with care and rigor, it unravels. The trains themselves dictate expanding the parameters of the postwar era.

On the one hand, the roots of the era really extend back into the late 1930s and early 1940s. Some of the locomotives, rolling stock, and accessories filling out the Lionel roster in the first years after the war represented updated versions of prewar items. On the other hand, the branches of the postwar era reached beyond 1969, stretching into the 1970s. General Mills put out motive power, railcars, and more based on models developed well in the past.

Unprecedented appeal

Getting bogged down in the temporal limits of the postwar era narrows vision. Instead, let's pay attention to trends at Lionel and in the general culture of postwar America. They shed light on why toy trains proved extraordinarily popular and how Lionel's leaders sought to capitalize on the skyrocketing appeal of its products.

The place to begin is with Lionel. Analyzing and appreciating what the engineers, advertising executives, production supervisors, and sales personnel at the corporation achieved during the postwar period are essential tasks. We must, as a consequence, direct our attention to different trends influencing how the largest and most important domestic manufacturer of electric toy trains made and marketed them between 1945 and 1969.

Overshadowing everything else were both the extraordinary popularity in America of those playthings in the 13 years after the war and the gradual decline of their appeal in the 12 years that followed. Public fervor for electric trains enriched Lionel well into the late 1950s and shaped its brilliant streak of answering with superb, highly entertaining models. Yet as consumers, especially young ones, lost interest, nothing seemed to work.

Never, though, should observers forget the unprecedented appeal of Lionel electric trains. People from every walk of life, every income level and educational level, and every region of the United States desired a train set. The urgency they felt rivaled their wish for a black-and-white television, a shiny new sedan, or the latest refrigerator or washer and dryer.

Lionel outfits from the middle of the 1950s, including the no. 1523, balanced toy-like qualities with realism. This train, like all the ones photographed, comes from the collection of Joe Algozzini.

Indeed, viewing a Lionel outfit less as a toy and more as an electric appliance aids in comprehending why Americans wanted one so badly. Folks everywhere believed owning a set was going to improve the quality of their life while testifying to their status as solid members of the growing middle class.

Necessary and not cheap

A train would demonstrate to neighbors a family's determination to provide generously for its children. As Lionel's advertising had long maintained, boys who played with an electric train grew up to become productive, hardworking, and intelligent adults. Parents who envisioned their sons as future accountants, dentists, factory foremen, scientists, and so forth accepted the responsibility to prepare them with the right tools. A train was thus paramount, as vital as textbooks and a blue suit.

From the 1940s well into the 1950s, families across the country, even ones struggling to make ends meet on a regular basis, invested in Lionel trains for their sons. They did so fully aware those toys were not inexpensive. An electric train should be viewed now as it was then: a luxury item treated with care and respect. No wonder many parents insisted trains be used only during the holiday season and then be carefully packed away.

Families had spent too much on the locomotives and railcars for them to be handled recklessly. Lionel pieces, even basic rolling stock, were not trivial in cost. To drive home that point, the original price of every item listed in this book has been adjusted for inflation. In each More Information box, retail values of long ago are translated into current dollars.

Magic for boys

How frustrating the rules about putting the beloved Lionel train back in the attic or closet must have been for youngsters who wanted to play with it all the time. They associated their set with fun and magic rather than personal enlightenment or a successful career.

Boys, especially those who lived near full-size railroads or had traveled on real passenger expresses, filled their heads with dreams of running their own network. After the war, no plaything meant more or seemed as sophisticated than an electric train. So what if that miniature railroad empire depended on track with an unrealistic three rails and spanned only a sheet of plywood or a rug on the floor.

Well into the 1950s, children prized an electric train as the finest thing they could own. They begged parents and grandparents for one and let displays in department stores and other retail outlets mesmerize them. Boys saved every dime and quarter they earned delivering newspapers and mowing lawns in hopes of affording more track or another boxcar or gondola.

Tastes keep changing

Unfortunately for Lionel, the confluence of social, cultural, and economic factors boosting the appeal of electric trains after the war simply couldn't last. Youngsters matured and so discovered pastimes and consumer goods more fascinating than miniature locomotives and stations.

No matter what Lionel did in hopes of retaining the loyalty of its customers, fickle youngsters in time came to prefer spending dollars and hours on baseball gloves and hockey sticks, used Impalas and fresh-off-the-lot muscle cars, and, of course, girls. Even earlier, their infatuation with speed and innovation caused male baby boomers to abandon railroads, full-size as well as miniature, for jet-propelled airplanes and rockets, along with slot cars.

Yet even if sadness and neglect tainted the final chapter of the postwar saga, no one should overlook the joy and thrills Lionel gave children of the postwar era and their parents for so many years. The slogan, "An Investment in Happiness," accurately characterized every train set Lionel sold. A new generation would never forget the pleasures of those toys.

Technological advances

The myriad pleasures and excitement Lionel trains and accessories created in their grateful audiences reflected noteworthy advances in how the company developed, mass-produced, and marketed its action-packed and magical playthings. No account of Lionel during its postwar glory should minimize the contributions made by ingenious designers, industrious production supervisors, clever advertising men, and tireless sales personnel. Those dedicated employees, often unidentified or ignored, deserve credit in some way for all the magnificent toys.

Improvements in tool design and breakthroughs in the molding of various kinds of plastics enabled Lionel, along with its domestic competitors, to manufacture more efficiently and at lower cost durable locomotives and rolling stock with greater detailing. The revolution in the production of consumer goods attributed to the amazing development of injection-molded plastics changed every facet of life in

Vivid colors, scale dimensions, ample details, and exciting performance combined in outfit no. 2235W and others from the middle 1950s.

Beautiful styling enhanced by realistic design and proportions still characterized some sets in the 1960s, including the no. 12800.

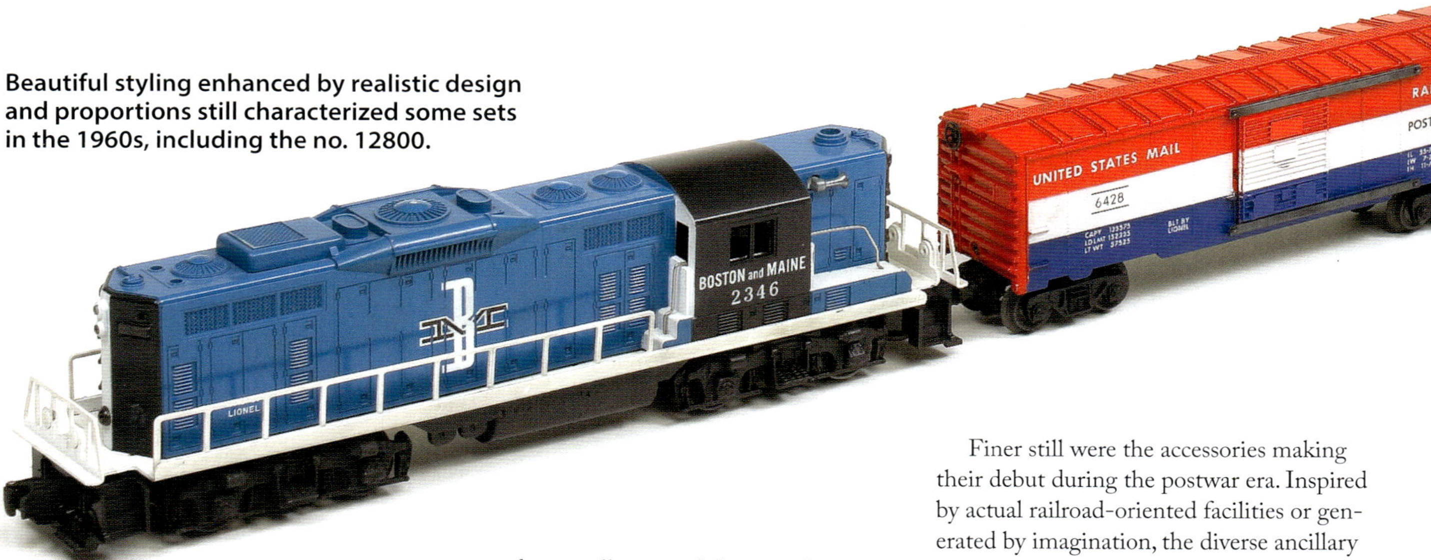

postwar America. Electric trains, like so many toys, would never be the same.

Two specific inventions changing the locomotives integral to Lionel's success helped make those models seem more like full-size motive power. Chemists as well as electrical engineers on the payroll labored for years to fine-tune those innovations.

First, in 1946 and 1947, came more reliable and safer mechanisms to create smoke so steam engines of all sorts could send whiffs out their stacks. Terrific visual effects of puffing smoke complemented the sound effects of a blaring whistle.

Then in 1949 and 1950, the debut of Magne-Traction, which depended on powder metallurgy and the use of magnets, allowed locomotives to dash faster and climb higher while holding on the track with more authority. Meanwhile, designers upgraded electrics and diesels with horns.

The technology behind adding sound effects to models of the latest cab units and road diesels hardly shattered barriers. The secret to their success involved how Lionel designers used batteries and simple horns, just as it did the installation of lightbulbs.

The same point characterized the ongoing use of solenoids, electromagnets, and vibrating motors to expand the range of animation on operating rolling stock, signals, and freight loaders. Members of the Engineering Department absolutely excelled at adding special effects to otherwise ordinary boxcars and gondolas to enhance their magic.

Finer still were the accessories making their debut during the postwar era. Inspired by actual railroad-oriented facilities or generated by imagination, the diverse ancillary items cataloged astounded consumers. Everything a model railroader might want to build a miniature empire appeared in the back section of the annual color catalogs.

Improved decoration

What advances in injection-molded plastics and powder metallurgy made possible and the clever use of familiar electronics carried further boiled down to the ability of Lionel to satisfy the growing demand for more realistic models. Consumers increasingly demanded their locomotives, railcars, towers, and loaders more closely replicate full-size prototypes.

One more innovation Lionel quickly came to depend on for making its trains look more like the real thing touched on decoration. To be precise, the introduction of paint masks meant substantial savings

in time and money when coloring plastic bodies. More elaborate railroad paint schemes could easily be duplicated, particularly as hot- and rubber-stamping machinery continued to improve. So also did screen-printing techniques.

Lionel heralded year after year superb locomotives and rolling stock with greater beauty and animation. Little wonder children and adults agreed that no toy was as sophisticated, thrilling, magical, or essential as an electric train. And for so long, those advances gratified them.

Realism grows

Demand for Lionel trains boomed throughout the late 1940s right into the 1950s. Standing tall as loyal customers were the fathers of baby boomers. Many of those dads had lost out on having their own sets. Economic depression in the 1930s and global war in the early 1940s denied them the greatest of toys. Now they could afford to buy a train and felt no hesitation about getting one to enjoy with their children.

Top executives at Lionel, all of whom had started working there prior to World War II, set out to revive the balance they had striven to achieve earlier between putting on the market both fanciful toys and realistic models. Men at the top of the corporate ladder, including Joshua and Lawrence Cowen, Arthur Raphael, Joseph Hanson, and Samuel Belser, had grasped how wide a variety of individuals were engaged in model railroading. From little children entranced by colorful and amusing playthings to adolescents and adults searching for faithful replicas of the latest and more interesting locomotives and freight cars. The Lionel line combined both.

Paging through the captivating full-color catalogs distributed between the launch of the first complete line of trains in 1946 and the corporation's golden anniversary in 1950 reveals how designers and sales leaders once more filled the line with both kinds of electric trains. As before the war, decision-makers appeared to aim toy-like engines and cars toward the lower end of the line and bigger, more realistic models toward the upper and more expensive end.

Short and colorful toys elicited smiles from children after the war, as did the little steamers puffing smoke. At the same time, new technology and market considerations encouraged executives and engineers to lean toward realism. They acknowledged the need for additional details on railcars and superior performance in locomotives.

Delicate balance

The prevailing trend pushing still greater realism moved forward in large part by how in the late 1940s and early 1950s devoted consumers responded to new entries into the marketplace. To be precise, competing manufacturers of O and S gauge trains built to scale dimensions with more details were challenging Lionel. The dominant player could not afford to be complacent or permit current offerings to define its reputation.

Starting around 1952 and 1953, Lionel answered challengers, including American Model Toys and A.C. Gilbert Co., with bigger and better-decorated models for every segment of its line. A delicate and exception balance between whimsical toys and realistic replicas took shape. Never was the postwar line better.

A commitment to enhancing the realism of Lionel trains motivated engineers to hunt for brand-new, often specialized types of rolling stock and unique rail equipment. Their research led to an array of wonderful freight cars unlike anything ever before seen on O-27 and O gauge layouts. Similar growth characterized the list of motorized units.

In plain terms, the different advances in how Lionel models were being produced and decorated during the first half of the postwar era helped decision-makers fill the market with the more realistic models consumers increasingly asked for. By the same token, advertising executives knew how to capitalize on media, such as television and mass-circulation magazines, to showcase those improved trains to bolster demand.

So what if consumers were modifying their approach to electric trains in the

Toy-like promotional outfits, such as the no. 19444, showed what Lionel did in the 1960s.

Compare the magnificent outfit no. 2211WS from 1953, which promised endless action.

As with the no. 11341, Lionel tried to give every set action and fun in the early 1960s.

1950s by demanding greater realism and more animation, executives and salesmen at Lionel appeared to be saying. Those corporate leaders felt confident they knew how to react with even finer, more attractive, and better running trains and accessories. They knew how to keep Lionel on top of the field while multiplying its profits.

Back to toys

Lionel read the market as tipping in the middle and late 1950s toward greater and more robust realism. The company had to acknowledge that shift. And it did.

Colorful and more detailed diesels and electrics based on modern motive power entered the product line. As did specialized freight cars, often with animated features. With them came fantastic motorized units unlike any ever cataloged before.

The trend toward enhanced realism and action kept accelerating. In 1957 alone, Lionel heralded a brand new kind of track looking less like it had three rails (Super O) as well as small models with consistently accurate proportions (HO scale).

Then, toward the end of the decade, the tide in the market turned again. From the late 1950s and into the 1960s, consumers acted as though Lionel and its rivals had offended them. Sales fell as youngsters, like many of their elders, dismissed railroading as old-fashioned and irrelevant.

Swift aircraft, sporty automobiles, and orbiting satellites captivated the youth of America. Boys reaching adolescence now clamored for replicas of the Boeing 707s, Corvettes, and Jupiters making headlines and filling their dreams. They wanted to race miniature cars, not load logs.

Leaders at Lionel, feeling nervous about the limitations of more realistic trains, adopted a different philosophy. They would dazzle consumers with fantastic playthings loaded with animation and sheer fun. Every model would promise children more to do than merely operate.

Designers crafted marvelous toys. The motorized units and operating freight cars entering the cataloged line boasted lights, sounds, and mechanisms to entertain boys and girls. Many had a military or space orientation, all in hopes of appealing to consumers who might otherwise overlook an electric train. The ingenuity shown by engineers astonished.

Not enough

The closing decade of the postwar era witnessed declining sales despite notable efforts to innovate. Creative minds now worked to broaden the animation of operating cars, motorized units, and accessories. They often did so by leaving behind the quest for realism, emphasizing instead the whimsical pleasures of imaginative toys. Reversing trends going back three decades would, inventors and salesmen thought wishfully, bring success.

How unfortunate that the waning allure of electric toy trains all but doomed their hard work to failure. Little that desperate executives tried as the 1960s wore on seemed able to revive the widespread appeal of Lionel's products. Too much had changed to save the company.

It is easy, therefore, to assume that the products being released lacked quality or interest. Yet as these 100 collectible Lionel locomotives, railcars, and accessories from the postwar era prove, the company never stopped inventing or marketing memorable pieces. Each item demonstrates greatness—whether in how it was developed, what it replicated, or why it was produced. Judge them as artifacts testifying to the glory of an American icon.

Steam Locomotives

Steam locomotives dominated the Lionel line for the first decade of the postwar era. Designers upgraded them with several innovations, in particular sight and sound effects, well into the 1950s. Eventually, as occurred on full-size railroads, diesel-electric motive power assumed prominence. But much of the glory Lionel knew after the war came from steam.

Serious infatuation

Lionel's infatuation with steam locomotives had several sources. First and foremost, co-founder Joshua Lionel Cowen prized those familiar engines. He saw them as beautiful and powerful, believing every boy in the land shared his views.

Second, while diesels and electrics were making inroads on American rail lines, steam still prevailed before and after the war. If anything, the 1930s and 1940s represented a landmark era for steam, with, awe-inspiring locomotives being built.

Third, children in every region of the country glimpsed steam engines daily. No wonder they dreamed of having miniature versions running on their tabletop layouts or ovals of track they laid on bedroom floors and living room carpets.

Notable advances in technology helped Lionel turn youngsters' dreams into reality. Until the early 1930s, engineers at the firm had no alternative to stamping and blanking thin sheets of steel to mass-produce toy locomotives. Those models could not be, as a consequence, scale replicas.

The advent of metal die-casting technology changed that situation. Now designers and production supervisors at Lionel found it possible to create rugged models built along scale proportions and loaded with more detail than imagined.

Another breakthrough, the invention of a reliable, realistic whistle in 1935, bolstered the appeal of Lionel's steamers. Authentic sounds easily controlled elevated those locomotives into a new realm.

Lionel had capitalized on its superior die-casting techniques and innovative use of electrical features to introduce O gauge models of contemporary steamers in the late 1930s. Having a cadre of draftsmen and model makers working under Chief Engineer Joseph Bonanno didn't hurt either, especially when they had at their fingertips blueprints lent by railroads.

"No compromises necessary!" declared a prewar catalog. "Lionel locomotives look right and are right. They're scale models in appearance as well as in performance." The conclusion was plain: If the engines pulling the trains were accurate and dependable, so was everything else Lionel offered.

Marvelous innovations

The same philosophy held sway when the war ended in August 1945. Having only a few months to prepare an outfit for merchants heading into the holiday season, Lionel needed a good-looking, reliable prewar locomotive and tender to update with its new staple-end trucks equipped with knuckle couplers.

Executives settled on the 224, a model with a 2-6-2 wheel arrangement whose main assembly was forged of a zinc alloy. Lionel had cataloged what was known as the Prairie between 1938 and 1941.

Momentum sparked in 1945 gathered speed over the next year. What made 1946 stand out? Let's note first the innovation eliciting praise from consumers and within the trade. A revolutionary mechanism produced whiffs of smoke!

The smoke unit from 1946 relied on a special bulb installed in top-of-the-line locomotives; smoke pellets were dropped onto the bulb, which heated them until they dissolved. Too bad the effect was disappointing because the amount of smoke wasn't great. Improvements came over the next year until Lionel had a safer, more dependable method of inducing smoke.

A second step forward in 1946 involved the introduction of an elaborate control, directional, and uncoupling system utilizing radio frequency waves. That system, developed by Bonanno, came installed in a four-car freight outfit known as the no. 4109WS Electronic Control Set. All components came equipped with receivers to respond to an operator's commands.

Greatness in 1946

Because Lionel's headquarters was located in New York City, its leaders and designers

had been well aware of which engines and passenger trains ran on the Pennsylvania Railroad and the New York Central. That trend influenced two of the new locomotives highlighting the line for 1946.

Just two years earlier, the Pennsy had ordered a huge turbine-driven 6-8-6 engine from Baldwin Locomotive Works. That beast, the sole member of the S2 class, never amounted to much. It pulled only scattered passenger trains prior to being retired in 1952. But all the publicity given the Turbine intrigued Lionel, and its designers announced O and O-27 gauge versions (nos. 671 and 2020, respectively).

That three-rail giant, with a whistle, smoke unit, and double worm-drive Atomic Motor, stood front and center when evaluating the line. Lionel adapted its Turbine to serve as motive power for the Electronic Control Set (no. 671R).

Engineers set their sights on updating the 226, a die-cast 2-6-4 painted black and cataloged between 1938 and 1941. They adapted its boiler, installed an extra set of drive wheels (to make it a 2-8-4), fitted it with the latest trucks and couplers, and put in an Atomic Motor and a smoke unit. They christened the no. 726 the Berkshire, after a prototype on the Boston & Albany, a subsidiary of the New York Central.

Continued greatness

The release of the Turbine and the Berkshire, plus updated versions of older switchers and midrange engines, expanded the O-27 and O gauge lines. Yet designers and marketing executives showed no intention of relaxing, even as Lionel, like prototype railroads, began diverting more resources toward diesels.

For example, 1947 saw some noteworthy developments at the toy giant. Its engineers ironed out problems with the Berkshire and Turbine and improved the smoke unit. They modified the 225 steamer, a 2-6-2 cataloged from 1938 through 1942. The new engine, which was assigned numbers 675 in O gauge and 2025 in O-27, was promoted (incorrectly) as a replica of the Pennsy's class K4 Pacific.

Low-end novelty

The exploding demand for toy trains was pushing Lionel from scale realism to toy-like items as the decade came to a close. Decision-makers emphasized the need to make and market playthings families could afford no matter what their budget.

The change in priorities influenced the creation of a steam locomotive and tender introduced in 1948. Designers, while completely ignoring the O gauge roster, gratified the wish of sales personnel for an inexpensive train to counter the advances being made by Louis Marx & Co.

The Engineering Department devised the no. 1001 Scout locomotive, a 2-4-2 with Lionel's first injection-molded plastic boiler. A year later, perhaps because leaders felt uncomfortable relying on inexpensive plastic, they substituted a die-cast metal boiler and renumbered that stripped-down steam model as no. 1110.

Unfortunately, as people operating the low-end steamer quickly learned, the Scout's real problems were mechanical and not aesthetic. Its plastic-case motor and unreliable reverse unit frustrated consumers. They inundated Lionel's service stations with repairs, grumbling about engineering and quality control at the firm.

Magne-Traction

As though to make amends for the Scout, Bonanno and associates George Jurasov and John Salles conducted experiments involving magnetism and powder metallurgy. Their labors led to the development of Magne-Traction, an innovation that advanced a model locomotive's pulling and climbing capabilities while enabling it to stay on metal track much better.

Magne-Traction became standard on locomotives. Or it was until the Korean Conflict and resulting shortages of Alnico magnetic material interrupted the process. As a consequence, Lionel felt compelled in 1952 to release versions of the Turbine as well as the Berkshire (nos. 671RR and 726RR, respectively) and a reissued 675 and 2025, all lacking Magne-Traction.

Hudsons galore

Pleased as Lionel's engineering and sales crews were about Magne-Traction, they could have guessed the return of a near-scale model of the New York Central's 4-6-4 Hudson would overshadow it. In 1950, to mark the firm's golden anniversary, Lionel brought back what many observers claimed was its finest O gauge steamer. The no. 773, even if not entirely to scale, still had the latest features, notably Magne-Traction and a smoke mechanism.

Also in 1950, Lionel added a modified Hudson to the O-27 line. The no. 2046 shared a New York Central heritage with its O gauge counterpart. Its boiler casting derived from one developed for the Berkshire. The 2046 ran through 1951. Then the no. 2056, a twin lacking Magne-Traction, replaced it for 1952, only to have Lionel revive the 2046 for 1953.

Hudsons stayed on the minds of engineering and sales personnel for the next few years. They began in 1953 by cataloging the new "Santa Fe-Type" 685 and its O-27 partner (2055), which captured the look of an Atchison, Topeka & Santa Fe Railway prototype. Those steamers had smoke, whistle, and a headlight.

Lionel replaced the 685 in the O gauge line in 1954 with the all-but-identical no. 665. That Santa Fe-type 4-6-4, cataloged through 1959, differed from its predecessor in having a feedwater heater in front. An O-27 version, the no. 2065, was available from 1954 through 1956. Lionel also introduced the no. 646, an O gauge version of the 2046. The 646 ran through 1958.

Last gasp

After 1955, which was the last year Lionel offered any sort of Turbine, corporate heads de-emphasized steam locomotives in the O gauge line. Diesels predominated as motive power for the biggest, most expensive outfits. Having a Berkshire, a Hudson or two, and occasionally something else seemed enough.

The situation was different in O-27. Lionel maintained a roster that included 2-6-4s with and without both smoke and Magne-Traction (nos. 2037 and 2016, respectively) and two Hudsons. Designers supplemented it in 1955 with a reissued 0-4-0 switcher (no. 1615) and next in 1957 with a 2-4-2 decorated for the Pennsylvania Railroad (no. 250).

But the biggest story about steam in broke in 1957, when Lionel announced the no. 746. Amid the diesels and electrics in the new Super O line, Lionel brought out a replica of the Norfolk & Western Railway's class J 4-8-4 Northern. Loaded with features, such as illuminated marker lights and a liquid smoke generator, the streamlined 746 proved that, as the Consumer Catalog insisted, "steam locos can be right up to the minute in power and design."

Through 1959, the 746, standing out thanks to brilliant red striping and yellow lettering, pulled top-of-the-line freight sets. Strangely, those Super O outfits usually included space- and military-themed rolling stock that hinted at a future world in which steam locomotives had no place.

End of the line

The same uneasy juxtaposition of yesterday and tomorrow appeared in 1959. Lionel, in the midst of proclaiming itself the toymaker of the space age, issued the General, its first model of a 19th century locomotive and tender. Two versions of a 4-4-0 American were cataloged through 1962. The superior Super O gauge 1872 had a smoke unit and Magne-Traction. Its O-27 twin, the 1862, did not.

The motive for offering an antique train stemmed from a wish to capitalize on the nation's interest in the Wild West and the upcoming centennial of the Civil War. Lionel knew Thomas Industries had made O gauge models of 19th century locomotives in the late 1940s and 1950s, but never viewed it a threat. Of more concern might have been news that rivals A. C. Gilbert Co. and Louis Marx & Co. planned to introduce old-time trains in 1959. Lionel had to respond in hopes of preventing the S gauge American Flyer Frontiersman or the O-27 Wm. Crooks set from enticing new customers.

Otherwise, the 1960s proved anticlimactic for Lionel's shrinking roster of steam locomotives. That was appropriate, remembering how nearly all the full-size steam engines still around were being dispatched to scrap yards or museums.

The high point undoubtedly came in 1964, when Lionel brought back the 773 for a final run, this time with the 773W tender. The classic Hudson lasted for two more years. Then it, too, went into retirement, a faded memory of greatness.

Steam locomotives dominated the Lionel line for the first decade of the postwar era. Designers upgraded them with several innovations, in particular sight and sound effects.

In every other respect, the 1960s deserved attention only because of the assortment of O-27 gauge 2-4-2s available. Those primarily plastic models, descendants of the Scout locomotives, appeared with a range of numbers and were coupled to different tenders. They led cataloged and promotional outfits.

Useful and plentiful as those small units were, they scarcely exemplify what was finest about Lionel's postwar steamers. Hobbyists must turn their gaze back to the late 1940s and into the 1950s to appreciate the heights of innovation and outstanding modeling the Lionel Corporation put into its replicas of steam engines.

221 Empire State 2-6-4 and Tender

Though the 221 steam engine was small and inexpensive, it really was a step forward at the dawn of the era. It reflected the influence of prewar design and technology while shedding light on where decision-makers wanted to proceed now that the market was perking up again.

Name is key

The 221, which Lionel cataloged in 1946 and '47, differed from other low-end steam locomotives because of its name. Lionel referred to it as the Empire State Locomotive because engineers had based its "gladiator-style" shroud and bullet nose on the 4-6-4 Hudson used by the New York Central for one of its passenger trains.

The *Empire State Express* blazed between New York City and Buffalo. Late in 1941, the New York Central inaugurated a new stainless-steel streamliner with a futuristic Hudson. The dynamo from industrial designer Henry Dreyfuss made headlines and starred in newsreels.

1946

Lionel might have planned to add a model in 1943. But a federal mandate curtailing production of consumer goods made with strategic materials forced it to halt development and marketing in 1942.

Evidently, decision-makers remained confident that a generalized replica of the Empire State steamer would appeal to hobbyists. The 221 made its debut, not in the Spring Catalog released first in 1946, but in the Advance Catalog that came out on its heels. The brief delay suggested it was not ready for mass production.

The emphasis given the 221 in the Consumer Catalog delivered in the fall shows Lionel viewed it with pride. "Powering many of the Lionel 'O27' Gauge Trains," the copy declared, "is this handsome, realistic 6-wheel drive Empire State Model—swift, sleek, beautifully designed."

Old with new

Engineers blended old parts with a new die-cast metal body to create the 221. Studying the components revealed some from prewar steamers (for example, nos. 250 and 1666), along with a host of new ones created especially for the 2-6-4 engine: metal handrails, crossheads, connecting rods, headlight, and drawbar.

Laborers dipped the body in gray paint (black was tried later). Then they rubber-stamped the three-digit product number on each side of the cab. A full complement of driving hardware as well as an ornamental sand dome and safety valve further enhanced the engine's appearance.

The drivers added typically were blackened at the factory. Occasionally, and perhaps early in the production run, they were cast aluminum. Some 221 models also featured aluminum front and rear trucks.

The silvery details distinguished the 221. So did its eye-catching shell, right down to "Lionel" cast in the pilot. Otherwise, it lacked anything smacking of deluxe. An operating headlight and a three-position reverse unit were about it. Not every one sold even came matched with a whistle tender. As for smoke, the grand news of the year, not a whiff would ever blow out from a 221.

Two outfits a year

The Consumer Catalog pictured 13 O-27 outfits. Only two passenger sets, each with two no. 2430 blue-and-silver Pullmans and a no. 2431 observation.

The 221 pulled the far more attractive passenger outfit. The steamer and its whistle or non-whistle tender with New York Central decaled lettering and stripes, which looked smashing leading the trio of cars, carried over from the prewar era.

Also available in 1946 and '47 was a three-car freight. Without straining, the 2-6-4 pulled nos. 2411 flatcar (with pipes in 1946 and logs in 1947) and 2465 Sunoco double-dome oil car both years. The Pennsylvania RR N5 caboose was a no. 2472 in 1946 and a no. 2457 in '47.

A two-year run exhausted demand for the 16½"-long Empire State combination. Sadly, Lionel gave up on the 221 a year before it brought out its first streamlined passenger cars. The green-and-gray plastic models in the no. 2400 series would have complemented the sleek steamer and burnished its reputation.

More information

- $19.75 with whistle ($243.73)
- Casting improved to strengthen pilot for 1947
- Designed for O-27 track; lost contact with power rail on O gauge switches and crossovers

671 Turbine 6-8-6 and Tender

Studying locomotives Lionel cataloged over many years reveals ongoing changes to the mechanisms and key assemblies. The 671 Turbine steam locomotive exemplified the commitment to developing trains that appealed to wide audiences and satisfied consumers with top-notch performance. Cataloged between 1946 and '49, the O gauge version of the Turbine underwent modifications until it rose to the upper echelon.

Ironically …

This account of the Turbine uses the word "ironically" because the models created to run over three rails proved more successful and lasted longer than did the full-size steamer. Lionel made thousands of Turbines; ironically, the Pennsylvania RR gave up on the inefficient beast after only one!

Executives at Lionel, bewitched by the publicity the Turbine had received at its splashy debut in 1944, pressed ahead with a replica to showcase as their first entirely new postwar locomotive. So confident did they feel about the model with a 6-8-6 wheel arrangement they decided all-but-identical versions would be valuable additions to both the O gauge and the O-27 cataloged rosters for 1946.

1946

Problems early on

"The New, Handsome Powerful Lionel 20-Wheel Pennsylvania Steam Turbine Locomotive," as it was anointed in the Consumer Catalog, thrilled for a handful of reasons. Count among its mechanical traits a horizontally mounted Lionel Precision Atomic Motor used in tandem with a worm shaft that turned two axles with worm wheels. Spur gears linked the worm shaft with the motor shaft.

Designers crammed the motor and worm shaft into so tight a space inside the die-cast metal casting they couldn't mount the reverse unit vertically. So they had to lay the unit flat and devise a plug-and-jack arrangement in the cab to handle lockout functions. No customary slot in the shell.

Another challenge was getting a model with 20 wheels to operate on track with a 31" diameter. Lionel chose to omit flanges from the two middle drivers on each side. Doing so tightened the turning radius yet compromised the pulling power.

One more drawback to the Turbines released in 1946 related to the smoke mechanism. A pioneering achievement fell short, due to its reliance on a special bulb used to heat the smoke pellet while serving as a headlight. Never did the unit work as dependably as advertised.

Upgrades galore

Here was where Chief Engineer Joseph Bonanno and his talented staff earned their salaries. Flaws and failures spurred them to upgrade the early 671.

Inside the Turbines marketed in 1947 and the following two years, they substituted a single worm drive for the double one. The updated design powered only the rear drivers and put the worm on the motor shaft. Those modifications shifted the motor to a 30-degree angle, leaving additional space so the reverse unit could be installed vertically. The familiar slot for the protruding lever appeared.

Meanwhile, Mario Mazzone, a brilliant member of Bonanno's team, put his mind to advancing how steamers could smoke. For the 671 and its kin, he made a superior element—a heat coil inside the boiler and independent of the headlight. The unit benefited from improved smoke pellets.

Aesthetic changes also took place. The thick nickel rims originally added to all drivers gave way to thin blackened ones on the first and fourth drivers in 1948. Designers elected to remove all rims on the 671 for the final year of production.

Tenders matter

Tenders paired with 671s took strides ahead, too. First was the no. 2466W, with a plastic shell dating from the prewar era housing the whistle. On its heels in 1947, arrived the no. 671W. Similar in appearance to the four-wheel 2466W, it also had "Lionel Lines" rubber-stamped silver or white across each of its sides.

A breakthrough came in 1948 with the new no. 2671W streamlined tender featuring a water scoop. "Pennsylvania" was rubber-stamped silver or white on it. Better still, early versions of the six-wheel tender had operating red backup lights.

Work and care upgraded the 19½"-long engine-tender duo until the 671 Turbine truly distinguished the O gauge roster. The fate of the toy sure diverged from that of its full-size prototype.

More information

- $35 ($431.93)
- Price for engine-tender duo raised to $37.50 in 1948
- Pennsylvania RR keystone on front could be red or black—6200 was the number of actual Turbine

675 Prairie 2-6-2 and Tender

How artificial and often meaningless is the division between prewar and postwar eras hobbyists assign to the history of Lionel. Admittedly, global conflict disrupted manufacturing and set the stage for new directions. But more continuity existed from the early 1940s to the end of the decade in terms of leadership, planning, and product.

Different postwar locomotives demonstrate this point. Their roots in the prewar period grew so near the surface that it takes little effort to grasp how they carried forward older designs. Even a model touted as brand new, in this case the no. 675 Prairie steam locomotive, owed a debt to the past.

Useful castings

The late 1930s represented a significant span for Lionel. The firm was rapidly escaping from financial difficulties, and its engineering staff was venturing boldly ahead with a commitment to developing more realistic trains.

1947

Designers completed a new group of boiler castings in 1938 to serve as the basis for a few die-cast metal steamers. Details added to the castings varied, as did the size of their cabs. Engineers fitted them with two leading trucks, four or six drivers, and two or four trailing trucks. And thus did the O gauge and O-27 fleets grow.

Riding amid the newcomers was a 2-6-2 steamer identified as the no. 224 or 224E, depending on whether an electronic reverse unit was installed. Using the so-called "medium" casting, that midrange O gauge racehorse led freight as well as passenger outfits from 1938 until Lionel had to curtail production after 1942.

When Lionel revived production of electric toy trains in 1945, the shebang did open with a Prairie. Curiously, the 2-6-2 guiding the sole outfit merchandised was the O gauge no. 224, which used the prewar boiler casting with a small cab. A year later the same casting created the no. 1666. Not a scrap tossed to the 225.

To the rescue

Lionel, eager to capitalize on the vintage casting, had offered Prairies void of key features. "Bottom of the line" described the 224 and 1666. Operating headlights, maybe whistle tenders, no smoke units.

Once leaders believed their feet were on firmer ground, they replaced the early Prairies with more respectable locomotives. To the rescue in 1947 dashed the 675.

According to the sheets written for servicing the locomotive, it was "an adaptation of the Pennsylvania Type K-5 passenger steam engine." Next came the caveat: "differing from it principally in having a two- instead of a four-wheel leading truck." A Prairie and not a Pacific.

Designers performed enough surgery on the casting to justify giving it a unique part number (675-6). Nonetheless, close examination left no doubt about its ancestry. Obvious were the cast-in details a 675 shared with a 225, notably the air lines, boiler bands, and sand and steam domes.

Alterations to the casting were essential if the 675 and its identical O-27 twin (no. 2025) were going to accommodate a smoke mechanism. There was no chance Lionel would risk sales by leaving out that special effect the way it had with the low-end Prairies cataloged the previous two years.

Key points

Decorative elements of the 675 as it was cataloged between 1947 and 1949 started with the casting painted black and the number rubber-stamped silver below the windows of the cab. Wire handrails and an ornamental bell looked sharp. So did the sparkling green marker lamps on the front. The smokestack was a separate part. In 1947, Lionel kept it unpainted aluminum; later a smaller, black piece became the rule.

Oddly, variations derived from the keystone cast into the boiler. Think of a hot-stamped silver "675," followed by a gold "5690" on a red decal and then an intertwined "PRR." How funny that Lionel opted for "5690." No idea what that number meant since the only Pennsy locomotive to use it was a boxcab electric!

All three years the 675 graced the cataloged line, it served as the motive power for the three outfits (two freight and one passenger) introducing the O gauge section. Prices for the sets ranged from \$35 to \$50.

More information

- \$25 (\$269.78)
- Price for 19"-long engine-tender duo raised to \$28 in 1948
- Matched with a no. 2466T or 2466WX whistle tender and later no. 6466WX whistle tender

1656 Switcher 0-4-0 and Tender

A steam switch engine and tender, which planners of the annual line had considered essential in the late prewar era, seemed superfluous a decade later. Not as many modelers showed interest in owning a model of the hard-working little locomotives responsible for shunting freight and passenger cars around yards.

Executives reluctant to ignore that area sought to win sales by introducing detailed replicas of a new diesel switcher, beginning in 1949. That trend gained momentum in the 1950s, with steam neglected until the no. 1615 arrived in 1955. Yet plenty of three-rail layouts still depended on the no. 1656, an 0-4-0 from 1948 and 1949.

Prewar beginnings

Despite the fact that Lionel added the 1656 to its line three years after inaugurating train production following World War II, the plucky switcher could trace its roots to the prewar era. Its ancestors were distinguished members of the stable of near-scale locomotives developed by Lionel engineers.

The trend to revamp the roster with O scale models gained momentum in the late 1930s and early 1940s. Among the classics created by Lionel during those years was a virtually perfectly proportioned replica of the B6 0-6-0 switcher used everywhere on the Pennsylvania RR. Models with slightly different product numbers made their debut in 1939, with a few cataloged in subsequent years.

For 1940, the Engineering Department modified the boiler and other parts to complete a series of small, scale-detailed steam switchers. Nos. 201 and 203 came with 0-6-0 arrangements and were assigned to the O gauge line; nos. 1662 and 1663 were given 0-4-0 arrangements and went to the O-27 roster.

The tenders linked with the different steam switchers ended up being shorter than their semi-scale relatives. They did use many of the same components, such as drawbars, coal piles, backup lamp housings, and rear steps.

1948

Revived after the war

The men in charge of reviving the Lionel line immediately after World War II wanted a relatively plain and simple steamer for the middle range of the O-27 product line. Updating the 0-4-0 in minor ways struck them as a solid answer.

Lionel announced the no. 1665 in 1946. The die-cast metal switcher came painted black with an operating headlight and three-position reverse unit. It came with a no. 2403B tender equipped with a bell that repeatedly clanged when the switcher traveled. The yard goat also came with a backup light on its short tender.

Decision-makers, who had selected the 1665 to lead a single set in 1946, dropped it from the catalog after just that year. The growing line offered in 1947 lacked a steam switcher. Perhaps the days of helping kids move rolling stock around their yards with little steam engines had ended.

Not so! In 1948, the year Lionel broke ground with Scout locomotives, it filled the slot above those low-end steamers with an 0-4-0 having an operating headlight and coil coupler in front. The catalog heralded the no. 1656 combination as a "powerful, realistic switcher locomotive and tender.…Just the thing for shunting your Lionel cars from sidings to main lines."

Better than expected

The 1656 looked just like the 1665, right down to the coil coupler on the front and the wire handrails on the sides. In fact, other than having an improved motor (characterized by double reduction gearing), the two 0-4-0s were identical.

Lionel paired the new 15¼"-long steam switcher with a no. 2403B or 6403B Lionel Lines slope-back tender equipped with a bell and backup light.

The 1656 and tender, priced separately at $25, led a three-car freight outfit in 1948 and 1949. In light of how much play value a switcher and cars might have provided, set no. 1425B disappointed. All Lionel included with the caboose were nos. 6456 Lehigh Valley hopper and 6465 Sunoco double-dome tank car.

The 0-4-0 steam switcher then vanished from the cataloged line. Lionel offered nothing like it until bringing out the decidedly inferior no. 1615 in 1955.

More information

- $25 ($249.63)
- Rubber-stamped silver cab number varied in size
- Slope-back tender equipped with backup light and bell

1110 Scout 2-4-2 and Tender

The announcement in the opening pages of the Consumer Catalog for 1948 still causes readers to stop and stare: "The biggest model railroad news in years!" Bigger than the smoke mechanism Lionel had created? Bigger than the realistic remotely controlled knuckle coupler? Bigger than the automatic milk car or the F3 diesels?

The bold copywriter dared tantalize designers and customers alike when he declared Lionel about to introduce something greater and more important.

The inaugural Scout outfit! A brand-new freight train intended to appeal to families without too much money to spend on a toy. Lionel stood poised to engage in battle with Louis Marx & Co. The chief weapon to be employed in combat ended up being the no. 1110 steam locomotive and tender new in 1949.

1949

Missing the mark

Common sense and the bottom line told Lionel's leaders they should attend to the low end. Selling basic outfits with few frills did much to pad the financial reports and put a smile on the faces of accountants and stockholders.

Demand for electric trains skyrocketed after the war. Lionel needed to respond because Marx with its low-cost sets and Hafner with its windups continued to snipe at the giant and steal customers.

Elementary O-27 trains retailing for around $20 apparently had failed in 1946 and 1947 to secure a key segment of the market for Lionel. Time, executives concluded, to devote resources to accomplishing that goal. The pair of Scout sets heralded in 1948 as news of enormous significance represented their best hope.

Not ready

Designers handed the task of forming the Scout roster reached a fateful decision. To save money and give the train a unique identity, they devised a new coupling system incompatible with every other regular-production model. What they deemed Manumatic Control relied on an ancillary piece to uncouple the cars. Operators had only to press the button on the controller to release one of them.

The brand-new no. 1001 steam engine and tender, derived from a 2-4-2 Columbia type, featured a puny motor. Cutting production costs dictated leaving off a three-position reverse unit.

Lionel packed the 1001 in two sets in 1948, each with a price below $20. One train consisted of two freight cars and a caboose; the second offered three cars. Minimal decoration covered the lightweight unpainted plastic rolling stock.

All too soon, many consumers felt they had been fooled by the so-called big news. The plastic motors in their Scout steamers quit working or proved too weak. Being unable to couple the cars to regular O-27 models left them frustrated.

An improvement

Angry customers and complaining repair personnel drove home the vital point that Lionel had to remedy the Scout debacle—fast!—without pushing retail prices higher. Exasperated designers left the rolling stock alone. They refused to disown Manumatic Control. Those aspects of the line carried forward into 1949.

Attention went to the locomotive, condemned as the culprit in the show. Gone was the 1001 and in its place rolled a better, more dependable performer.

Even before 1948 had ended, engineers had finished an upgraded steamer, the no. 1101. That uncataloged 2-4-2 had a die-cast metal body instead of the plastic one used for the 1001 steamer, a metal motor, and a three-position reverse unit.

Further tinkering with an eye on holding down costs brought forth the no. 1110. Lionel cataloged that 2-4-2 and its no. 1001T non-whistle tender in 1949 and again in 1951 and 1952. The 1110 retained the die-cast body painted black. But designers had no choice but to revive the plastic motor and two-position reverse.

Where it fits

The 1110 earns a spot as part of Lionel's strategy for conquering the market. Consider the slightly modified Scout engine as an artifact with historical significance rather than a solid O-27 performer.

More information

- Illuminated but lacked headlight lens; also lacked smoke unit
- Whistle tender not included
- Replaced in 1950 by no. 1120 equipped with Magne-Traction
- Sold only as outfit component

736 Berkshire 2-8-4 and Tender

Style paired with steel, reliability leavened by hints of wonder—exactly what you want in a close friend, a favorite entertainer, and a superb Lionel steamer symbolizing all the magnificence of its postwar success. The Berkshire. Different versions of this 2-8-4 powerhouse rose to the peak of the cataloged roster over a tenure spanning virtually the entire era. From 1946 through 1968, modelers always had a Berk.

Make a pick

History-minded individuals crave the first Berkshire, the no. 726 brought out in 1946. Raising it to significance, as I explained in my book *101 Classic Toy Trains: Best of the Postwar Years*, were its innovative motor and smoke unit. Mechanical improvements distinguished the versions of the Berk manufactured over the next three years. Operators therefore seek a later 726.

The no. 736, which carried forward the legacy of Lionel's 2-8-4 from 1950 on, also merits attention, especially for hobbyists with tighter budgets. This Berkshire boasts virtually all the elements making the 726 so sweet. Thanks to Magne-Traction, it climbs harder and pulls more.

1950

A little background

The tale celebrating the long run of the 736 opened long before 1950. Remember how the roots of the 675 Prairie wound back to 1938 with the creation of boiler castings for new O gauge and O-27 steamers? The same sequence of innovation led eventually to the Berkshire.

The largest and most detailed of the designs finalized enabled Lionel to develop the prized no. 226/226E, a locomotive with a 2-6-4 wheel arrangement. That classic injected the line cataloged between 1938 and 1941 with greater glory.

The same casting led Lionel during the war to envision a grander steamer for the future. Designers modified it to accommodate extra drive wheels and thereby introduce a 2-8-4. They kept intact the steam chest and pilot casting from the 226/226E.

Within a year, engineers had overcome the shortcomings of the double worm drive powering the motor put on the 726 and its faulty smoke mechanism. A better operating yet still handsome Berkshire proved to be their triumph.

New era

The advent of Magne-Traction in 1949 transformed the fleet of locomotives Lionel championed for its golden anniversary a year later. A major step forward promised the finest performances yet. In response, the product numbers of leading engines changed. The Berkshire became the 736.

Lionel developed a new casting to fit the ingredients required for Magne-Traction, including a permanent magnet and iron pole piece plates. The boiler door, ornamental whistle and movable bell, wire handrails, and die-cast pilot truck lived on.

Minor alterations did take place. The four-window frame on the cab went to a three-window style, presumably so the 736 appeared different from the 726. Lionel reverted to the older look in 1953. Also in 1953 the large number rubber-stamped silver below the window yielded to a smaller one. Generally hot-stamped white, the three-digit number shifted back to rubber-stamping in the late 1960s.

To date a 736, note the boiler front (two reinforcing wedges cast onto the plate below the headlight in 1952 added stability), trailing truck (changed from die-cast metal in 1955 to sheet metal with plastic side frames), and flagstaffs (removed from the pilot bar around or after 1956).

On top

The parade of top-of-the-line outfits with a 736 went on for years, including the first Super O set. All were freights. The 736, unlike the 726, was not enlisted to head a passenger train. Still, every one of the 16 sets cataloged between 1950 and 1966 had terrific rolling stock and animated models.

Marketers coupled the 736 to the finest streamlined whistle tenders. The best might have been the no. 2671WX Lionel Lines selected in 1950 and 1951. After skipping 1952 due to the Korean Conflict, they adopted no. 2046W Lionel Lines in 1953. It remained the stalwart through 1960. Then, or in 1961, no. 736W Pennsylvania complemented the 736, as it did through 1968.

More information

- $37.50 ($374.45)
- Price for the 20½"-long duo had risen to $60 by 1968
- Replaced by no. 726RR in 1952 due to shortage of magnetic materials caused by Korean Conflict

2026 Adriatic 2-6-4 and Tender

When investigating the locomotives developed by Lionel during the first years of the post-World War II era, we discover how often engineers used designs dating from the late prewar years. They also borrowed assemblies and key parts from popular models to create new ones. The later version (1951-53) of the no. 2026 steam engine, with a 2-6-4 wheel arrangement, showed that process at work.

Not the first 2026

Lionel had to provide steady performers at a variety of price levels. Top locomotives could carry hefty tags, but smart marketing dictated offering reliable models at mid-range and low points.

After the war, Lionel introduced nos. 671 Turbine and 726 Berkshire for the upper end of its roster. At the opposite extreme went steamers with 0-4-0 and 2-4-2 wheel arrangements. Occupying the middle were 2-6-2 and 2-6-4 locomotives.

For 1947, Lionel developed the no. 2025 steam engine for its O-27 roster. That 2-6-2 represented a modified version of the no. 225 cataloged before World War II. The updated locomotive (assigned number 675 for the O gauge roster) was promoted as a replica of the Pennsylvania RR's famed class K4 Pacific. Nice idea, except that the full-size steam engine came with a 4-6-2 wheel arrangement.

A year later, Lionel's designers put a different boiler on the 2-6-2 chassis to create no. 2026 for the O-27 line. The die-cast metal shell featured the smokestack and steam chest in different locations; other than those cosmetic changes, the pair of 2-6-2 steamers scarcely diverged. Both came with a smoke mechanism and an operating headlight, plus they were coupled to a whistle tender.

The 2026 returned for a second year in 1949. Again, it had a black-painted body with rubber-stamped silver cab numbers, an ornamental bell and whistle, wire handrails, a die-cast metal trailing truck, and a three-position reverse unit. It typically had spoked drivers; scarce examples came with Baldwin disc drivers.

New model of the 2026

1951

Lionel dropped the 2025 and the 2026 after 1949. Replacing them in the middle of the O-27 group of steamers for 1950 was the no. 2035, which had a 2-6-4 wheel arrangement. The 2035, equipped with Magne-Traction, took over the spot held by the 2-6-2 steamers. (No. 2036, another new 2-6-4 in 1950, was at the low end because it didn't have a smoke unit.)

Then came the troublesome year of 1951, when Lionel had to drop some locomotives to cut production costs. Out of nowhere, or so it seemed, emerged the familiar 2026. But designers had revamped it, transforming it from a 2-6-2 to a 2-6-4 and installing the die-cast metal boiler developed for the 2036 a year before.

The 2026 still came with a black-painted die-cast metal body, spoked wheels, a smoke unit, an operating headlight, and a three-position reverse unit. So far, so good, until consumers were shocked to discover the newcomer lacked Magne-Traction.

Whereas the initial 2026 had been given a full complement of driving hardware, the new model had only drive rods and side rods. Instead of a die-cast metal trailing truck, there was now a cheaper one fashioned out of sheet metal.

Whistle or not in 1951-1953

Lionel used the later version of its 2026 steamer as the motive power for a trio of three-car freight sets placed at the low end of its O-27 roster in 1951-1953.

Set no. 1477S (cataloged in 1951 and 1952) included a non-whistle tender (no. 6466T) with its nos. 6012 gondola, 6014 boxcar, and 6017 caboose, all making their debut in 1951. In 1953, set no. 1501S (with nos. 6032 gondola, 6035 tank car, and 6037 caboose) also had a tender without a whistle (no. 6066T).

With outfit no. 1463WS, a midrange entry from 1951, the 2026 jumped a notch. Lionel upgraded the 2-6-4 by pairing it with a no. 6466W tender with a two-tone whistle. The steamer, behind because it lacked Magne-Traction, for once did more than merely smoke and beam its headlight.

More information

- Spoked drivers equipped with drive rods and side rods
- Cab number rubber-stamped silver (1951-1952) or hot-stamped white (1953)
- 6466W whistle tender (1951 only)
- Sold only as outfit component

2037 Adriatic 2-6-4 and Tender

The brain trust overseeing sales and engineering grappled in the 1950s with a problem unlike anything it had seen before. Steam locomotives, the bread and butter for the corporation for more than a generation, mattered less and less on full-size railroads.

If Lionel developed new models of steam locomotives, it risked losing the allegiance of modelers eager to operate replicas of the most modern equipment. But Berkshires, Hudsons, and their kin could be equipped with more special effects than diesels. Smoke units and two-tone whistles beat dull-sounding horns. Nothing looked slicker than side rods driving up and down.

Escaping that dilemma meant devoting fewer hours and dollars to developing new castings and assemblies for steamers. Instead, the men at the helm searched for reliable locomotives to serve as the centerpieces of the O-27 and O gauge rosters. For the former, no. 2037 filled that role to a tee.

Good casting

The most time-consuming and costly aspect to adding a steam locomotive to the line was developing the primary casting. The boiler, with its assorted details and openings, demanded research and precision. It had to be able to accommodate the motor and other internal mechanisms, the drive and other wheels, and the cab.

Lionel advanced when its engineers finished work on different new boiler castings for steamers making their debut in 1938. They used the smallest of those tools for two newcomers with 2-6-2 wheel arrangements: nos. 224 and 1666.

Both of those Prairies returned with slight modifications after World War II. Even after Lionel deleted steamers with those product numbers from its line after 1947, designers exploited the casting.

The 1666 boiler brought about, with minor modifications, the 2026 in 1948. That 2-6-2 then brought about the 2036 in 1950.

1953

A venerable casting again underwent a few changes to create a new steamer (the 2036 had a 2-6-4 arrangement). Lasting only one year, the 2036 resulted in the second iteration of the 2026, which returned as a 2-6-4.

Finest yet

Too bad that neither the 2036 nor the later 2026 had a smoke mechanism. Worse, the second steamer also lacked Magne-Traction. Designers, pledging to assemble the perfect middle-of-the-road steamer, set out to add both features.

Out emerged no. 2037 in the line announced for 1953. Another 2-6-4, it hit the deck fully loaded: Magne-Traction, smoke, headlight, three-position reverse unit, and often a whistle tender.

The die-cast metal body looked terrific painted black with a white number rubber- or hot-stamped below the cab window. Add in the ornamental bell, whistle (a reworking of the tooling), and spoked drivers with drive and side rods.

Fair to say the 2037 had two lives. Between 1953 and 1955, it rose to only middling rank when all the steamers were accounted for. It led a couple of O-27 freight outfits each year. Yet those sets consisted of ordinary rolling stock.

Mature years

Lionel surprisingly removed the 2037 from the line cataloged for 1956. A puzzle because the 2-6-4 returned with a roar the next year and occupied a notable spot in the O-27 roster through 1963. Like a Chevrolet Impala or Ford Fairlane, the 2037 grew to be a familiar sight, one promising excellent performance.

The best-known version of the steamer from its second stage was the one painted pink and designated motive power for the notorious Girl's Train. Outfit no. 1587S aimed to appeal to females with cars done up in pastel hues. No. 2037-500 and its matching no. 1130T-500 non-whistle tender hauled five freight cars in 1957 and 1958, but couldn't make the set a hit.

Following were year after year of pure reliability. Lionel put a 2037 (back to being painted black) on the point of at least one freight between 1959 and 1963. In addition, more than 40 promotional sets included the hard-working 2037 during those years. No question that 2-6-4 steamer deserved all the applause.

More information

- $25 ($224.48)
- Locomotive and tender measured 18½" long
- Sold separately in 1955 for $25
- Reported with three non-whistle tenders and three whistle tenders

2065 Hudson 4-6-4 with Tender

The array of wheel arrangements characterizing Lionel's postwar fleet of steamers turns out to be more diverse than many observers think. Yet one rises above all others. The 4-6-4 has been synonymous with greatness at Lionel since the no. 700E O scale replica of a New York Central Hudson awed the world in 1937.

And, although Lionel reached towering heights with its Turbines and Berkshires, the first Hudson and the near-scale, beautifully detailed versions that followed epitomized the finest engineering Lionel did. Among the worthy successors of the 700E should be counted the no. 2065.

Varied plans

Lionel cataloged the 2065 from 1954 through 1956 as both a component of nine O-27 outfits and a separate-sale item. When planners removed it from the roster, they decided to nail shut the coffin for O-27 Hudsons. Only the O gauge grouping included a 4-6-4 in the second dozen years of the postwar period.

1954

To be sure, the Hudson was reserved for the O gauge motive power stable for much of the era. Decision-makers thought initially of reviving a near-scale model based on the prewar no. 763 for 1946, but then abandoned the planned no. 703.

Momentum stalled until the company celebrated its golden anniversary in 1950, when the no. 773, a near-scale replica, graced the O gauge line. Key features added to that instant classic ranged from a smoke mechanism to a whistle tender, Magne-Traction to an operating headlight and a three-position reverse unit.

Executives wisely elected to develop an O-27 Hudson for their 50th year. Designers did so with a wink and a nod at the accountants. They saved cash by fitting the 4-6-4 arrangement to the boiler casting already used for the Berkshire. Out strolled the no. 2046 with Magne-Traction, a smoke unit, and a whistle tender.

Lionel proved its allegiance to the Hudson despite dropping the 773 for 1951. The 2046 returned for a second year and again in 1953. During the interval, the no. 2056—identical except for the absence of Magne-Traction—rigidly upheld the Hudson standard.

Something different

The Engineering Department put the finishing touches on a different sort of Hudson in 1953. Rather than another replica of a New York Central 4-6-4 or a hybrid with Berkshire traits, they sired a superb Hudson whose roots could be traced to the Atchison, Topeka & Santa Fe Ry.

The O gauge no. 685 and its O-27 gauge twin, no. 2055, departed from what Lionel had shown previously mainly due to the plain front of the boiler. A unique look sufficed. For the first time, the company had two distinct Hudsons.

That noteworthy if minor trend went forward for 1954, when designers added an external feedwater heater tank on the front of the otherwise plain front. With that change they created the no. 665 for the O gauge line to supersede the 685.

O-27, too

Anyone modeling O-27 trains discovered a newcomer with the same new auxiliary feedwater heater on the boiler front. The 2065—identical to the 665 and using the 2055 casting—made its debut in 1954 as the principal O-27 steamer.

Everything desirable was there on the 2065: Magne-Traction, a smoke mechanism, an operating headlight, and a three-position reverse unit. The black-painted die-cast metal body shell boasted an ornamental bell and whistle, wire handrails, lots of driving hardware, and a trailing truck with plastic side frames.

Definitely the finest Hudson crowning the O-27 motive power roster, the 2065 came with a whistle tender to stretch out over 19½". Either the no. 2046W streamlined model or the no. 6026W square type of tender complemented the outstanding Santa Fe-inspired 4-6-4.

Times were changing, though, and the commercial appeal of steamers was slipping. Of the 10 O-27 outfits offered in 1954, Lionel made seven of them steam. A year later, the proportion shrank to seven out of 15. And in 1956, the last year Lionel cataloged the 2065, a steam locomotive led a mere five out of 16 sets.

More information

- $32.50 ($290.74)
- Price raised to $35 in 1956
- White cab number could be rubber-stamped or hot-stamped
- Led seven outfits between 1954 and 1956

746 Streamlined Northern 4-8-4 and Tender

The steam era on American railroads, as well as on the Lionel Lines, was coming to an end by the middle of the 1950s. With diesels predominating on full-size lines, Lionel had little reason to devote engineering resources and expertise to develop another large and expensive steam locomotive and tender after 1956.

Yet one of the top locomotives Lionel introduced in 1957 was a model of a streamlined steam engine and tender on the Norfolk & Western Ry. The no. 746 earned praise for its beauty and smooth operation. It revealed how individuals not closely associated with Lionel could shape the line.

Inventive outsider

John Van Dyck, a metalworker and model railroader from Virginia, loved his O gauge trains. And he loved the Norfolk & Western, whose main line ran near his home. He watched the N&W's streamlined 4-8-4 class J locomotives roar past, leading publicized passenger trains, particularly the *Powhatan Arrow*.

Familiar with how to shape sheet metal and solder components, Van Dyck took a no. 726 Berkshire and refashioned it in 1955. He created a bullet nose for the boiler, added two wheels to the pilot, and moved the drive rod to the second wheel. He brushed red stripes across it to complete a credible O gauge version of the J.

Van Dyck contacted the N&W and then the Engineering Department at Lionel. In 1956, he shipped his modified Berkshire and tender to New Jersey. Chief Engineer Joseph Bonanno and his aide, John DiGirolamo, scrutinized the model before offering minimal compensation but no assurances that Lionel would add the J.

Meanwhile, Bonanno instructed his staff to duplicate what Van Dyck had done. Certain details—metal running lights, pressure release valves, and a handrail on the nose—were omitted to keep down production costs. Still, what those engineers achieved was the 746 locomotive and tender.

1957

Size and elegance

More than any previous Lionel steamer, the 746 and its companion tender mixed size with elegance. "The Grand Daddy of All Steamers" boasted a worm-geared motor, complete with a three-position reverse unit and Magne-Traction. The operating headlight, blasting whistle in the tender, and improved smoke unit (it used liquid and not tablets) enhanced that newcomer to the train line in 1957.

The 746, although not a scale model, never appeared compact or out of proportion. Components blended wonderfully, perhaps because of the rounded nose, curves on the boiler, silver wire handrails, and recessed cab windows.

The red-painted stripes outlined in yellow gave the black-painted die-cast metal locomotive a sense of warmth. Those sweeping decorative elements brought sophistication to the J and its tender.

Lionel knew it had a winner in the 746 and placed it in five superb Super O outfits between 1957 and 1959. Those top-of-the-line sets featured near-scale freight cars and operating items; four sets even had an accessory or two, so any boy lucky enough to receive one of them had a railroad empire at his fingertips.

Despite its beauty and power, the 746 never quite won over the public. Perhaps the demise of steam felt across America was reverberating among Lionel fans. Or maybe the general decline in interest in toy trains made it impossible for the Super O to thrive. Had Van Dyck brought his prototype to Lionel five years earlier, who knows how successful it might have been?

Class by itself

The streamlined steamer—the sole 4-8-4 cataloged by Lionel during the postwar era—was the firm's crème de la crème. The gift of an outside contributor, the Norfolk & Western J epitomized the blend of realism and fancy that made the line great.

Collectors and operators laud its stature, grace, and power. Touches as simple as the elegant striping and the shiny driving rods leave them in awe. To own a 746 is to join an exclusive club of those most appreciative of Lionel glory.

More information

- $49.95 ($427.77)
- Locomotive and tender were 21½" long
- Led Sears, Roebuck promotional outfit no. 9694 in 1960
- Striping on no. 746W whistle tender could extend across entire side

1872 General 4-4-0 and Tender

Designers, pushed to develop three-rail models of the latest diesel locomotives during the second half of the 1950s, received different instructions sometime after 1956. They were asked to create a replica of an old-time steam locomotive and tender in response to widespread interest in the Old West. Motion pictures and television shows fed a frenzy toy firms like Lionel aimed to exploit in hopes of driving up sales.

Ironically, as sales executives discovered when they attended the American Toy Fair held in New York City during the beginning of March 1959, designers at Lionel's competitors—A.C. Gilbert Co. and Louis Marx & Co.—had been handed similar requests. Both of those toy manufacturers unveiled old-time steamers and cars. Their S and O gauge trains also sought to capitalize on the craze for boots and saddles.

1959

But Lionel's models, differing in their product number and mechanical features, went further. By referring to the locomotive and tender as the General, marketing men connected the new nos. 1862 and 1872 with an incident from the Civil War.

Movie about Andrews' raid

What Lionel was promoting as an old-time train might have been inspired more by a motion picture about a daring episode during the Civil War than by nostalgia for the Wild West. In 1956, Walt Disney Productions released *The Great Locomotive Chase*.

That 85-minute film dramatized the attempt by Union soldiers commanded by James Andrews (played by Fess Parker) to infiltrate Confederate lines in April of 1862 and steal a Western & Atlantic Railroad freight train in Georgia. The raiders managed to capture the train and start driving it toward federal lines in Tennessee while destroying the rails behind them. The crew failed to reach its destination before being apprehended. Still, they gained fame, as did the wood-burning locomotive on the train named the General.

Aware of the favorable response given *The Great Locomotive Chase*, executives at Lionel thought a model of the General would be a positive addition. Its appearance would appeal to Civil War enthusiasts as well as the millions of people, young and old, who loved the Old West and the cowboys and lawmen associated with it.

Lionel models the General

The catalog for 1959 introduced the no. 1862 old-time steam locomotive Lionel called the General. (It can't be mere coincidence that the item's number was identical to the year of Andrews' raid.) The 4-4-0 steamer came with a two-position reverse unit and a lantern with a bulb, but without Magne-Traction. The engine's ornamentation delighted consumers, although they discovered to their dismay that the whistle was quite fragile.

The 1862 went with a tender lettered for the Western & Atlantic RR. Designers duplicated those markings on passenger cars to create an O-27 set and a gift pack.

A deluxe old-time outfit designated for the Super O group introduced what Lionel proclaimed the "5-Star General"—the no. 1872. That locomotive had Magne-Traction, a three-position reverse unit, and a smoke mechanism. The smokestack was painted black in contrast to the gray one on the 1862. The front lantern went from tile red to black. A no. 1872T non-whistle tender was paired with the locomotive.

Besides the smoking 4-4-0 engine (a feature that enhanced the realism), outfit no. 2528WS came with a no. 1877 flatcar with horses and two illuminated passenger cars: nos. 1875W coach with an on-board air whistle and 1876 mail-baggage car. There were also plenty of sections of Super O track and a bottle of smoke fluid but not a transformer.

The Super O version of the General, which retailed separately for $25, remained in the catalog through 1962. By then, youngsters seemed to have forgotten the Civil War and were a bit bored with the Old West. Space travel and atomic warfare, not to mention GI Joe and a slew of slot-car racing sets, had caught their fancy. Once again, it would be up to the ingenious engineers and marketing people at Lionel to find ways of appealing to them.

More information

- $25 ($206.74)
- Tender too small to hold whistle
- Handrail forms key part of circuit powering headlight
- Led promotional outfit no. X-677 in 1959

Diesel and Electric Locomotives

The O and O-27 gauge models of diesel and electric locomotives captured the color and detail of all sorts of prototype engines manufactured by virtually every major builder of the time. As never before, Lionel depended on dazzling children and the families who bought train sets. Reliable performance was only part of what the company promised with its diesels and electrics. More to the point, they offered style and elegance. Multiple-color paint schemes and flashy graphics represented something novel and modern for Lionel.

Diesel and electric engines reflected a more aggressive marketing approach on the part of Lionel. Sales executives saw in them rich opportunities to reach more consumers. They weren't content to market one or two kinds of prototypes or offer limited, even generic decoration.

Instead, Lionel invested in tooling and painting equipment that enabled it to catalog several types of diesels and electrics in a variety of road names and paint schemes. It sought to represent the latest locomotives used on railroads in every part of the United States. Further, the firm brought out models that were aimed at every price level. Diesels and electrics showed how forward thinking both Lionel's engineering staff and its sales force could be.

Away from steam

Times were changing on American railroads after 1945. Lionel would have to change, too, if it wanted to dominate the market. Progress on most railroads meant purchasing diesel-powered engines and relying less on steam. On selected lines electric locomotives gained in importance.

Children expected toy train makers to provide detailed, dependable models of what they saw. Should Lionel hesitate, other firms, particularly A. C. Gilbert Co., would intervene in hopes of conquering the market.

In 1947, Lionel picked up where it had left off about 20 years before. It cataloged a model of a highly publicized electric locomotive workhorse. Before the Great Depression, that tactic had entailed offering Standard and O gauge replicas of the bipolar used by the Milwaukee Road.

Lionel aimed to stay ahead by again mass-producing an O gauge locomotive based on an electric receiving acclaim from designers and travelers. The full-size legend that inspired a miniature legend was the Pennsylvania Railroad's GG1 electric.

Next advance

The real break with the past occurred in 1948, when Lionel released the first models of the F3 diesel manufactured by the Electro-Motive Division of General Motors. The F3 represented a gamble, one Lionel might not have taken had ample support not come from outside.

Joshua Cowen didn't care for diesels and might have been reluctant to bless the decision of his son, Lawrence, newly installed as president, to add an O gauge replica. They had no idea how kids would react to a model of a locomotive missing the action and drama of a steamer.

Several breaks encouraged Lionel to proceed. General Motors agreed to underwrite a portion of the tooling costs in exchange for seeing its emblem on the model. The New York Central was willing to meet the same conditions, as long as the new no. 2333 featured its name. That satisfied Lionel, so an F3 painted in the Central's scheme made its debut in 1948.

What transformed the 2333 into a lovely swan was the decision of the Atchison, Topeka & Santa Fe to contribute to its development. In return for that assistance, representatives requested that Lionel catalog a version with its road name and herald. Nothing could have benefited Lionel more.

More and more

Once the Cowens had climbed on the diesel bandwagon, they refused to jump off.

In 1949, Lionel released O and O-27 gauge versions of another Electro-Motive Division diesel, this time an NW2 switch engine (nos. 622 and 6220, respectively). The choice was curious. Perhaps General Motors had inserted stipulations in its agreement that compelled Lionel to roster a second EMD prototype. As important was the action of a competitor. General

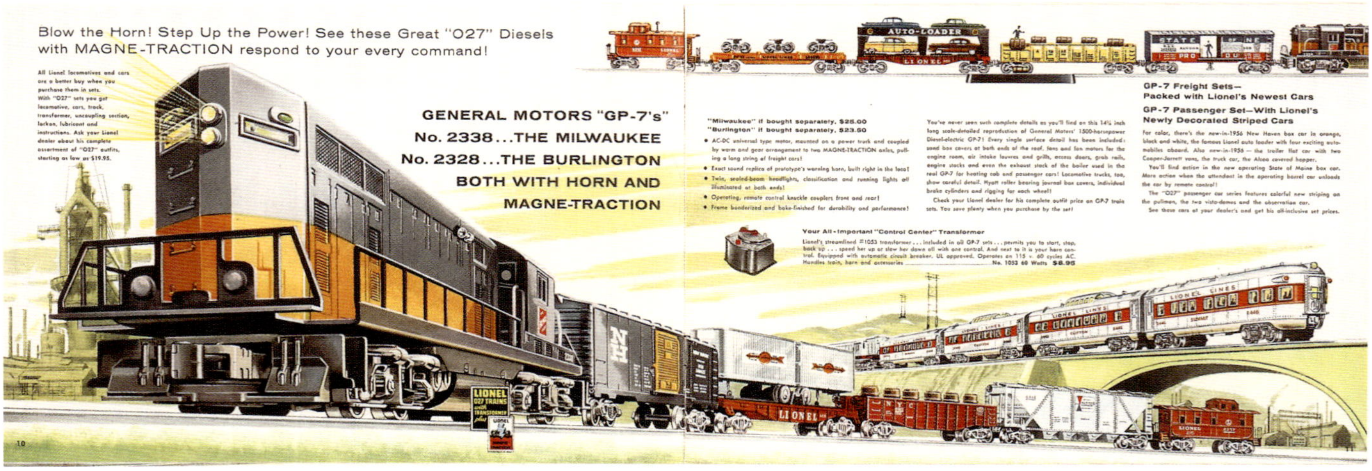

Models Corp. had introduced an O gauge model of the NW2 in summer 1948. Worried about losing sales to this newcomer, Lionel sent examples of the GMC switcher to its factory for engineers to study and recreate.

More than its chiming bell, what set the 622 apart from its peers (including the 6220) was a brand-new feature Lionel called Magne-Traction. Engineers had been conducting experiments involving powder metal in hopes of reconstructing the wheels and axles used on locomotives. They wanted to bolster the magnetism of those parts and thereby endow engines with greater pulling power. Success with the 622 in 1949 inspired Lionel to add this feature to more engines the next year.

Besides Magne-Traction, Lionel's golden anniversary year of 1950 heralded the introduction of a new diesel. This time designers concentrated on broadening the O-27 line with a replica of the FA type manufactured by the American Locomotive Co. (Alco). As was true of Lionel's F3s, the no. 2023 came in an A-A combination of identical powered and non-powered units. Decorated for the Union Pacific, their injection-molded plastic bodies were painted yellow (the roof was gray) and hot-stamped red. Lionel equipped these diesels with Magne-Traction and operating lights and a horn.

After bringing out new diesels for three consecutive years, Lionel rested from its labors in 1951. Perhaps sales executives doubted the wisdom of expanding the roster, or restrictions caused by the Korean Conflict had limited their options. The only new product was a modified 2023 in silver and gray.

Busy rivals

Such minimal activity contrasted with the actions of Lionel's rivals. In 1950, Marx capitalized on the popularity of the Santa Fe's warbonnet scheme, lithographing it on an O-27 model of a different Electro-Motive diesel, the FT. Marx also offered an F3 decorated for the Southern Pacific.

Gilbert, too, trusted the warbonnet to sell diesels. Starting in 1950, it cataloged S gauge models of Alco's sleek PA and PB painted and lettered for the Santa Fe. (Lionel also introduced a B unit for its diesel in 1950.) Meanwhile, Gilbert's American Flyer line forged ahead of Lionel with the first toy version of a diesel road switcher. Modelers praised the dashing silver Electro-Motive GP7.

Lionel answered only indirectly in 1952 and 1953. Instead of bringing out brand-new models, it expanded its roster by decorating diesels for more railroads. For example, nos. 2031 Rock Island and 2032 Erie A-A units joined the Union Pacific engines (renumbered as 2033) in the FA stable. All three were cataloged from 1952 through 1954, as were a pair of NW2 switchers that were overshadowed by another F3. Arriving in 1952 was the no. 2345, a silver-and-orange A-A combination for the Western Pacific.

Consumers found Lionel's competitors extremely busy. Marx announced an O-27 model of Electro-Motive's popular E7 and added a Baltimore & Ohio unit to its list of F3s. Gilbert offered new versions of its S gauge PA, this time painted and lettered for fictitious yet exciting passenger trains.

The most significant of Lionel's rivals in 1953 was American Model Toys, which brought out its own O gauge diesel, a model of an Electro-Motive Division F7. That handsome piece came decorated for several railroads, including the Chicago & North Western, New York Central, Pennsylvania, Santa Fe, and Southern Railway. The most attractive AMT diesel might have been the one painted and lettered for a specific train, the *Texas Special*.

Bursting ahead in 1954

Lionel responded fiercely in 1954 with an outstanding line. Leading the way was the no. 2321 Fairbanks-Morse Train Master. Dual-motored, it came decorated for the Delaware, Lackawanna & Western and featured operating lights and couplers, a horn, and Magne-Traction.

Also making their debut in 1954 were F3s whose decoration indicated how seriously Lionel took AMT. First there was the no. 2245, a single-motored O-27 painted and lettered for the *Texas Special*. The fact that Lionel had decorated an A-B combination for a specific train left no doubt it wanted to counter AMT. Next came the no. 2356, which consisted of an A-A combination painted green and gray for the Southern. Cataloging those F3s, along with New York Central and Santa Fe models, meant Lionel's diesels represented almost every region of the country.

Still active

The 1954 line proved Lionel could pursue the twin goals of designing toys and building near-scale models. In fact, it showed again and again over the next three years how skillfully it accomplished those aims.

In 1955, engineers unveiled a road switcher to counter the American Flyer unit. Like Gilbert's model, the no. 2028

Pennsylvania Railroad was designated a GP7. Along with that O-27 model, Lionel released two other EMD road switchers: no. 2328, decorated for the Chicago, Burlington & Quincy and no. 2338, which represented the Milwaukee Road.

For Lionel, 1955 stood out in other ways. More F3s and NW2s were available, as was a version of the Train Master decorated for the Virginian Railway. Moreover, following an absence of four years, it cataloged a GG1. The no. 2340 came in Brunswick green or Tuscan red; either way, it was a gorgeous addition, especially when pulling the streamlined cars packed with the no. 2254W *Congressional* outfit.

A year later, Lionel directed its attention to small niches in the toy train market. It filled them with models of General Electric locomotives, an occurrence suggesting decision-makers had negotiated some kind of licensing agreement with their counterparts at General Electric.

To start, there was the no. 520 80-ton electric, whose appearance hearkened back to the boxcabs Lionel had made in the second and third decades of the century. Another electric, the no. 2350 New Haven EP-5, broadened the O gauge line with the elegance of its black, orange, and white scheme. The third GE prototype was a 44-ton diesel pulling freight or passenger cars. Three versions were offered in 1956, including nos. 628 Northern Pacific and 629 Burlington Route.

Peak performance

With those General Electric locomotives, Lionel reached the peak of its diesel production. By 1956, it was cataloging models of virtually every major type of modern locomotive. Its depth became even greater when nos. 41 U.S. Army gas turbine and 51 New York Navy Yard Vulcan switcher were cataloged. Lionel didn't offer a model of a Baldwin prototype as Gilbert did or an Alco switcher as Marx did. All the same, it couldn't have expanded its line without hurting its own sales.

What became clear was how quickly and completely models of diesel and electric locomotives had superseded steamers at Lionel. The assorted newcomers, distinguished by their variety and color, had leapfrogged to the forefront of the motive power roster. Designers, challenged to revamp the line so Lionel would remain ahead of all competitors, had responded with vigor and brilliance. The 1950s at Lionel unquestionably belonged to the models of the different electrics and diesels enthralling the public.

Diesel and electric engines reflected a more aggressive marketing approach on the part of Lionel. Sales executives saw in them rich opportunities to reach more consumers.

About finished

At the end of the 1950s, Lionel held the line on diesel development while cutting corners on models in the locomotive roster. New road names were available for the O and O-27 F3s, for example, including nos. 2373 Canadian Pacific A-B combination cataloged in 1957 and 2379 Denver & Rio Grande Western A-B duo cataloged in 1957 and 1958.

Then Lionel dropped those beauties and kept only nos. 2242 New Haven and 2383 Santa Fe (both new in 1958 with many details missing). Details also were removed from the NW2 diesel switchers, beginning in 1955, although the number of road names cataloged increased significantly over the next six years.

Nowhere was the procedure of eliminating details, simplifying decoration, and adding road names more evident than with the Alco FA. Lionel had discontinued that fine O-27 diesel after 1954, only to reissue it in a less elaborate form three years later.

Alco locomotives produced from 1957 through 1969 had thinner, less durable bodies than their predecessors. Engineers plugged the locomotive's portholes and marker light slots and removed the headlight lens. Not surprisingly, the FAs cataloged during the 1960s looked cheap and performed poorly, suggesting how quality had slipped in importance at Lionel.

Although inexpensive FAs came to dominate the Lionel line during the 1960s, a few premium diesels and electrics remained in the catalog. Still, when compared with the finest years of diesel and electric locomotive development at Lionel, the 1960s lose most of their luster. The ingenuity and expertise demonstrated by the engineers who designed the earlier locomotives were unparalleled. No finer testaments to their work survived than did the F3s, Train Masters, and GG1s manufactured by Lionel.

2332 Pennsylvania GG1 Electric

The O gauge models of the Pennsylvania RR's iconic GG1 electric-profile locomotive now range from toy-like to scale replicas in every paint scheme used by every railroad that has ever owned a GG1.

Circumstances were simpler during postwar times. O gauge enthusiasts had only a handful of Lionel models bearing the name and keystone of the Pennsy to consider. Brunswick green or Tuscan red and five thin stripes or one broad one, a list that began in 1947 with the no. 2332.

1947

Cowen votes

Lionel had, since the 1920s, augmented its catalog with models of locomotives that made news. Particularly electric units, with their whirring motors and delicate metal pantographs drawing current from criss-crossing overhead lines.

Joshua Cowen paid attention when the Pennsylvania RR heralded a new electric in the mid-1930s. The swift and sleek GG1, painted Brunswick green, had five thin stripes reminiscent of a cat's whiskers.

After World War II, someone, perhaps Cowen, suggested a model of the GG1. The Pennsy gladly cooperated. Chief Engineer Joseph Bonanno took on the project, asking Development Engineer Frank Pettit to obtain needed materials.

Instant classic

Pettit told the saga behind the 2332 in the July 1997 issue of *Classic Toy Trains*. He wrote about the decision to design the model for three-rail track with a 31" diameter rather than the 72" type a scale replica would have required.

Next in importance, according to Pettit, was selecting the right motor for the GG1. Bonanno preferred the long-nosed, twin-bearing motor installed on the 671 Turbine. Pettit disagreed. He believed the vertically mounted motor he had devised for the 726 Berkshire was the better candidate. Bonanno carried the day.

Yet a third chapter should be devoted to the operating horn. The sound produced by the initial device hardly excited Pettit. He spent hours experimenting with what he termed "a plastic sound box of resilient material." To it, he added an iron core and coil windings until, when activated electrically, it vibrated to create a blaring sound that the elderly Cowen approved.

Odd number

Pantographs completed the preliminary piece Pettit and his model maker, Henry Niemann, presented early in 1947. That mock-up, which the Advertising Department depicted in the Consumer Catalog, bore the number "4911," which Pettit liked because the Pennsy used it on a GG1.

But Victor Nigro, who handled production scheduling at the plant, grumbled that 4911 wasn't consistent with anything in the line. Worried it would cause confusion, he changed the number after noticing that the new electric came with a 2-3-3-2 arrangement of axles on each side.

Two colors

Advances in technology enabled Lionel to form the GG1 shell by casting a molten alloy consisting of iron and zinc instead of having to stamp sheets of steel. Consequently, the 2332 looked more realistic, especially with its elegant curves, than had previous electrics.

The Pennsy provided samples of the Brunswick green paint. That hue, already dark, ended up indistinguishable from black on the first group of models. Subsequent paint showed more of a green tint.

Decoration of the 14½"-long 2332 included small keystones (rubber-stamped and then decaled) and five stripes (usually gold) applied with a special roller machine.

The first GG1s ascended to the peak of the O gauge line in 1947 and remained there for the next two years. The retail price of a 2332 rose to $37.50 in 1948.

More information

- $32.50 ($350.72)
- Could take current from overhead wires through pantographs
- Operating headlight at each end
- Led outfit no. 2144W heavyweight passenger train in 1948 and 1949

2333 New York Central F3 A-A Units

The post-World War II era for toy trains opened chronologically with Lionel rushing to market an outfit for the holiday season of 1945. But focusing on technological, aesthetic, or even economic considerations suggested the era began in 1948, when Lionel developed its F3 diesel.

Lionel committed its reputation, along with ample resources, to bringing out a replica of a diesel locomotive whose look and mechanics exemplified what was happening on American railroads. The no. 2333 team of powered and non-powered A units represented a departure from the steam and electric motive power Lionel long had depended on to generate sales.

Less celebrated

The single product number referred to two versions of the same diesels. Lionel released simultaneously F3s painted and lettered for the New York Central and the Santa Fe. Such a step demonstrated a change in marketing strategy. Executives believed they could woo customers across the country by offering two road names.

1948

Ever since, the Santa Fe units, brilliant in their silver-and-red warbonnet scheme, have held center stage. Yet there's no purpose in overlooking the New York Central F3s. Technically, they were mirror images of the Santa Fe units. Their two horizontally mounted motors and three-position reverse unit duplicated mechanical features of their comrades. All the F3s gratified kids with their working headlights, knuckle couplers, and operating horn.

Only in decoration might the New York Central diesels drop into second place. Although not in the Northeast and Upper Midwest, where that railroad ruled. Residents revered the two-tone gray paint scheme with its "lightning stripe" pattern.

Outside help

Lionel cataloged its F3s for two nationally renowned railroads for reasons other than commercial. Leaders had reached out to both the manufacturer of that type of diesel cab unit and a pair of the Class 1 lines investing in it for their assistance.

Collaborating with the Electro-Motive Division of General Motors as well as the New York Central and the Santa Fe lifted economic pressure off Lionel. All three contributed financially to the creation of necessary tooling. When called on, they provided blueprints, photographs, painting diagrams, and other materials.

Joshua Cowen remained an advocate of steam engines for his line. But his business acumen and competitive spirit overshadowed sentiments favoring older locomotives. He recognized the need to diversify.

Working overtime

Marching in front as months passed away in 1948 were Chief Engineer Joseph Bonanno and the draftsmen and model makers under his supervision. They consulted regularly with their counterparts at General Motors until completing near-scale replicas of the F3 loaded with details and built for solid performance.

More than ever before, designers were capitalizing on the breakthroughs being made in the burgeoning field of injection-molding new thermoplastics. The detail on the body shells of F3 diesels would otherwise not have been possible.

Late yet great

Lionel, it appears in retrospect, finished the development of its 2333 units later than expected. As a consequence, it postponed delivery until early 1949.

Consumers proved to be quite forgiving, so impressed were they with the 2333 models. Lionel used the combinations in identical four-car freight outfits pushed to the upper end of the line for 1948. A year later, it placed the F3s at the head of five-car freight sets with two animated models.

The New York Centrals, like the other 2333 pair, reflected Lionel's deep commitment to improving its O gauge roster with models of contemporary trains. The stylish diesels symbolized confidence in the present and hope for the future.

More information

- $42.50 ($424.38)
- Combination measured 26½" in length
- General Motors decal and stamped lettering varied
- Open portholes with plastic lenses

624 Chesapeake & Ohio Electro-Motive NW2 Switcher

The noteworthy trend at Lionel during the early postwar era of decorating models in eye-catching color schemes took a giant step forward in 1952. Along with the orange-and-silver Western Pacific F3s (no. 2345), the firm introduced the elegant yet brawny no. 624 Chesapeake & Ohio NW2 switcher. The blue-and-yellow diesel impressed viewers and became a strong member of the locomotive roster.

Not the first

The 624 wasn't the first O gauge model of an Electro-Motive Division NW2 diesel switcher to join Lionel's roster. That honor went to no. 622 Santa Fe, added in 1949 with its twin, no. 6220 for the O-27 line.

1952

Lionel's designers were more than likely to have copied the work of a competitor and not developed their own model of this switcher. General Models Corp. had already put an O gauge model of the NW2 on the market. Personnel at Lionel, according to former employees, had bought one to see how they could create something similar.

However, the 622 and 6220 were not mere imitations of the GMC model. They were the first Lionel locomotives to feature Magne-Traction. And they came with a bell that rang automatically as they traveled. Too bad they weren't pretty.

Lionel brought back the black-painted locomotives in 1950. Minor changes in decoration occurred, but otherwise what Lionel offered in its jubilee year hardly differed from what it had sold in 1949.

During the critical year of 1951, Lionel deleted its Santa Fe diesel switchers. Perhaps executives had given up its value.

Based on a real engine

Whatever decision-makers might have been thinking about the NW2, they still cataloged it again in 1952. Besides a modified version of the Santa Fe (no. 623, issued without a ringing bell), they produced a far more colorful switcher, the 624, loudly decked out in blue with yellow details and lettered for the Chesapeake & Ohio.

Some traditionalists protest that the 624 was unlike anything then plying the rails. Sorry folks, but Lionel based its blue-and-yellow diesel on a Chesapeake & Ohio prototype. That railroad had painted its 57 NW2 units in that gaudy style. Blame the C&O for breaking the mold of black switchers.

To Lionel's credit, it followed suit and presented an O gauge model that stood out in a world dominated by black steamers and dark electrics painted a single color. The 624 carried forward the notable trend launched by the company in 1948 with the no. 2333 Santa Fe F3 in silver and red and advanced with the no. 2023 Union Pacific Alcos in bright yellow in 1950.

Appreciation of the 624 C&O switcher's beauty starts with its vivid blue-painted body on top of a matching die-cast metal frame. Highlights include a bright yellow stripe painted at the edge of the frame and twin smokestacks molded out of yellow plastic that was left unpainted. Also on the roof are an unpainted black ornamental bell and an unpainted black radio wheel in front.

Yellow decals with the name of the railroad and its herald steal the show. Beware of flaked or scratched decorative elements, including the yellow number hot-stamped on each side of the cab. Examine the silver horns and handrails for problems.

The 624 came equipped with two-axle Magne-Traction, a three-position reverse unit, and dual operating couplers. An operating headlight at each end helped the 624 stand out, particularly because Lionel had eliminated the bell from its NW2.

Separate only

Lionel cataloged the 624 through 1954, yet it never used this handsome and rugged diesel switcher as the motive power for an outfit. The C&O diesel switcher appeared as only a separate-sale item during those three years, priced at $25.

Too bad because the 624 would have looked great with a silver or orange boxcar, a red gondola, and a silver tank car as a low-end freight. Or better with a searchlight car, a crane car, and a work caboose as the components of a work train.

Designers eliminated seven of the 10 stanchions on each side of the body shell for 1953 and 1954. They also deleted a small General Motors decal on later versions. Otherwise, the 624 never changed during its years in the cataloged line.

More information

- $25.00 ($227.76)
- Wire handrail along hood
- Silver ornamental horn
- Coil knuckle coupler at both ends

2031 Rock Island Alco FA A-A Units

Youngsters operating O-27 trains in the late 1940s felt blessed and cursed. Heartened by the expanding roster of novel rolling stock and animated cars. Disheartened by the superior locomotives filling up the O gauge stable. Only big kids got a Berkshire, a GG1, or an F3.

Until the golden anniversary year of 1950! Years of having to be content with nothing beyond the same Turbine and NW2 switcher culminated in a brand-new diesel added exclusively to the O-27 line. Kids delighted in the Lionel rendition of an Alco FA-1 diesel in Union Pacific colors. They were more pleased three years later when the no. 2031 Rock Island units arrived.

Something new

Lionel had collaborated with General Motors and the New York Central and Santa Fe railroads on O gauge models of an F3 diesel. The powerful and elegant powered and dummy replicas turned the hobby upside down. Lionel could brag about having something unique.

1952

Which it did in catalogs and advertisements in 1948 and 1949. O gauge modelers, thrilled by the steam locomotives and GG1 electric leading the finest sets, wondered at the riches pouring down on them.

Yet the need to build the motive power roster never declined. Lionel wanted to reach out to a different manufacturer and secure the loyalty of other railroads. So it looked to the American Locomotive Co. and the mighty Union Pacific.

The way that nationally renowned railroad painted its diesels Armour Yellow and Harbor Mist Gray made them appealing. Better still, those colors would remind Lionel enthusiasts about the toy company celebrating 50 years since its founding.

Thus emerged the no. 2023 Alco FA-1 units handsomely dressed for the Union Pacific. The O-27 roster finally claimed a model unlike what O gaugers had.

Incidentally, circumstantial evidence suggested Lionel might have been considering something other than an Alco for its O-27 line. The yellow injection-molded plastic bodies used on a few F3s in 1950 and 1951 might have been for proposed UP versions of the O gauge model. In addition, two General Motors E7 six-axle A units lettered for the UP appeared in a Lionel advertisement in the December 1950 issue of *Railroad Model Craftsman* magazine.

More to come

Regardless of what Lionel planners might have been debating, they ended up adding Union Pacific Alco diesels to the O-27 line in 1950. They brought them back a year later, although they chose to shift from yellow paint to silver in 1951.

The next phase followed logically and smoothly. Offer consumers Alcos painted and lettered for other railroads. How else might Lionel boost sales while reaching modelers enamored with regional lines running near their communities?

Cataloged for three years starting in 1952 were powered and dummy Alco FA units decorated for the Erie RR (no. 2032) and the Rock Island (no. 2031).

Looking under the hood of the powered diesels revealed Magne-Traction, a three-position reverse unit, a horn activated via remote control, and a working headlight. The non-powered FA units came with only a working headlight.

Powered and dummy Alcos used a die-cast metal frame painted black with a narrow stripe at the bottom (yellow on the Erie and white on the Rock Island). Other cosmetic highlights included an ornamental horn, a headlight lens, and marker lenses with their four-digit number (not found anywhere on the shell).

Like a rock

The 2031 Alcos represented a major step by Lionel. The black-painted bodies with broad red-painted stripes and white hot-stamped lettering introduced a midwestern line to three-rail trains. Lionel likely negotiated a deal with the Rock Island because near-scale boxcars decorated for that line joined the roster in 1953 and 1954.

Lionel advanced in a similar direction with the Western Pacific in 1952, bringing out diesels with its name (no. 2345 F3 A units). Yet executives selected neither the WP engines nor the Rock Island Alcos to lead a set—both were sold only separately.

More information

- $38.95 ($353.71)
- Operating couplers at both ends
- A-A combination measured 22" long
- Retail price increased to $39.95 in 1954

2245 *Texas Special* Electro-Motive F3 A-B Units

Marketing possibilities multiplied after designers completed work on the first replicas of an F3 diesel. Initially, though decision-makers cataloged models with just the names of the two railroads whose investment had underwritten the research and development. New York Central and Santa Fe were all from 1948 through 1951.

A significant trend took off a year later, when Lionel brought out the next F3s. They came decorated for a western railroad, perhaps reflecting a campaign to bolster sales in a different part of the country. From then on, Lionel gambled with its diesels. They featured road names with regional appeal at best. A key example of what Lionel hoped to achieve was the no. 2245 *Texas Special* F3 A and B duo.

Indiana rival

Intense demands for electric trains after the war ignited fierce competition. Lionel acted to counter some of what its major rivals—Gilbert and Marx—were doing. Smaller companies, content to nip away at less-prosperous segments of the market, annoyed but hardly threatened the giant.

American Model Toys, based in Auburn, Ind., initially bewildered Lionel. AMT's streamlined passenger cars and near-scale freight cars eventually sparked serious responses as Lionel refused to concede important and profitable fields. In time, AMT also introduced O gauge models of Electro-Motive F7 diesels that bothered Lionel, although it already ruled the roost with its more reliable F3s.

Members of the Engineering Department, like their peers in Lionel's sales offices, tallied the diverse road names AMT used on its diesels. One, in particular, intrigued them. Red-and-white F7s came decorated not for a railroad but for a passenger train crossing the Southwest.

1954

Something different

Not since the prewar period, with the introduction of the Standard gauge *Blue Comet*, had Lionel cataloged a model based on a full-size passenger train. But competition with AMT explained the decision to paint and letter F3 A and B units for the *Texas Special*, which ran between St. Louis and San Antonio over the St. Louis-San Francisco Ry. and Missouri-Kansas-Texas RR.

Cautious marketers proved reluctant to pair the 2245 combination brought out in 1954 with streamlined passenger cars bearing *Texas Special* markings. Yet they did take a few bold steps with the F3s.

To start, the non-powered unit they matched with the powered A unit ended up being a B unit. Never before had Lionel done that with its F3 diesels.

Second, planners designated the *Texas Special* A and B units as O-27 entries. Making them the first F3s assigned to the less prestigious half of the train line.

The 26"-long duo led a freight outfit and a passenger set in 1954, besides being offered for separate sale. Lionel put them in only a passenger outfit in 1955.

Real beauties

The 2245, in spite of being equipped with only one motor (horizontally mounted in 1954 and vertically a year later), muscled boldly ahead with Magne-Traction and a three-position reverse mechanism. The A unit presented a blinding headlight and an operating knuckle coupler on its pilot.

Terrific looks distinguished the *Texas Special*. Early production featured a silver-painted chassis with a red-painted pilot and silver side frames with steps. Then the pilot evolved to silver, and the side frames were blackened chemically.

The plastic shells dazzled with their glossy red paint. Laborers masked the lower portion by hand before screen-printing each side white, with lettering and details carefully cut out of the tape to remain shiny red.

A white five-pointed star on the nose and two-piece ornamental horns on the roof added class. As did decals of the heralds of the sponsoring Frisco and MKT.

More information

- $39.95 ($357.39)
- Price dropped to $29.95 in 1955
- Drawbar pull of 8 to 10 freight cars
- B units with closed portholes released late in 1955

2321 Lackawanna Fairbanks-Morse H-24-66 Train Master

Lionel, the diesel kingpin when it came to "covered wagons" and switchers, fell behind with heavy-duty road units. Gilbert scooped its rival in 1950 by releasing no. 370, its S gauge model of an Electro-Motive Division GP7. Executives and engineers at Lionel plotted revenge. The only issue was which road diesel they would model in O gauge. Something else from General Motors would have been logical, and in 1953, an advertisement showed a preliminary model of what looked like an EMD SD9.

Yet that engine never entered discussions for mass-production at Lionel. Instead, the toymaker took its cue from a massive 2,400-horsepower, six-axle hood unit Fairbanks-Morse began shopping in 1953. This powerhouse, designed for freight and passenger service, carried the impressive title of "Train Master."

1954

Auspicious debut

Despite the efforts of public relations personnel with Fairbanks-Morse, the boxy yet powerful H-24-66 Train Master tempted only a few railroads to place orders.

Regardless, Lionel took notice of the Train Master. Their "scale-length" replica, 15½" long, made its debut in 1954—one more reason collectors laud that year's line as among the best in history.

The 2321 Train Master is one of the landmark O gauge locomotives of the era. Mechanically, it lived up to its billing in the Consumer Catalog as a "Power Giant." Designers packed two worm-drive motors equipped with Magne-Traction plus a three-position reverse unit inside the injection-molded body shell. No wonder the Train Master was capable of pulling as many as 24 freight cars.

Don't forget the other outstanding components. A beaming headlight at each end, along with operating knuckle couplers and a blasting horn delighted owners. The six-wheel passenger trucks featured "delicately molded springs and hand brake connections," according to the description in the Consumer Catalog.

Picking a name

Key people on the engineering and sales staffs saw the wisdom of starting with one of the railroads owning Train Masters. Therefore, factory personnel painted and lettered preliminary O gauge samples for the Delaware, Lackawanna & Western, the Reading Lines, and the Southern Pacific.

Those attractive mock-ups went on display at national and regional toy fairs. Evidently, industry insiders voted for the Lackawanna. Lionel fell in line and offered a model with a simplified scheme.

The process began with the body shell being painted maroon. Then, after workers masked selected areas by hand, they sprayed on gray, like Lackawanna Train Masters. Originally, they left the roof maroon. Undoubtedly an aesthetic benefit, that step demanded additional painting to cover overspray. To save pennies and minutes, supervisors opted for a gray roof.

Consumers praised the rubber-stamped yellow stripes and maroon lettering. Gratifying them as well were the decaled Fairbanks-Morse medallions on the sides and the Lackawanna heralds on each end. Those details, not to mention the wire handrails, enhanced the 2321.

Solid sets

The Train Master looked confident, bold, and strong. Planners used the 2321 as the motive power for a pair of excellent freight outfits in 1954 and another in 1955.

Five-car outfit no. 2223W, nicknamed "Big Haul" in the 1954 Consumer Catalog, stood out with its two animated cars (3461 log car and 3482 milk car) and no. 6417-25 color-coordinated porthole caboose. The star was no. 6464-100 Western Pacific boxcar with its orange body and short blue feather.

The 2321, like the other two models of a Train Master added in 1955 and 1956, exemplified the commitment at Lionel to merging toy-like elements with scale realism. No other O gauge locomotive, not even the F3, raised the line to such greatness in the middle of the postwar era.

More information

- $43.50 ($389.15)
- Separate sale only in 1956
- Priced reduced to $39.95 in 1955
- Front end equipped with headlight and Mars light

6250 Seaboard Electro-Motive NW2 Switcher

The emergence of diesel-powered locomotives represented as much a challenge and shift for toy train makers as it did for railroads across North America. Each firm, no matter how large or small, had to decide how much to invest in the new technology and when it ought to turn its back for good on steam locomotives.

An advantage for businesses whose heads understood they were marketing toys was the shift in how locomotives looked. Steamers traditionally had been painted black, so models should be black. But with railroads adopting multi-hued schemes for diesels, toy firms felt free to experiment in hopes of attracting buyers.

How else to explain the no. 6250 Seaboard NW2 diesel switcher? Its blue-and-orange scheme replicated not the full-size locomotive but the Lionel box!

Old switcheroo

The transition to motive power dependent on diesel fuel rather than coal commenced in the 1930s and accelerated through the next decade. Toy train makers also moved into the diesel age. Lionel plunged forward in 1948 with its F3 covered wagons.

1954

How fast Lionel meant to dip another toe in the diesel waters eludes us, due to a lack of evidence. All we know is that a competing firm may have been responsible for the next Lionel diesel because it debuted another diesel from Electro-Motive's fleet.

General Models Corp. made an O gauge model of a NW2 switcher in 1948, the same year Lionel finished its F3. Rather than lose business to that challenger, Lionel moved on with an NW2 of its own.

Black times two

Lionel introduced its NW2 switcher in 1949. Black-painted models, each with Santa Fe and General Motors markings, joined the O gauge and O-27 lines. The diesels were identical except in number (622 versus 6220).

The Santa Fe switchers came equipped with a ringing bell and a new feature called Magne-Traction. Using powder metal and magnets produced an innovative alloy, engineers made it possible for miniature locomotives to run faster and climb higher while staying on the track better.

Lionel dropped its first NW2s after 1950. Shortages of critical materials caused by the Korean Conflict curtailed its ability to add Magne-Traction. A new Santa Fe switcher and one decorated for the Chesapeake & Ohio filled out the line in 1952.

Look south

The various Santa Fe models as well as the C&O switcher offered young engineers faithful images of what those railroads were then running. The black and white of the first units and the blue and yellow of the latter did copy reality.

Not the garish 6250 bursting into the O-27 roster as a set component in 1954 and departing as a separate-sale item in 1955. The eye-popping scheme was like nothing on the Seaboard, which used the black-and-red pattern seen between 1956 and 1958 on nos. 601 and 602 NW2s. The 6250 imitated colors used on Lionel's component boxes ever since the 1930s.

Putting the Seaboard Air Line name and round medallions on the shell was promising. Lionel had thus far in the postwar era ignored southern railroads. Now the South rose with Southern Railway F3s (no. 2356) and Seaboard NW2 switchers.

Tough enough

Fancy looks shouldn't disguise how hard the 6250 toiled with its worm-drive motor, two-axle Magne-Traction, and three-position reverse unit. An operating headlight and working couplers completed a great package. And the Seaboard unit led the first NW2 set since 1950.

More information

- $25.00 ($223.65)
- 11⅝" long
- Led no. 1523 Gandy Dancer four-car work outfit in 1954
- Described in 1955 catalog as being modeled after an SW1 switcher

2338 Milwaukee Road Electro-Motive GP7 Road Diesel

Much as postwar fans may want to believe Lionel blazed every key trail, history tells a different story. It missed with a road diesel. The A.C. Gilbert Co. announced a model of a GP7 in 1950, which was a long five years before Lionel added a version for three rails.

Once inspired to deliver a replica of the locomotive built by the Electro-Motive Division of General Motors, engineers at Lionel delighted their bosses and consumers. The finest of their new Geeps, as judged by its features and performance, was the no. 2338 Milwaukee Road GP7.

Motley trio

The Milwaukee Road unit entered in 1955, one of three GP7s. It, along with no. 2328 Burlington Route, earned the title of deluxe. Both road diesels came with a horn, headlights, and working couplers. Not the third newcomer. No. 2028 Pennsylvania RR was, noted the *Lionel Service Manual*, "a stripped-down model, without headlights, warning horn or certain decorative features such as railings around the cab...."

1955

Further distinguishing each deluxe road diesel were a vertically mounted motor, three-position reverse unit, and Magne-Traction. Designers used what they learned from creating the Train Master model of the year before and applied it to the GP7.

The 2338 had an unpainted orange plastic shell whose upper half, roof, and cab were spray-painted black. The orange band continued across the cab on the earliest models and typically didn't bisect it.

Graphics included hot-stamped lettering (black and then white product number and black built data). A rubber-stamped Milwaukee Road herald (brown or red) went beneath the window on each side.

Something else planned

Lionel unveiled a classic unit with its 2338 Milwaukee Road GP7. Yet the Engineering Department originally had another rugged road diesel on the drawing board before that EMD Geep or even the Train Master made a splash in the field.

A color photo in an ad in the November 14, 1953, issue of *The Saturday Evening Post* suggested Lionel considered a different diesel. That image showed Frank Pettit, Lionel's development engineer, and a plaster model of a road switcher with the features of an EMD six-axle SD7 diesel rather than its four-axle GP7.

Was Lionel, perhaps encouraged by EMD, contemplating adding a miniature version of the new six-axle "special-duty" diesel and not the four-axle "general-purpose" unit that had been out since 1949?

Still, an SD7 never entered Lionel's postwar line. Slow sales of the SD7 might have led EMD to push the GP7. Or the costs associated with fabricating the longer shell of an SD7 and designing and producing its larger trucks came into play at Lionel. To save money, estimators and production supervisors had advised going with a GP7.

The idea makes sense considering Lionel intended the GP7 for the low end of the line, where it wouldn't compete with the Train Master. The firm adhered to a strategy of offering deluxe and basic locomotives with similar looks.

Ho-hum sets

Individuals planning the cataloged roster for 1955 relegated the 2028 and 2328 to the O-27 line. The Milwaukee Road GP7 they elevated to the O gauge line.

The 14½"-long 2338 pulled a basic work train in 1955 and was available for separate sale. For 1956, the Milwaukee Road GP7 fell to O-27 status to lead two better five-car outfits. Set no. 709/1559W even boasted a pair of operating cars.

Lionel deleted the Milwaukee Road GP7 after a second year. By then, a different diesel decorated for that railroad (the no. 2378 F3 A and B duo) held sway.

More information

- $25.00 ($224.48)
- Scarce one has full orange band
- Early translucent shell gave way to opaque one as light shone through
- Accessory Catalog for 1956 showed model with tilted railroad herald

2240 Wabash Electro-Motive F3 A-B Units

Wouldn't you have loved to spend some time with the brain trust at Lionel during the postwar era? Only then might we have learned why prototype railroads, ignored for generations, suddenly found their names and heralds on new items.

1956

Take the Wabash Ry. Overlooked throughout the prewar era and for the first decade of the postwar, it inspired four diesels and an operating boxcar over four years in the late 1950s. Among them were the no. 2240 F3 A and B units.

Introducing the Wabash

The Wabash was one of several lines crossing the heart of the Midwest. At its peak, the railroad boasted main lines stretching from Buffalo, N.Y., in the east as far west as Kansas City, Mo. Tracks reached Detroit and Chicago and down to St. Louis to form a compact and busy network.

While the Wabash operated freight trains, it gained renown for passenger trains, in particular beauties between Chicago and St. Louis during the streamliner era. Stainless-steel coaches and dome cars looked elegant behind diesels dressed in deep blue with white and gray details.

Lionel jumps in

Executives at Lionel seized on the Wabash in 1955 as the inspiration for one more F3 A-B duo. The no. 2367 graced the O gauge line as a set component and a separate-sale item. The A unit came with a three-position reverse unit and twin vertically mounted motors. Magne-Traction and a horn were there, too.

A year later, Lionel shifted the Wabash A-B combination to its O-27 roster and renumbered the pair as 2240. Available separately, the F3 duo also served as the motive power for outfit no. 712/1563W, a five-car freight train.

The basic mechanical features of the 2240 diesel remained unchanged from those installed on the 2367—with one notable exception. Like other F3s placed in the O-27 line, the powered A unit had only a single vertical motor.

Pretty in blue

The decoration of the 2240 A-B combination scarcely differed from that of its predecessor. As stated in the Consumer Catalog for 1956, "deep-sea blue and gleaming white combine to make a symphony of color and power on wheels."

Lionel painted the blue-plastic shells a rich shade of blue. Masks enabled laborers to finish the roofs and upper portion of the bodies in gray. Screen-printing added white to the lower section of each side. Lastly came the eye-catching broken white stripes on both units.

Of course, most loved was the decal emblem on the nose replicating the flag herald used by the Wabash. The name of the railroad came emblazoned in yellow on the white section, thanks to hot stamping.

Additional features included the blue-painted chassis and pilot, chemically blackened side frames, and one-piece ornamental horns on the roof. By this time, portholes on the mold of the F3 had been closed up. Lionel installed an operating knuckle coupler on the pilot and fixed "self-centering" couplers at all the ends.

One other element deserves attention because it differentiated the 2240 from the 2367. The ladder on the door of the cab—which was raised on the 2367 A unit—was molded into the shell for the 2240. Otherwise, they looked identical.

Only a year

Lionel cataloged the 2240 combination for just one year. The A and B units vanished from the line as fast and mysteriously as had the O gauge models. Did a provision of the company's agreement with the Wabash limit their runs to a single year? Had the toy train market snubbed them?

Questions about the 2240 refuse to die. No explanation has ever surfaced about why Lionel didn't put a matching no. 3424 Wabash brakeman car in the set it pulled. What a striking tribute that would have made to a once-famous railroad.

More information

- $29.95 ($264.98)
- B unit came fully painted
- Center stripe on B unit extended only partially across each side
- Duo measured 26" in length

2350 New Haven General Electric EP-5 Electric

Two noteworthy trends shaping the line heralded for 1956 coincided in one of the three impressive locomotives depicted on the front cover of the Consumer Catalog. Between a smoking Berkshire and a gleaming GG1 the artist poised a new electric by General Electric, decked out in a stylish new scheme from the New Haven RR.

Lionel's embrace of GE gave an interesting twist to its roster. Executives negotiated a deal with the New Haven that yielded locomotives and rolling stock over the next few years. The magnificent electric launching both trends was the no. 2350.

Jets for Lionel

Excuse leaders at Lionel if they were obsessed with jets in 1956. Not airplanes but the EP-5 electric-profile locomotives the New Haven had purchased from GE. These fast flyers under catenary were nicknamed "Jets" by public relations firms and journalists. Executives, hypnotized by the Jets' coverage in regional newspapers and national television, made adding an O gauge model a priority. Copywriters proclaimed the black-orange-white EP-5 "The Most Colorful 'O' Gauge Loco In Lionel's History."

Borrowed parts

Designers, studying GE blueprints of the 4,000-horsepower Ignitron Rectifier, fabricated a body using the cutup shells from F3 diesels. Then model makers formed a unique assembly for the 15¾"-long EP-5 electric. Supervisors cast the bodies using black, gray, or yellow plastics.

The vertically mounted motor installed on each 2350 had been born a year before. Engineers at Lionel had fine-tuned it for the no. 2028 Pennsylvania RR GP7 unveiled for the 1955 line.

Relying on die-cast metal trucks developed for F3 and GP7 models might seem like a boo-boo. After all, General Motors and not General Electric manufactured those diesels. But engineers always hunted for shortcuts that might save money. So they searched through their cupboards in search of other parts to add to the EP-5s. Chief Engineer Joseph Bonanno must have smiled when he learned the new model was going to use the well-tested three-position reverse unit and operating horn. His GG1s would donate their pantographs!

1956

Color variations

The modernistic paint scheme—its bold orange and white stripes jumping off the black body plus the gigantic railroad initials—fueled demand. Diagrams of the scheme linked to the short and controversial tenure of Patrick McGinnis as president of the New Haven influenced the look of the O gauge EP-5. Lionel began by spraying the plastic shells black. Laborers put on the orange and white bands with silk-screen printing. Breaking them at spots (access doors and sand ports) was unavoidable due to the process adopted.

Paragraphs have been written about differences in the arrangement of colors and letters and the type of nose trim on the 2350 during its three years in the catalog. Let's stick to the most common and least expensive. The "N" was white, and the "H" was orange. The railroad name was hot-stamped white. An adhesive-backed decal did the trim on the nose at each end.

Good uses

After the time and money allocated to the development of the EP-5, Lionel would have been foolish to limit its impact. Capitalizing on the electric proved important to decision-makers once they learned A.C. Gilbert Co., their chief rival, was bringing out its own New Haven EP-5.

The 2350 led two five-car freight sets in 1956. Both 802/2259W and 804/2263W included a new boxcar decorated for the New Haven. In 1957, so did outfit no. 818/2279W, the last one cataloged with that EP-5. Featuring a car matched with the locomotive was a wise tactic Lionel had seldom used with its sets.

More information

- $29.95 ($264.98)
- Price raised to $35 in 1957
- "375" in number plate came from actual New Haven EP-5
- Vertical cracks appeared on cab noses over time

2368 Baltimore & Ohio Electro-Motive F3 A-B Units

The turning point in the history of Lionel's F3s came toward the close of 1955. Until then, sales executives and designers had been limited in the railroads they could recommend because the paint schemes had to be simple enough for the shells to be masked by hand.

A longtime employee envisioned a better solution. His experiments succeeded, much to the joy of engineers and salesmen.

Models from the late 1950s attest to the importance of this breakthrough. The best may be the no. 2368 Baltimore & Ohio F3 A and B units.

Paint masks

The breakthrough came from General Foreman Romualdo Camuso. He fashioned a contraption consisting of metal sheets on hinges that could be lifted to fit around a blank plastic body. With this device, a laborer could spray paint on a designated area of the shell without marring anything that wasn't being exposed.

Thanks to Camuso's invention, shells could be spray-painted in less time and have more colors added. Lionel could look at virtually any prototype scheme and consider adopting it for F3 or GP7 rosters.

1956

Members of the Engineering Department proceeded to research dozens of American railroads. Joseph Bonanno and others initiated the conversations, and Louis Melchionne would, if asked, create paint diagrams and preliminary models. Lionel's archives contain mock-ups of F3s decorated for the Atlantic Coast Line, Bessemer & Lake Erie, Minneapolis & St. Louis, Texas & Pacific, and others.

Try the B&O

Executives went out of their way to solicit aid from regional lines eager to splash their heralds and slogans across models of their rolling stock, diesels, and electrics.

Already on board by 1954 were the Western Pacific and the Rock Island. Next to arrive was the Wabash. The New Haven climbed on the bandwagon in a big way in 1956 with an electric locomotive, a boxcar, and an automobile car.

The Baltimore & Ohio made a deal with Lionel that led to two near-scale boxcars, a compact diesel from General Electric, and the first member of a small fleet of Rail Diesel Cars—all in 1956.

Above everything else shone the latest entry in the group based on the F3 diesel built by General Motors. The 2368 A and B units pleased with their blue-gray-white scheme, which would have been prohibitively expensive before Camuso's masks.

Quiet beauties

To decorate each 2368, workers typically began with a blue plastic shell they painted step by step until they had a roof done in gray, a nose and upper portion done in white, and side stripes done in black. Over each stripe went accents, the road name, and built data hot-stamped yellow.

Additional care went into rubber-stamping blue and yellow stripes across the nose of the powered A unit until they kissed painted side stripes. One-piece ornamental horns, number boards, and headlight lenses heightened the realism.

The greatness of the 26"-long A-B combinations extended from their beauty to their operation. The 2368s benefited from a second advance made in 1955.

Lionel went from horizontally mounted motors to vertically mounted ones. The change not only reduced the "growl" produced by the reverse units, but it also improved the quickness of the F3s. Combined with Magne-Traction, those advances under the frame helped Lionel's top diesels pull more cars at faster speeds.

One and done

Lionel placed the 2368 A-Bs in a superb O gauge freight set for 1956. Among the most prized outfits of the period, the no. 807/2269W failed to include either of the new Baltimore & Ohio near-scale boxcars.

Odd as the omission of a matching car was, it was surpassed by the decision to delete the B&O A-B duo after one year.

More information

- $39.95 ($353.45)
- Blue-painted bodies likely were replacement shells
- Black chassis with black-painted pilot and chemically blackened side frames

625 Lehigh Valley 44-Ton Center-Cab

By 1956, deciding which models to add to Lionel's motive power roster was taxing the imagination of designers and sales personnel. They had finished miniature versions of cab units, road diesels, and switchers from American Locomotive Co., Fairbanks-Morse, and General Motors, among the largest domestic manufacturers.

Members of the Engineering Department studied publications about modern railroading and perused annual reports released by railways across the U.S. Model makers and draftsmen observed real trains.

Inspiration might come after consulting other locomotive makers. Thus an often-forgotten General Electric diesel sparked the development of a new model for the O-27 grouping of locomotives that included the no. 625 Lehigh Valley unit.

A trio of stars

Press releases from GE introduced Lionel to three newcomers. First, an 80-ton electric ordered by a mining firm in the South American country of Chile led to the creation of the no. 520 box-cab. A larger and sleeker electric soon to ply the New Haven RR inspired the no. 2350 New Haven EP-5 (followed over the next three years by three more models with different paint schemes and railroad names).

1957

The third locomotive derived from a GE prototype was a diminutive 44-ton center-cab diesel whose roots could be traced to a labor agreement made in 1937. That pact mandated the presence of a fireman on any locomotive weighing at least 90,000 pounds or 45 tons. In response, GE developed a model rated at 44 tons.

Between 1940 and 1956, GE built about 350 of those diesel units. Ironically, Lionel introduced its model the same year GE discontinued its 44-tonner.

Lionel models in four colors

Once the Engineering Department had fastened on a 44-ton center-cab as a logical addition to the low-end of the roster, it began exploring how to assemble a replica quickly and inexpensively. The answer involved utilizing existing parts and tooling, mostly from Lionel's NW2 diesel switcher. The body shell of the 44-tonner was, however, newly done.

Designers called for a single vertically mounted motor, Magne-Traction on one axle, a three-position reverse unit, and operating couplers on the four center-cabs making their debut in 1956. They saved money by omitting a working horn.

Cutting corners explained why the 625, new in 1957, had an unpainted red plastic shell on its black-painted sheet-metal frame. To gussy up the second 44-tonner decorated for the Lehigh Valley (after no. 627), designers specified painting the middle black. Hot-stamped white graphics and a white stripe painted across the lower portion of the body duplicated what had been done with the 627.

Simplicity dictated an ornamental bell and an ornamental whistle on either side of the cab. Fortunately, the 625 had a working headlight.

Too small

The Consumer Catalog for 1956 had claimed the 44-tonners were given "the same unique 'steeple cab' as the GE prototype" with "complete and accurate" body details. What wasn't discussed was the fact that Lionel's model was grossly oversized. If the 625 and its kin had been scale models, their dimensions would have approximated those of a motorized unit.

Lionel's marketing plan for 1957 called for the 625 Lehigh Valley to pull an O-27 five-car freight outfit (no. 726/1571). Planners relegated the diminutive diesel to the list of separate-sale items a year later before eliminating it from the line.

Curiously, the men setting out what Lionel would offer in 1957 had thought it prudent to introduce a second center-cab decorated for Lehigh Valley.

Imagine that Lionel had two Lehigh Valley 44-tonners on its O-27 roster and the prototype railroad owned only three!

More information

- $18.95 ($162.29)
- 11¾" long
- Instruction sheet claimed it could pull eight lightweight cars
- Equipped with fixed plastic knuckle couplers

228 Canadian National Alco FA A Unit

Devoting special energy to penetrating the Canadian toy market had never been a pressing need at Lionel for one simple reason. Children north of the border felt the same love for electric trains as did youngsters in the U.S. Therefore, the firm needed to do little more than advertise its products across Canada, make them available to retail accounts, and offer transformers certain to operate there.

Even so, executives sensed in the 1950s they should take more action to ensure Lionel's dominance in Canada. A passenger outfit came about in 1957. Later came a pair of little-known diesel locomotives as motive power for a few promotional sets. These engines, nos. 227 and 228 Canadian National Alcos, deserve more attention.

1960

Looking to Canadian railroads

After World War II, Lionel strengthened its presence in Canada by working closely with the heads of its sales office in Toronto. Roy Clarke and his son, William, represented the toy giant and made sure displays of its trains and accessories occupied places of prominence in department stores and retail chains across Canada.

A notable change occurred in November 1955. Chief Engineer Joseph Bonanno contacted the Canadian National and the Canadian Pacific. In his correspondence, he stated that Lionel was exploring the addition of Canadian passenger equipment to its O gauge line. He requested photos and information.

Files in Lionel's archives revealed all subsequent correspondence originated from the Canadian Pacific. Nothing to indicate how the Canadian National responded to Bonanno's appeal. The CP sent drawings, paint diagrams, and a booklet about the *Canadian*, a transcontinental train that made its maiden trip in 1955. Those materials led to the development of F3 diesels and matching streamlined cars decorated for the CP. They filled the no. 2296W Super O set cataloged in 1957.

Another effort in 1960

Lionel offered the Canadian Pacific locomotives and streamlined cars only for that year. Likely believing demand had been met, executives failed to advise another production run or additional equipment painted and lettered for the CP.

The Canadian National finally had a moment—nothing more—in the sun.

Two virtually identical Alco FA units arrived in 1960. Neither the no. 227 nor the no. 228 appeared in the Consumer Catalog. The latter did get brief note as a separate-sale item in the Advance Catalog for 1961.

Both diesels had plastic shells (black, blue, and gray plastic are known) painted a medium shade of green with two narrow yellow stripes across the upper third of the body. The railroad name, catalog number, and "Built by Lionel" finished the graphics, which were hot-stamped yellow.

Interestingly, the 227 had a closed pilot while the 228 had an open pilot.

Inside the shell, fastened to a blackened stamped-steel frame, the two diverged. The 227 lacked a reverse unit and any traction aid except for the weight riveted to the rear of the body. The only feature this diesel boasted was a headlight. The 228 came with a two-position reverse unit and two-axle Magne-Traction. It was equipped with a working headlight but not a horn.

Promotional uses only

Lionel used the CN diesels only as the motive power for promotional outfits. The 227 handled more assignments than did the 228, being packed in 10 uncataloged sets. Outfit nos. 1113 and 1115 from 1960, both aimed at Canadian markets, included a 227. Four additional promotional outfits used a 227 Alco FA in 1961, followed by three in 1963 and then one in 1964.

The 228 pulled two promotional sets in 1960, nos. X-533NA and X-550NA (both marketed in the U.S.). This relatively scarce diesel appeared in another outfit in 1961 (and might be substituted in cataloged set no. 1643) and one more in 1962.

More information

- $19.95 ($160.57)
- Open pilot with small or large ledge
- Packed in corrugated cardboard box stamped NO. 228P on ends
- Led promotional sets X-625 in 1961 and 19203 in 1962

2322 Virginian Fairbanks-Morse H-24-66 Train Master

No greater challenge exists for postwar experts than trying to explain actions that appear now to be inconsistent and without logic or business acumen. Examples abound from the 1960s. That decade offers case after case of Lionel adopting courses that seem puzzling.

1965

A matter as simple and straightforward as which locomotives to keep in production leaves knowledgeable collectors shaking their heads in confusion and dismay. Santa Fe F3 diesels and Lionel Lines 2-8-4 Berkshires survived, and various Geeps went in and out of the cataloged line with no rhyme or reason. In 1965, out of nowhere, the Train Master came out of retirement.

Three to zero

Between 1954 and 1958, the O gauge roster had included at least one replica of the Fairbanks-Morse H-24-66 Train Master. Lionel had released models decorated for three railroads and designated them as the motive power for at least one outfit.

In real life, the 2,400-horsepower road diesel equipped with six-wheel axles was met with indifference in 1953. Within a year, Lionel had finished a model. The no. 2321 Lackawanna arrived first, followed by the nos. 2331 Virginian Railway in 1955 and 2341 Jersey Central in 1956. The Virginian Train Master lasted longest—until 1958.

Then nothing for half a dozen years. None of the FMs went into a promotional set. Inventory must have dwindled to zero.

New Virginian

Then a revival! Who advocated bringing back a Train Master in 1965? Why the Virginian and not the other road names from the past or a brand-new one?

Another question touched on whether anyone recognized the shortcomings of the first grouping of Train Masters. First, the paint schemes used on the three were not faithful representations of what their prototypes had adopted. Second, the plastic shells had been cast a bit too small, so when they were screwed to the metal chassis the holes eventually developed cracks. Certainly not a big problem, but still one that ought to have been avoided.

Viewed from a positive perspective, the revived Virginian Train Master, now given the number 2322, boasted all the deluxe features of its namesake. To be specific, it had two motors, Magne-Traction, a three-position reverse unit, operating lights at the ends, a horn, and operating couplers. Can't forget the applied wire handrails and two ornamental horns.

The new Virginian looked identical to the most common version of the 2331. Both had a blue body shell with wide yellow-painted upper and lower stripes, ends painted in a crisscross fashion, and rubber-stamped yellow lettering. A decal of the railway's herald appeared at each end. Decals of the Fairbanks-Morse emblem brightened the cab sides.

By the way, scarce variations of the 2322 have been reported in reference books. According to those guides, an unknown number of blue or black shells came painted both blue and yellow.

Slight difference

Removing the shells revealed a minor difference between the older Virginian units and the 2322. Lionel substituted green wire for the black it originally used for the armature winding. Sadly, designers didn't improve the casting. Cracks at the screw holes showed up.

Planners, either ignorant or dismissive of flaws in the shells, assigned the 2322 to a pair of freight outfits in the two years it was cataloged. They crammed the same rolling stock into the boxes for no. 12820 in 1965 and no. 12850 in 1966: two animated cars, four non-operating cars, and an illuminated porthole caboose. The sole difference? More track and a pair of remote-controlled switches went into the later outfit.

Only the return of Super O outfit no. 13150 (the Hudson freight) for a third year surpassed the 12850 in 1966. Neither set survived another year, which essentially slammed the door on postwar glory.

More information

- $65 ($496.57)
- 16½" long
- Used in promotional outfit no. 12820-100 in 1965
- Led promotional outfit no. 12850X in 1966

2346 Boston & Maine Electro-Motive GP9 Road Diesel

Learning about the corporate history of Lionel during the postwar era sheds light on how executives shaped the products being manufactured and marketed. Plainly, they did nothing arbitrarily or thoughtlessly. The notion that Lionel was making mere toys and therefore hardly cared what left its factory holds no water and insults its leaders.

A locomotive cataloged toward the end of the period illustrates more than initially assumed. The no. 2346 Boston & Maine GP9 road diesel shows how three sales tactics converged to influence the men struggling in the 1960s to bring out successful electric trains.

1965

Meet the Geep

Lionel placed the 14¼"-long 2346 in its line in 1965 and 1966. The road diesel, described as "Scaled to perfection" in the 1965 Consumer Catalog, had a black plastic body painted blue. Standing out were the cab and ends, both painted black, and the white-painted frame with railings.

The colors exuded elegance and dignity. The graphics heightened the appeal. Designers specified hot-stamping the road name and product number white; the modernistic Boston & Maine logo should be hot-stamped both black and white.

Inside the shell, technicians installed the best package available for any O gauge Geep. A single horizontally mounted motor with a three-position reverse unit supplied ample power. Magne-Traction upgraded the performance of the diesel.

A richly bellowing horn complemented the ornamental horn added to each side of the shell. Operating headlights illuminated the number boards at each end.

First the railroad

Two regional railroads dominated the scene in New England during postwar days. Lionel had introduced motive power and rolling stock decorated for the New Haven RR in 1956. It turned to the Boston & Maine the next year with a boxcar. Over the next few years, Lionel honored the B&M, whose network of track exceeded 1,500 miles, with Alco diesels as well as a Southern Pacific-type caboose.

The 2346 GP9 carried forward the toymaker's intention of keeping B&M models in its line. Consumers praised the B&M's sophisticated paint scheme and slick herald. Many were familiar with its passenger trains, including the *Flying Yankee*, which had inspired a model from Lionel in 1935.

Then the model

Engineers and marketing executives faced the challenge in the late 1950s and into the 1960s of building a broad and up-to-date roster while keeping down costs. They succeeded by making wise use of tooling.

Lionel had required a new mold for the GP7 introduced in 1955. Thereafter, however, it had only to select road names and color schemes to increase the list of road diesels. They went from the Pennsylvania RR to Milwaukee Road to Wabash.

Cleverly, engineering figured out how to broaden the roster with another road diesel in 1958 without having to invest in massive tooling. They stuck a molded piece of plastic on the roof of the shell and declared the part a "dynamic brake blister." The presence of such a component meant, Lionel insisted, the diesel was now a GP9.

Need to reuse

A third trend—in addition to a focus on regional railroads and a push to increase the roster at little expense—assumed importance. Planners revived models customers had prized in the past (a scale Hudson steamer or near-scale boxcars) or had more recently underestimated. They hoped a second chance would bolster the bottom line.

Lionel had tried its luck with a Boston & Maine GP9 in 1961 and 1962. The no. 2359 had led a space-themed Super O outfit each year. Then the Geep vanished.

Returning as the 2346 three years later. The two B&M road diesels were identical, except for the numbers. Same paint scheme. Same operating features. Were folks glad—or indifferent—to see the GP9 return?

More information

- $40.00 ($305.58)—2359 had been priced at $29.95 in 1961
- Led outfit no. 12800 in 1965 and 1966 (included Boston & Maine boxcar and caboose)
- Included in promotional outfit no. 12800X in 1966

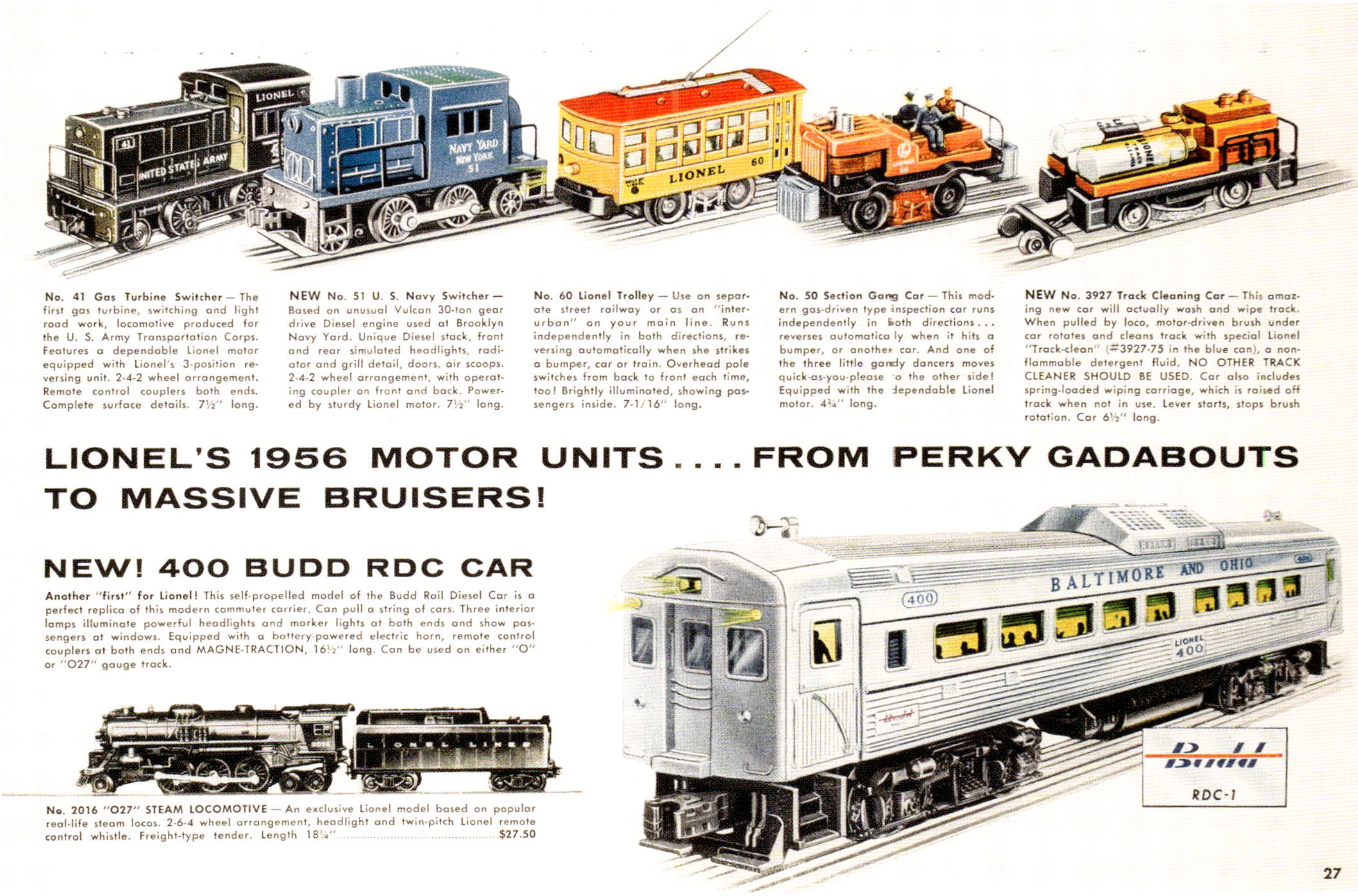

No. 41 Gas Turbine Switcher — The first gas turbine, switching and light road work, locomotive produced for the U. S. Army Transportation Corps. Features a dependable Lionel motor equipped with Lionel's 3-position reversing unit. 2-4-2 wheel arrangement. Remote control couplers both ends. Complete surface details. 7½" long.

NEW No. 51 U. S. Navy Switcher — Based on unusual Vulcan 30-ton gear drive Diesel engine used at Brooklyn Navy Yard. Unique Diesel stack, front and rear simulated headlights, radiator and grill detail, doors, air scoops. 2-4-2 wheel arrangement, with operating coupler on front and back. Powered by sturdy Lionel motor. 7½" long.

No. 60 Lionel Trolley — Use on separate street railway or as an "interurban" on your main line. Runs independently in both directions, reversing automatically when she strikes a bumper, car or train. Overhead pole switches from back to front each time, too! Brightly illuminated, showing passengers inside. 7-1/16" long.

No. 50 Section Gang Car — This modern gas-driven type inspection car runs independently in both directions . . . reverses automatically when it hits a bumper, or another car. And one of the three little gandy dancers moves quick-as-you-please to the other side! Equipped with the dependable Lionel motor. 4¾" long.

NEW No. 3927 Track Cleaning Car — This amazing new car will actually wash and wipe track. When pulled by loco, motor-driven brush under car rotates and cleans track with special Lionel "Track-clean" (#3927-75 in the blue can), a non-flammable detergent fluid. NO OTHER TRACK CLEANER SHOULD BE USED. Car also includes spring-loaded wiping carriage, which is raised off track when not in use. Lever starts, stops brush rotation. Car 6½" long.

LIONEL'S 1956 MOTOR UNITS . . . . FROM PERKY GADABOUTS TO MASSIVE BRUISERS!

NEW! 400 BUDD RDC CAR

Another "first" for Lionel! This self-propelled model of the Budd Rail Diesel Car is a perfect replica of this modern commuter carrier. Can pull a string of cars. Three interior lamps illuminate powerful headlights and marker lights at both ends and show passengers at windows. Equipped with a battery-powered electric horn, remote control couplers at both ends and MAGNE-TRACTION, 16½" long. Can be used on either "O" or "O27" gauge track.

No. 2016 "O27" STEAM LOCOMOTIVE — An exclusive Lionel model based on popular real-life steam locos. 2-6-4 wheel arrangement, headlight and twin-pitch Lionel remote control whistle. Freight-type tender. Length 18¼" $27.50

RDC-1

27

Motorized Units

Developing motorized units, along with creating operating accessories, assuredly provided the most fun for the ingenious members of the Engineering Department. Like the youngsters buying their products, they felt free to play with trains. They combined disparate parts and discovered what they could make flip, flash, or fly!

Inspiration from outside

Start with a definition. A motorized unit is any toy able to propel itself on two or three rails thanks to the motor installed in it. Technically speaking, the item envisioned stands apart from a steam or diesel locomotive, which served to pull railcars. A motorized unit, whether based on an actual rail vehicle or derived from a toy designer's imagination, should be viewed as an independent model.

The recipe for success does begin with a measure or two of realism. Most of the motorized units introduced in the 1950s and early 1960s were derived from what could be seen on full-size railroads or industrial lines. Engineers did plenty of research and studied piles of photographs.

Then designers dumped into their mental mixing bowls dollops of whimsy and crazy. Their imaginations ran wild, as they madly experimented with spinning parts, twirling wheels, sparking motors, twisting figures, and blinking lights.

Long history

The golden age of motorized units encompassed the 1950s. Lionel, along with manufacturers major and minor, brought out amusing and exciting models. Though not alone in the market during the postwar era, Lionel could claim with justification it had been first. No one in the United States did motorized units better!

After all, didn't the wood gondolas Joshua Lionel Cowen equipped with an electric motor to use in window displays in 1900 qualify as motorized units? The painted steel models of streetcars and interurbans crowding the early line fit the fundamental description. So did mechanical handcars seemingly operated by Mickey Mouse, Donald Duck, or Santa Claus during the middle 1930s. Lionel had embraced the concept since its inception.

Even with such a rich background, Lionel seemed reluctant to return to the field after World War II. Perhaps executives feared introducing models people might deride as cute little toys at the moment when their company sought to associate its electric trains with power, size, and realism.

Hesitant or uninterested in acting to fill a gap, Lionel all but invited a few others to

do so. Pretty soon, several motorized handcars from competitors were fighting for space in toy and department stores.

Various railroad equipment

Did the appearance of many motorized units startle and anger decision-makers at Lionel? Development Engineer Frank Pettit, who had contributed to the design of windup handcars in the 1930s, hastily gathered his tools and materials, working until he had finished a prototype for the no. 50 Section Gang Car released in 1954. Lionel entered the arena with a bang!

Chief Engineer Joseph Bonanno tricked out the 50, putting a motor on its chassis. The unit spun ahead until it smacked into a train or another obstruction. Then the rubber bumper absorbing the force of the impact activated the reversing slide assembly, causing the gang car to reverse direction and dash off again.

Folks fell in love with the gang car. Its success pushed Lionel to make it a mainstay through 1964 and to accelerate development of additional units. A traditional trolley came next. The no. 60 Lionelville Rapid Transit made its debut in 1955, sticking around for the next three years.

Motorized units of a different sort—models of little diesels—joined the line in 1955. Remember how engineers kept searching for modern equipment to replicate for three-rail enthusiasts? The curiosity and determination leading them to investigate novel motive power also guided them to odorous gas-turbine yard pushers and Vulcan industrial switch engines.

Punched off the assembly lines like cookies from a sheet of dough came pint-sized switchers. The parade took off in 1955, launched by the no. 41 U.S. Army 2-4-2 gas turbine. The barely different no. 51 Navy Yard 2-4-2 Vulcan burst in a year later. The no. 42 Picatinny Arsenal, a knockoff of the 41, followed in 1957.

Also in 1957, clever designers exploited the motor and body shell they had fabricated for their switchers and, after fastening a new part to the nose, proudly announced something new. Specifically, by securing a miniature plow to the front of a Vulcan switcher they introduced the no. 53 Rio Grande Snow Plow.

Ballast, missiles, and more

The array of motorized units accompanying the 53 boggles the mind. By then, Lionel was showcasing no. 3927, a unique item that, besides entertaining viewers, cleaned and polished the track it traveled over. Complementary units simulated actual vehicles whose functions involved pressing down stones for ballast and unloading wood ties. The cataloged roster even contained a specialized automobile that had been fitted with flanged wheels to drive over railroad lines.

Rail Diesel Cars, motorized streamlined coaches from the Budd Company, had interested toymakers for years. Credit Auburn Model Trains and Louis Marx & Co. with the first O gauge RDCs. Lionel arrived late, but soon led with two motorized and two non-powered units that it cataloged between 1956 and 1958.

The gallery concluded with a few space- and military-oriented motorized units and then what was a genuine throwback. For 1959, engineers strapped on their thinking caps to devise the no. 44 U.S. Army Mobile Missile Launcher, a true accessory on eight wheels. A year afterward, sales personnel advised adding the no. 45, a missile launcher decked out in olive green for the U.S. Marine Corps.

Momentum ebbed in the early 1960s, and the final units sputtered out of the cataloged line. Other than the gang car and the ballast tamper, fans of the cool and creative self-propelled items had nothing to amuse or amaze them after 1963.

With the exception of an auxiliary piece arriving in 1962. The no. 65 Hand Car hearkened back to an earlier era because of its appearance and operation.

If anything, the 65 represented a retreat from everything contemporary in the area of motorized units. It had more in common with the models rival firms pioneered a decade before or the mechanical handcars Lionel marketed three decades earlier than it did with mobile missile launchers and Vulcan units.

The short yet notable tale of motorized units may have closed on a conservative and not an innovative note. Yet it told a lot about how designers added animation and invention to the postwar train line.

41 U.S. Army Gas Turbine Switcher

Barriers existed when executives contemplated how to broaden the postwar line. They respected unwritten rules when thinking about rolling stock or accessories to add. Everything should earn the approval of parents and other adults buying trains.

Any product advertised on a railcar must be safe and appropriate. Alcoholic beverages and cigarettes had no place on Lionel Lines. Neither did military items. Not since 1917, when the U.S. entered World War I, had Lionel blurred the distinction between its educational toys and equipment for armed forces.

1955

First to cross the line was the no. 41 U.S. Army Gas Turbine Switcher. The 2-4-2 broke ground for a virtual onslaught of cars, accessories, and more in the military camp.

No war toys

Lionel's leaders had long ago adopted a firm stance on the need for their enterprise to avoid manufacturing what critics called "war toys." Everything changed in 1955, probably because the mood of the country and boys' tastes in playthings were shifting.

To maintain sales and appear as up to date as any toymaker, Lionel started labeling models with the names and insignia of branches of the American armed forces. That trend continued through the rest of the decade and accelerated in the 1960s.

Creating motorized units

Although the gas turbine should be interpreted as a break with a tradition at Lionel, it also represented the next stage in a trend launched in 1954. Lionel had brought out with great fanfare the first of its motorized units. Those compact, self-propelled models were intended to bring in sales from modelers who owned outfits and sought eagerly to expand their rosters.

The same approach to marketing that portrayed signals, freight loaders, bridges, switches, and tunnels as purposeful secondary purchases, promoted the nos. 50 Section Gang Car and 60 Lionelville Rapid Transit Trolley as additions to an O or O-27 roster. The choices were ingenious, yet a bit fanciful. The gang car derived from maintenance-of-way equipment, and the trolley captured the look of streetcars. But the extent to which they duplicated full-size vehicles would have been hard to prove.

The 41 U.S. Army switcher followed a different path. Designers had explored railroad publications to learn about the newest and somewhat exotic items being developed and sold. Among the newcomers gaining traction was an experimental unit from Davenport Locomotive Works with a gasoline turbine motor. Its limited power was perfect for maneuvering around a yard and handling a few cars.

In the army!

Engineers sought in 1955 to broaden the types of motorized units available when they came up with the 41. Further, they hoped to lure kids entranced with the military and its latest equipment. How simple to hot-stamp "United States Army" white across the side of the black cab and then add the name and stylized emblem of the Transportation Corps to forge a unique piece to build up the roster.

So was born the 7½"-long Gas Turbine Switcher. It performed steadily, thanks to a reliable motor and three-position reverse mechanism. No point in adding Magne-Traction; greater pulling power and climbing ability were not in the cards.

The abbreviated list of features included an ornamental horn, a headlight lens at each end of the unit, and chemically blackened metal railings along the sides and ends. Operating knuckle couplers front and rear got the okay; a work headlight didn't.

In 1957, Lionel took the same tooling to create the no. 42 Picatinny Arsenal, which also had a 2-4-2 wheel arrangement. The name came from a facility in New Jersey, not far from the Lionel factory. The train maker had contracts to design precision instruments for the military that were carried out at the Picatinny Arsenal.

More information

- $11.50 ($103.26)
- Scarce versions came with black-painted shells
- Cataloged 1955 to 1957
- Instruction sheet described normal load of three or four freight cars

60 Lionelville Rapid Transit Trolley

Sometimes the best ideas are actually revivals of old ones. Manufacturers, including businesses producing miniature electric trains, return to what has worked for them or even a competitor in the past, and breathe new life into it.

Lionel accessories and motorized units seemed ripe for revivals. A station or loader could, if modified slightly, be made a worthwhile addition. More telling were those small items equipped with a motor whose form or function hearkened back to what Lionel had done before. A terrific example was the no. 60 Lionelville Rapid Transit Trolley.

Old business

When Lionel introduced the 60 in 1955, grizzled veterans of the toy train fraternity might have been excused for grumbling about how the little plastic trolley paled in comparison to what the company had marketed almost half a century earlier.

The text in the Consumer Catalog for 1955 claimed the model of a Birney type of trolley was "new!" The Lionelville Rapid Transit Trolley could be used, the copywriter claimed "on a separate street railway, or as an 'interurban' on your main line."

1955

"New"? Didn't anyone remember how, 40 or so years earlier, Lionel had cataloged trolleys or, more accurately, streetcars? They had been big business, right from the time Lionel introduced Standard gauge trains in 1906. The firm had offered sturdy models fabricated out of sheet steel and equipped with four or eight wheels and featuring open or closed platforms through 1916.

True, Lionel had not made an O gauge trolley during the decades immediately preceding and following World War I. Neither had it endeavored to do so during the first part of the postwar era.

Back in

But in 1955, a year after Development Engineer Frank Pettit devised the no. 50 Section Gang Car, something clicked. Perhaps he just showed how the mechanism he had developed could be adapted to a trolley.

Pettit had equipped the 50 with a special motor and drive mechanism. When the Gang Car rammed a bumper or another train, a shifting metal plate slid backwards. That briefly broke the motor's electrical circuit before reconnecting it, but in a way that caused the motor's armature to reverse direction. The back-and-forth bumper action generated interest and laughs.

Quickly, Pettit figured out how to use the same mechanism on a trolley. On making contact, the 60 shifted course and the pole on its roof swung around. None of the prewar trolleys ever did anything like that.

Younger executives with no memory of Lionel's old trolleys, would have enjoyed the animation. The elderly Joshua Cowen must have been pleased at how they were using an old concept to invigorate the line.

Few changes

Most of the features on the Lionelville Rapid Transit Trolley stayed the same during its four years in the catalog. The unit had an unpainted yellow plastic body and unpainted red roof, a rotating overhead pole, and internal lighting. Window strips secured to the interior depicted the silhouettes of passengers.

The earliest examples had hot-stamped black lettering (a few rare examples had red markings), roof slots, two-part spring bumpers, and metal motorman silhouettes. Soon the motorman silhouettes were eliminated. Then hot-stamped blue lettering became the norm over the remaining years.

Later variations used a solid one-piece bumper. Then designers added four more clerestory vents. The lamp, once partially painted silver, was left unpainted once the underside of the roof was fitted with an aluminized paper reflector.

Watching a Lionelville Rapid Transit play bumper cars on a main line or a separate track was a joy. That motorized unit likely put a smile on the face of Cowen as he recalled how Standard gauge trolleys and interurbans had helped his fledgling business grow into a national institution.

More information

- $7.95 ($71.39)
- 7 1/16" long
- Cataloged from 1955 through 1958
- Variations related to lettering, clerestory vents, and bumpers

3927 Track Cleaning Car

Motorized units served an important purpose for sales executives. Individuals at the helm never imagined someone would buy a lightweight diesel, a snowplow, or another item as a primary purchase. An outfit, including a locomotive and railcars, should be first. But to keep tempting consumers, there had to be a diverse assortment of auxiliary items. Accessories were obvious; then came motorized units.

Designers and marketing men wanted to appeal to Lionel fans in different ways to entice them to acquire a motorized unit. Entertaining them opened doors. So did promising prototype realism. A third method, one used infrequently, related to need. Offer modelers something necessary to improving the operation of a train. For that reason, in 1956, Lionel introduced the no. 3927 Track Cleaning Car.

A bit late

How often did Lionel operators worry about the cleanliness of their track? Not a concern to cause them to lose sleep. But designers and marketers imagined they could boost sales if they planted the idea in the minds of enthusiasts.

Already, the clever if insidious scheme had helped a competitor. The A.C. Gilbert Co. had introduced a novel piece of rolling stock intended to clean and buff its American Flyer S gauge track. Engineers had for 1952 modified a 10½"-long depressed-center flatcar by installing four felt track wipers. Two were saturated with cleaning fluid to wash the rails; the other wipers dried and seemed to polish them.

1956

The ploy succeeded magnificently. Any S gaugers focused on maintaining sidings and main lines would couple the no. 648 Track Cleaning Car to the engine guiding a freight or work train and let it traverse the layout a time or two.

A version of the specially equipped flatcar equipped with knuckle couplers followed the 648. That model, the no. 948, gave way to the no. 24533 Track Cleaning Car, which lasted through 1966.

Motorized cleaner

Members of the Engineering Department at Lionel, observing how S gauge operators responded to the campaign for cleaner, shinier track, felt strongly motivated to surpass their counterparts at Gilbert. Instead of devising a unique railcar for the task, they upped the ante in 1956 by inventing a motorized track cleaner.

How it did its job was straightforward. Integral to operation, of course, was the motor. Unlike the Flyer car, whose wipers merely rubbed over the rails, the Lionel unit featured a brand-new mechanism that, once manually switched on, rotated a sponge on the no. 3927-47 plate assembly.

Meanwhile, cleaning liquid in the plastic bottle secured to the cab assembly passed from a well on top to the rotating sponge below. The Track Cleaning Car, securely coupled to a locomotive, washed the rails as the saturated sponge turned.

Seconds after washing was done, the procedure ended with the track being dried. The absorbent cotton cylinders attached to the spring-loaded wiping carriage at the rear of the unit dried the rails. Layout owners liked seeing all three shine brightly.

Fresh start

Engineers developed every major component used on the 3927 specifically for that novel motorized unit. Key pieces, notably the frame assembly, handrail and switch assembly, cab assembly, sponge and plate assembly, and wiper carriage assembly, were invented for the 8¼"-long unit. Other parts were borrowed from other motorized items.

Nobody painted the orange plastic body. Laborers did hot-stamp Lionel Lines and the four-digit product number black. The fixed die-cast metal coupler meant the 3927 needed to be coupled to a locomotive or whatever railcar finished the train.

Once designers had completed their part of the process, the advertising and sales teams took over. They avidly pitched the novel unit to Lionel loyalists. Nothing could be more essential for superior performance, they contended, than clean track.

Should consumers agree and put a Track Cleaning Car high on their list of what to buy next, executives were more than ready to sell refill items. They insisted that only Lionel's cleaning fluid would work with a 3927. Soon, the line included cans of no. 3927-75 Track-Clean plus packs of no. 3927-50 track wipes.

More information

- $12.95 ($114.57)
- Cataloged from 1956 to 1960
- Price reduced to $10.95 in 1959
- Listed with "Operating Action Cars" in catalogs

52 Firefighting Car

Scrutinizing the list of motorized units cataloged for 1958 reveals breaks in the story. Gone were the trio of little switchers whose names linked them to the U.S. armed forces. Emphasis shifted from items tangentially connected to the military to some different models with a function related to the maintenance of rights-of-way.

1958

The nos. 53 Rio Grande Snow Plow and 55 Tie-Jector returned. Joining them was an innovative unit combining the pleasures of two toys: trains and fire engines. The no. 52 Firefighting Car dashed over track while helping kids protect their three-rail empires from brush fires and blazes in yards and depots.

Lots of plans

Parents knew boys dreamed of growing up to become firemen. They knew their sons begged for miniature pumper trucks and hook-and-ladder vehicles, almost as passionate about those toys as electric trains.

Obviously, then, a novel plaything blending firefighting equipment with toy trains would have ignited public demand! Yet none of the manufacturers released anything of that nature during the first dozen years of the postwar period.

But, judging from pamphlets and pictures filed away at the Lionel factory, plans for such an item began simmering around 1955. Ronald Saypol, who had moved from selling trains to assisting Executive Vice-President Alan Ginsburg, saw the commercial potential of a firefighting item.

Saypol contacted America LaFrance Corp., which made fire apparatus and vehicles. The idea hatched involved putting models of that equipment on flatcars.

Nothing happened, so in September and October of 1957, Chief Engineer Joseph Bonanno and one of his aides, John DiGirolamo, requested that the Woolery Machine Co. and the John Bean Division of the Food Machinery & Chemical Corp. send them plans of the firefighting equipment they made.

Bonanno mailed the drawings and photographs to an outside firm doing design work for Lionel. At Van Dyck Associates, in Westport, Conn., Kenneth Van Dyck and Ray Wheeler studied the materials with care.

Very different

Van Dyck and Wheeler eventually brought two different notions to Lionel. A flatcar loaded with firefighting equipment and figures constituted one course of thinking. It would give birth to the no. 3512 Fireman and Ladder Car in 1960. The other line of thought involved a motorized unit intended to extinguish small fires.

The minds sketching away in Connecticut learned soon that full-size railroads combated smoldering brush and blazes along their main lines with tank cars adapted for that purpose with hoses often put on extendable arms. Self-propelled equipment of the sort Van Dyck and Wheeler envisioned hardly existed and certainly not for fighting conflagrations threatening stations and industries.

Who cared? A terrific idea resulted in 1958—the 52 Firefighting Car. Almost tongue in cheek, its instruction sheet acknowledged the new motorized unit had emerged from vivid imaginations: It "does not have a precise prototype but incorporates the outstanding features of several pieces of railroad fire-fighting equipment."

Bold features

The 52 operated in a manner like the 50 Section Gang Car and 60 Trolley. Also equipped with a double-wound field motor, it scooted around a layout until its bumper smacked into a solid object. The impact altered the connections of the field winding relative to the armature, thus causing it to change directions and head off. Meanwhile, a rack-and-pinion arrangement spun the water cannon and the seat into which the tiny fireman had been plopped

Kids could have more fun by unraveling the hose on a reel at the opposite end. Too bad the warning light on top of the unpainted red plastic shell didn't flash.

More information

- $12.95 ($107.83)
- 7" long
- Cataloged from 1958 to 1961
- Included in three "bulk outfits" purchased by Madison Hardware Co. of New York City in 1960

54 Ballast Tamper

An extraordinarily fine line existed in the realm of electric trains between what an operating model could be designed to do and what it could be made to appear to do. Individuals envisioning a new animated car or accessory or a motorized unit shifted back and forth between replicating prototype practices and hinting at them.

Consider two revolutionary Lionel accessories from the late prewar era.

The no. 97 Coal Elevator made it possible to transfer chunks of coal from a trackside tray up to a storage bin and down a chute to a railcar. The no. 45 Automatic Gateman simulated safe passage at a grade crossing by having a figure moving out with an illuminated lantern in his hand.

1958

Motorized units fell into the same categories. The no. 3360 Burro Crane let a modeler lift and move cars. The no. 54 Ballast Tamper tickled an observer's imagination to suggest maintaining trackage.

Always suggesting

The dichotomy between the motorized units intended to perform actions and those developed to suggest activity took form long before the postwar era. If anything, it existed from the moment the first such pieces hit the toy train market.

Joshua Lionel Cowen launched his business by creating displays for merchants to arrange in their windows to attract customers. The self-propelled gondolas captured on a tiny scale what full-size rolling stock did—transport goods. By contrast, Lionel's early trolleys and interurbans only helped their owners pretend they were taking commuters to and from work, school, and home.

Jumping from the 1900s to the 1950s saw the division remain. The no. 50 Section Gang Car elicited smiles from operators, even though they had to imagine it bringing laborers to finish tasks along a main line. The no. 41 U.S. Army Switcher could actually move a freight car or two to an assigned site.

More entertaining and more dependent on the mind of its owner or onlooker was the 54 Ballast Tamper. Making its debut in 1958, that 7"-long piece stuck around for a few years only to return during the homestretch of the period. In fact, it was the final motorized unit Lionel then cataloged.

What it was

The instruction sheet told the truth. The Ballast Tamper "does not have an exact prototype but has been developed from several self-propelled machines used for railroad road-bed maintenance."

Chief Engineer Joseph Bonanno and his aide, Morris Zion, compiled information about ancillary equipment owned by railroads. Magazines, industrial ads, and promotional brochures opened their eyes to all the cool stuff possibly duplicated.

No idea was out of bounds when engineers discussed additions to the list of motorized units. From research and time spent at drawing boards and the model shop emerged novel items, some dependent on a child's knack for pretending.

Like the Ballast Tamper. Once energized, the 54 traveled until it hit a track trip. Suddenly, the unit slowed dramatically and the row of six red plastic tampers activated. They churned up and down as though packing down crushed rock to stabilize the rails and improve drainage. Striking a second trip halted the tampers.

Few details

Few modelers in the 1950s laid miniature stones between O gauge rails and ties to imitate the appearance of track. Even if they had, the 54 could hardly be expected to press down the little pieces of ballast.

Yet the animation delighted. Adding a standing figure to the cab made the illusion more believable. The ornamental horn on the roof looked smart. Too bad Lionel didn't install a working horn or light.

Perhaps minimizing the special effects was the goal. The 54 was a hit because its activity needed to be imagined rather than experienced. It depended on an imagination, as a motion picture or TV show did.

More information

- $12.95 ($107.83)
- Cataloged from 1958 to 1961 and 1966 to 1969
- Price increased to $14.95 in 1960 and to $15 in 1966
- Shown in Advance Catalog for 1962

56 Minneapolis & St. Louis Mine Transport

The practice of painting and lettering the same body shell with names and heralds of various railroads—an absolute for toy train makers now—became the standard during the postwar era. Not until the advent of injection-molding plastics and sophisticated paint masks could workers guarantee accurate and efficient reproductions year after year.

Lionel refined that practice with its diesels, starting with its replica of an F3 cab unit and moving forward with its NW2 switchers. The same process influenced the list of motorized units. Only in that way was Lionel able to bring out a diesel claimed to have been adapted for mining. Consider the no. 56 Minneapolis & St. Louis engine, cataloged in 1958 only.

Odd switcher

The Engineering Department, on the lookout for new and possibly unusual motive power, discovered an experimental unit with a gasoline turbine motor. They liked the 2-4-2 switcher from Davenport Locomotive Works, using it as the prototype inspiration for the no. 41 U.S. Army engine Lionel released in 1955.

Designers went on searching for specialized locomotives. They hit the jackpot with a 30-ton gear drive diesel switcher recently introduced by Vulcan Iron Works.

Engineers would take the motor and other mechanisms developed for the 41 and pack them in a shell given only minor modifications. Thus in 1956 was born the no. 51 Navy Yard/New York 2-4-2.

New railroad

No longer could executives trust consumers to be content with locomotives and cars lettered for only nationally known railroads, such as the Pennsylvania or the Santa Fe, or the fictitious Lionel Lines. Children wanted to own models decked out with the names they saw frequently.

Consequently, Lionel had campaigned to broaden the range of regional lines promoted by its trains. Engines decorated for the Rock Island and the Southern vied for space in yards with rolling stock advertising the Western Pacific and the Boston & Maine. The trend continued to pick up speed as the 1950s wore on.

1958

Scattered among the cars on O gauge layouts were boxcars labeled for the Minneapolis & St. Louis Ry. That midwestern line, established in 1870, spread south and then east and west from Minnesota into Iowa, South Dakota, and Illinois. Regardless of the name, the railroad never stretched as far south as Missouri.

The M&StL caught the attention of executives at Lionel. A plain near-scale boxcar with its name and slogan entered the line in 1953. Four years later arrived a similarly proportioned model blinding in the railway's new red-and-white scheme.

Somehow, leaders became obsessed with the M&StL. For 1958, they added a road diesel and an open quad hopper with its name. Lionel decided to repaint its Vulcan switcher for the railroad—meet the 56.

Mining power

Bright red paint covered the familiar body shell (typically maroon), with the sides of the cab sprayed white. The hot-stamped simple red graphics stood out boldly.

Lionel declared the 2-4-2 was used to transport ore from mines, to which owners lifted an eyebrow in skepticism before saying, "Okay—why not?" Meanwhile, white-painted side rails and chemically blackened end rails injected touches of style.

Like the 51, the Mine Transport came with a tough motor and a three-position reverse unit so it could pull three or four lightweight cars. An operating knuckle coupler at each end let the switcher latch on to whatever might be at the site.

Soon gone

How long did the 56 Vulcan switcher last in the line? Only a year. Probably the lettering limited its popularity. The M&StL was hardly a household name. The railroad's total trackage ranked it only 37th among domestic lines at the time; total operating revenue dropped it even lower.

Kids glimpsed the so-called mining locomotive and wondered who or what M&StL stood for. Stumped, they likely went on to the play-oriented units.

More information

- $12.95 ($107.83)
- No operating headlight
- 7½" long
- Catalog illustration mistakenly lettered: Mining Company

68 Executive Inspection Car

A few motorized units from the postwar era hearkened back a generation or two to what designers had done in the distant past at Lionel. Certain models brought to mind the windup handcars offered during the 1930s. Other units seemed descended from the large and colorfully painted steel trolleys and interurbans made available 20 years before. Yet another chapter from the narrative provided by Lionel comes to life when turning a spotlight on the no. 68 Executive Inspection Car.

Racing cars

Almost half a century before the 68 boldly made its debut in 1958—going back to 1912—co-founder Joshua Lionel Cowen had presented something else to a toy world already infatuated with his locomotives and railcars. Fascinated by other current means of transportation, Cowen had introduced Lionel Racing Automobiles.

1958

The four outfits came with one or two circles of curved metal track on which rode models of a Stutz Bearcat. Motors enabled the cars to dash ahead like demons. Owning concentric loops and two racers let a child hold contests for speed records.

Sales figures must have disappointed Cowen because the outfits vanished after 1916. How could he have known a similar toy—slot-car racers—would turn the world upside down in the 1960s? The forerunners of that fad were the Lionel sets.

New Haven car

Whether Chief Engineer Joseph Bonanno or anyone on his staff in the 1950s remembered what Cowen had invented remains uncertain. Probably not. Instead, the men responsible for devising the 68—an O gauge replica of a DeSoto station wagon capable of zipping around loops of three-rail track—had been thinking of something else. They were familiar with a full-size contraption receiving publicity.

Patrick McGinnis, president of the New York, New Haven & Hartford RR from 1954 to 1956, liked inspecting his fiefdom. But he didn't think a private train or a business car, the typical means for executives to tour their domains, was suitable for the short trips he had in mind.

In September 1954, the New Haven bought a seven-passenger Cadillac and had the car fitted by its shop technicians with retractable railroad wheels, a third headlight, and rear marker lights. Thus was born "New Haven number 2."

Three-rail version

Lionel's engineering team couldn't have missed the press accounts. Inspired by the modified Cadillac, someone conceived of what became the 68.

The 7½"-long Executive Inspection Car combined two playthings that boys have loved forever: an automobile and a train. The *Lionel Service Manual* noted that this model ran on electrical current and its four flanged wheels did not retract.

Designers installed a two-position reverse unit with the motor. Current hit the rails, and the inspection car shot ahead or reared back. Twisting the knob that protruded through the roof switched the little speed demon to one-direction travel.

Illustrations in the Consumer Catalog for 1958 accurately depicted the 68 with its headlights and taillights brightly lit. Illumination represented the limited special effects. Too bad no one considered wiring the unit with an electric horn.

The catalog correctly depicted the bright red paint scheme (sprayed over a gray plastic shell) with cream side panels. However, it showed the roof of the 68 as a matching red. As produced, the Executive Inspection Car had a cream roof.

Why Lionel decided on that color scheme can't be determined. At least three preliminary models painted light blue with cream details have been verified.

Possibly someone proposed selling both models so kids could race them. The toymaker that had pioneered racing automobiles in 1912 might have wanted to try again. Nothing happened, and Lionel struggled to promote the 68, which could have been a neat component in a top set!

More information

- $12.95 ($107.83)
- Cataloged from 1958 through 1961
- Part of promotional "bulk outfit" no. X-572NA linked to Madison Hardware Co. for 1960

44 U.S. Army Mobile Missile Launcher

The operation of the 50 Gang Car had lost a bit of its novelty by 1956. Bored or mischievous youngsters dared Lionel to improvise. Maybe by combining the motive power of a locomotive with the animation of an accessory—all in the form of a single motorized unit!

Quite a challenge! Needless to say, the ingenious gentlemen working under the supervision of Chief Engineer Joseph Bonanno were more than up to the task. Check out the no. 44 U.S. Army Mobile Missile Launcher for proof.

Small starts

Starting with the Section Gang Car in 1954 and continuing with the no. 60 Trolley a year later, designers made good use of the mechanism devised to send a motorized unit in the opposite direction after its bumper struck a barrier of some kind.

A series of compact industrial or military switchers followed. Definitely slices of modern railroading, they still promised little action beyond pulling a few cars.

1959

Giving engineers the benefit of a doubt means praising the no. 3360 Burro Crane brought out in 1956 as a neat approximation of an accessory on motorized wheels. It cruised along before braking to hoist a fallen railcar along the right-of-way. Yet it had more in common with a crane car than it did a magnetic crane.

New heights

The breakthrough didn't occur until 1959, but when it did the world of toy trains changed. According to the instruction sheet packed with the new motorized unit, Lionel was offering "the prototype of an armored, self-propelled launching platform which could be used for tactical defense of railway lines and installations."

From fertile minds had sprung the 44 U.S. Army Mobile Missile Launcher. That unit, like its twin in olive green (no. 45 U.S. Marines launcher first cataloged a year later), rewarded consumers with motive power capable of pulling cars and carrying out a task worthy of a separate toy.

Until that moment in Lionel's history, the best its locomotives could offer were lights, sound (in the form of a whistle or horn), and puffing smoke. Emphasis went toward improving motors, allowing engines to go faster and pull more, as well as to enhancing external details for added realism.

But the 44 took Lionel's motive power to a higher level. It could toil as a locomotive, ready with a three-position reverse unit. The launcher drove forward or backward while coupled to a railcar grasped by a fixed knuckle at the rear.

Because engineers had beefed up the 12½"-long Mobile Missile Launcher by installing Magne-Traction, it could pull a few railcars. Its pulling power equaled if not surpassed the compact switchers.

More action

Luckily for consumers, there was more to evaluating the 44 than checking its speed and counting the cars it led. They understood the "mobile" in its name; more appealing to them was discovering how it became a "missile launcher."

Designers attached to the blue-painted plastic shell a gray plastic apparatus formed to hold four white plastic projectiles. The firing activator made it easy to manually launch individual missiles at targets located about 12" away. Or a young soldier might fire them via remote control if he had installed the proper Super O blade, O gauge or O-27 contactor, or any uncoupling track section.

The capability to launch missiles transformed the 44 from just a puny if dangerous-looking locomotive into a fantastic accessory on wheels. One cool feature was the red warning light on top of the shell. Another was the figure (unpainted blue vinylite when the 44 made its debut, but improved with a white-painted face and hands after 1959) at its control panel.

Rightly optimistic about the sales potential of the 44, Lionel used it as the motive power for a military-themed Super O set in 1959 and 1960. During those years and through 1962, it also cataloged the missile launcher for separate sale.

More information

- $17.95 ($148.44)
- Price raised to $25.00 in 1962
- Included envelope with six missiles
- Targets included nos. 943 Ammo Dump and 6470 Exploding Car

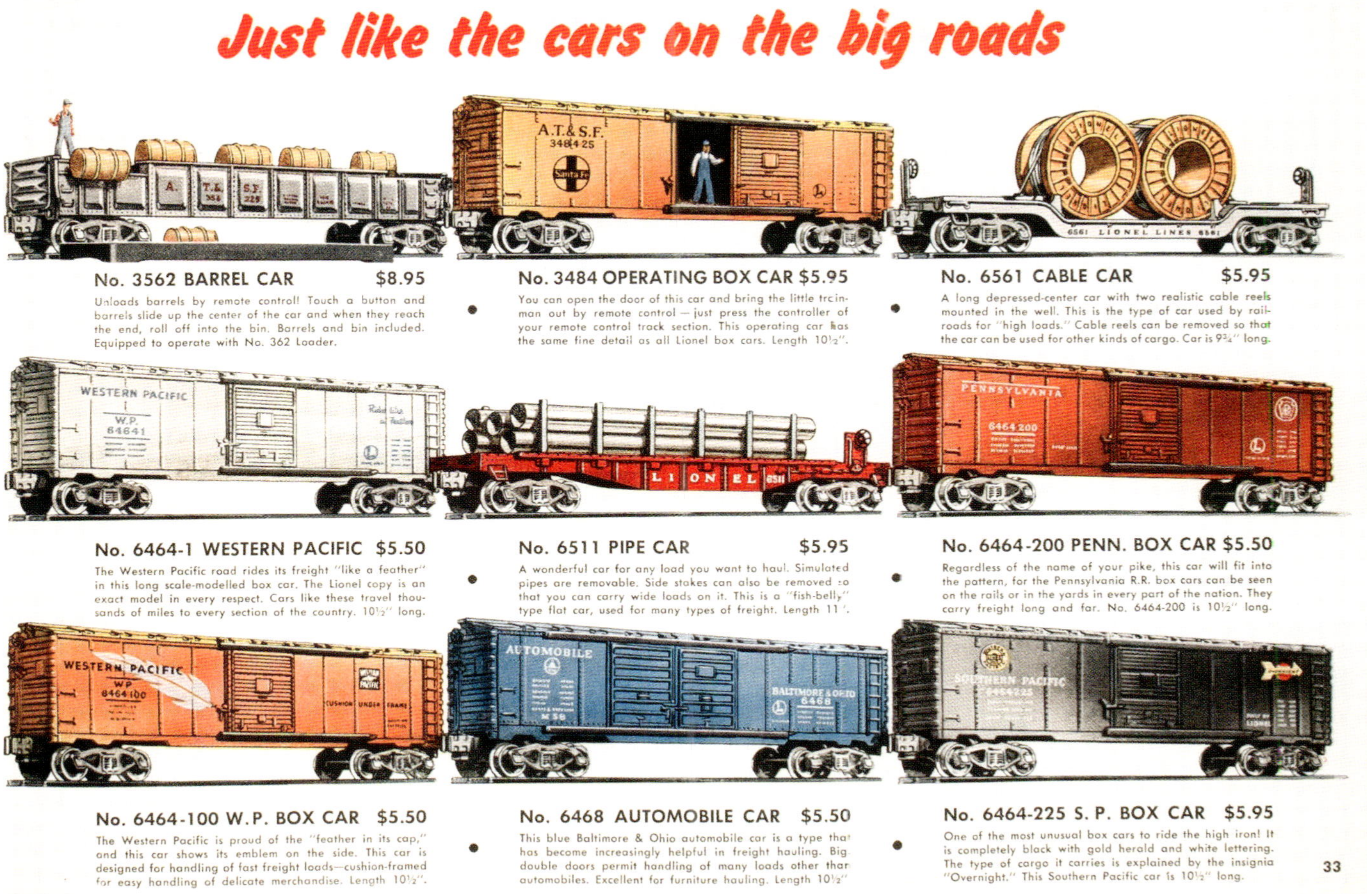

Just like the cars on the big roads

No. 3562 BARREL CAR $8.95
Unloads barrels by remote control! Touch a button and barrels slide up the center of the car and when they reach the end, roll off into the bin. Barrels and bin included. Equipped to operate with No. 362 Loader.

No. 3484 OPERATING BOX CAR $5.95
You can open the door of this car and bring the little train-man out by remote control — just press the controller of your remote control track section. This operating car has the same fine detail as all Lionel box cars. Length 10½".

No. 6561 CABLE CAR $5.95
A long depressed-center car with two realistic cable reels mounted in the well. This is the type of car used by railroads for "high loads." Cable reels can be removed so that the car can be used for other kinds of cargo. Car is 9¾" long.

No. 6464-1 WESTERN PACIFIC $5.50
The Western Pacific road rides its freight "like a feather" in this long scale-modelled box car. The Lionel copy is an exact model in every respect. Cars like these travel thousands of miles to every section of the country. 10½" long.

No. 6511 PIPE CAR $5.95
A wonderful car for any load you want to haul. Simulated pipes are removable. Side stakes can also be removed so that you can carry wide loads on it. This is a "fish-belly" type flat car, used for many types of freight. Length 11".

No. 6464-200 PENN. BOX CAR $5.50
Regardless of the name of your pike, this car will fit into the pattern, for the Pennsylvania R.R. box cars can be seen on the rails or in the yards in every part of the nation. They carry freight long and far. No. 6464-200 is 10½" long.

No. 6464-100 W.P. BOX CAR $5.50
The Western Pacific is proud of the "feather in its cap," and this car shows its emblem on the side. This car is designed for handling of fast freight loads—cushion-framed for easy handling of delicate merchandise. Length 10½".

No. 6468 AUTOMOBILE CAR $5.50
This blue Baltimore & Ohio automobile car is a type that has become increasingly helpful in freight hauling. Big double doors permit handling of many loads other than automobiles. Excellent for furniture hauling. Length 10½"

No. 6464-225 S. P. BOX CAR $5.95
One of the most unusual box cars to ride the high iron! It is completely black with gold herald and white lettering. The type of cargo it carries is explained by the insignia "Overnight." This Southern Pacific car is 10½" long.

33

Rolling Stock

Trying to figure out what kinds of electric trains consumers wanted probably kept salesmen and engineers at Lionel awake late into many nights. They struggled to satisfy youngsters and adults who could be maddeningly fickle about purchases yet deeply loyal to the brand they preferred. Top leaders at Lionel, much like their counterparts at movie studios, record labels, and automobile makers, sought valiantly to keep up with and even shape changing tastes during the postwar era.

The rolling stock developed and marketed by Lionel, even more than the locomotives, reflects the battles being waged at the time in the booming domestic marketplace. Examining the freight cars and cabooses released between 1945 and 1969 enables observers to gain insights into how decision-makers aimed to balance the public's intense if conflicting desires for both colorful and entertaining toys and realistically detailed scale or near-scale replicas.

The range of innovative and memorable items proves how successfully designers met the goals set by men overseeing the corporation. Lionel managed though not always with confidence or seamlessness to move back and forth between whimsy and realism—as consumers wished. For much of the era it accurately read the public and made superb rolling stock that let it dominate a market long captivated by trains.

Different approach

The rolling stock showcased and analyzed here serves as a representative sample of what Lionel released during the era. It illustrates the major trends in product development and marketing characterizing the company over the course of that quarter-century. Several pieces shed light on advances made in adding animation to freight cars, advances that revolutionized the hobby from the late prewar period through the final years of the postwar era.

When deciding how to treat those models, I elected to separate them according to general categories arranged alphabetically. Cabooses, however, went at the end of the chapter because they typically rode at the end of freight trains.

Ordinarily in books of this nature, each different type of Lionel rolling stock receives its own introduction. There are, in other words, brief histories of the boxcars, gondolas, hoppers, and so forth manufactured during postwar times. In addition, those summaries of how Lionel developed

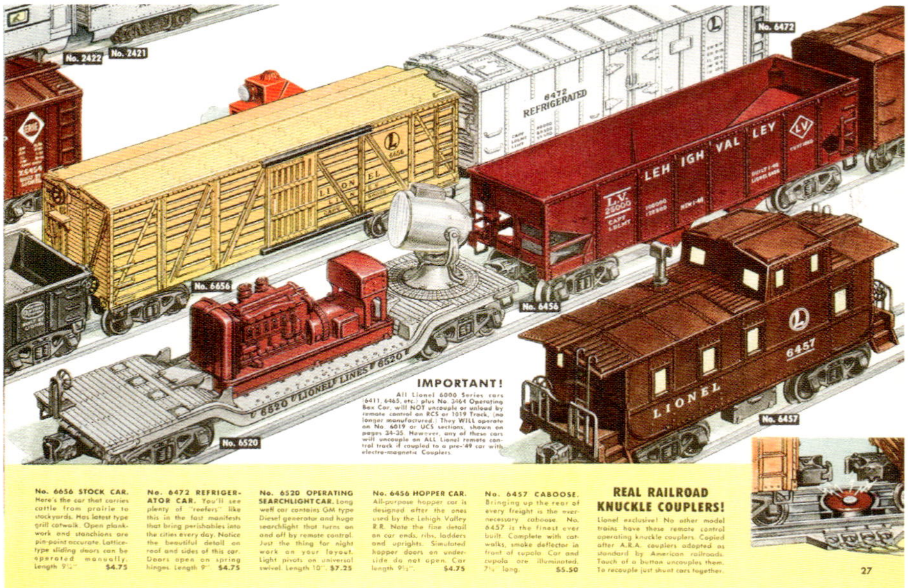

and improved freight cars include nostalgic recognition of their greatness. Such an approach has been the rule in reference guides and overviews of what Lionel made.

Not so here. Something different seems more appropriate and worthwhile. Following the pattern set earlier with locomotives and motorized units, I'll give a general understanding of and appreciation for the range of rolling stock cataloged.

Taking a broader, overarching approach to postwar rolling stock should make it possible for readers to see the entire group of freight cars and cabooses being offered, the way executives did throughout that era. Viewing these diverse models as a whole provides a better and fuller understanding of what engineers, production supervisors, and sales personnel built and peddled.

Stages on wheels

Truth be told, freight cars have a great deal in common. Namely, their form and appearance dictates their function, which proved critical in helping infuse Lionel's models with widespread appeal and enormous value as playthings.

Every freight car, from a design perspective, starts with a solid framework meant to ride over track on wheels (or more precisely, trucks consisting of wheels attached to axles). This foundation may be likened to a theatrical stage on which hands erect and situate props to develop convincing scenes for action to occur.

Install on the framework a closed rectangle with opening doors, and you have a boxcar. Modify it with thin openings along each side to get a stock car. Or install special equipment to cool whatever is packed inside to develop a refrigerator car.

Build up the long sides and short ends of the framework, and you have a gondola. Replace the solid bottom with bays whose doors can be opened and shut to construct a hopper. That type of freight car may be open at the top or covered.

Things becoming clear? Good, because the most basic freight car turns out to be the most diverse. Leaving the framework alone creates the humble flatcar. Of course, Lionel was no more likely to do nothing with that piece of rolling stock than were the full-size railroads its engineering crews kept using for inspiration.

Recall how Lionel added to flatcars with regular or depressed centers all the apparatus needed for manually operated derricks or electrically powered searchlights. Rudimentary stakes along the side held in place miniature logs and pipes. More elaborate loads multiplied the enjoyment of flatcars. Still later arrived a fleet of models equipped with animated effects and awesome operating features.

Yes, the array of freight cars Lionel cataloged during postwar days offered children countless ways to stay entertained. Better to perceive them not so much as stages on wheels but, especially if they had operating features, as playgrounds.

The vast range of innovative and memorable freight cars cataloged by Lionel proves how successfully designers met the goals set by the men overseeing the corporation.

Competing demands

The brain trust administering Lionel from the late prewar period well into the postwar acknowledged the demands conveyed from consumers interested in their electric trains. They knew as well how those demands might contradict and so force designers and sales personnel to expand the line to satisfy customers.

On one hand, kids, and often the parents buying the sets and accessories children received, expected Lionel to merchandise playthings. They trusted those toys to be entertaining, exciting, safe, dependable, and instructional. Adults spent money on trains with the belief that those toys would nurture proper habits.

On the other hand, youngsters maturing with Lionel trains inevitably came to expect more serious models faithful in proportion to full-size prototypes. They, like the legions of hobbyists embracing model railroading, dismissed the toys and minimized the appeal of animated effects. Realism overshadowed everything else.

Lionel's leadership had responded to a changing and expanding market at the end of the prewar period by supplementing its roster of wonderful toys with a growing number of scale and near-scale replicas of contemporary locomotives and railcars. They had also aimed to bring out models blending the best elements.

The same challenge—balancing fanciful and entertaining toys with detailed and convincing replicas—influenced leaders in the postwar era. How they overcame challenges stemming from commercial trends pulling them in different directions tells a lot about what Lionel made and sold.

Toys first prevail

Right after the war, skyrocketing demands for electric trains pushed Lionel to emphasize toys at the expense of accurate models that might have been more expensive and consumed more time to manufacture. Small and colorful freight cars and cabooses largely filled the O-27 and O gauge sets the corporation cataloged through the 1940s.

Some of the rolling stock cataloged plainly had roots in the prewar era. A few items, to be honest, had been carried over from the early 1940s. The sole difference being how brand-new knuckle couplers had been substituted for out-of-date kinds.

Other freight cars represented updated versions of familiar types, such as short boxcars, cabooses, and gondolas. Lionel redesigned them to capitalize on advances in plastics technology, in particular, injection-molded polystyrene.

Amid the obvious toys appeared a handful of near-scale models indicating that the commitment to realism had not disappeared. Deluxe single-dome tank cars and an excellent representation of a modern gondola hinted at what could be done.

Push from rivals

What might be considered the second phase of freight car development in the postwar era began as early as 1949 and continued over the following six years. Little by little, engineers replaced shorter, less-detailed and more fanciful rolling stock with impressive models that faithfully replicated what railroads were using.

Driving a major transformation of the Lionel roster were both internal wishes and external worries. Put simply, anxious marketing executives refused to allow the line to stagnate or fall behind. Meanwhile, competing businesses were striving to circumvent Lionel by introducing more realistic and detailed models.

Already, the A.C. Gilbert Co. was proving to be a formidable competitor with its S gauge brand of American Flyer trains. Built to scale proportions, those smaller locomotives and cars operated over realistic two-rail track, much to the chagrin and disappointment of Lionel enthusiasts less comfortable with mere toys.

American Model Toys posed a threat of a different sort. This newcomer was bringing out similarly realistic versions of contemporary rolling stock for the O gauge market. Its variety of boxcars, stock cars, and more surpassed the small and traditional models Lionel sold.

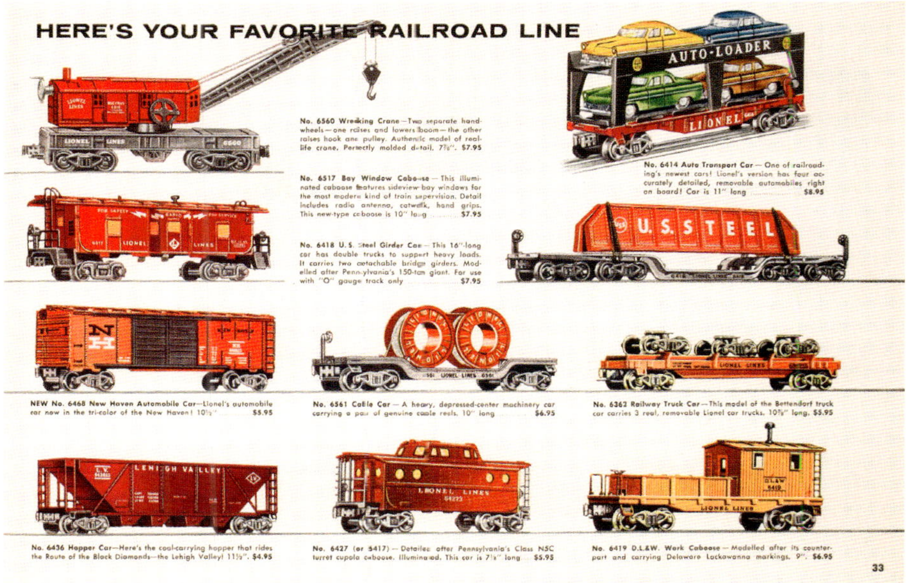

Heights of realism

Fretful executives pressed the Engineering Department to develop more realistic freight cars. A trickle launched by a gondola burst into a flood with near-scale boxcars, along with a porthole caboose, flatcar with pipes, automobile boxcar, and triple-dome tank car in 1953.

The torrent surged forward over the next couple of years. Lionel balanced whimsy and color with realism and detail as the no. 6464 series of near-scale boxcars increased. Also significant were a new refrigerator car, open hopper, stock car, and bay-window caboose. Can't forget operating versions of a few of those neat models.

Animated breakthroughs

Throughout the opening decade of the postwar period, Lionel had made headlines, revolutionized the toy industry, and boosted sales with its outstanding animated freight cars. Those amazing playthings thrilled youngsters by enabling them to simulate the activities associated with the movement and transfer of raw materials on full-size railroads. They were, in short, toys that enhanced realism.

Remote-controlled rolling stock capable of unloading barrels, logs, and coal had transformed the Lionel product line in the years before World War II. Then, afterward, it was a matter of updating most of those models to expand the roster. Pairing operating cars with static ones benefited Lionel in significant ways, most of all suggesting it was far ahead of the field.

That impression of outpacing every rival, muscular and puny, gained credence with the arrival of the landmark automatic milk car in 1947. Kids and adults watched breathlessly or gleefully handled the unloading of cans. Only slightly less marvelous was a similar operating car designed to mimic how cattle paraded in or out of stock cars. Modelers spent time completing tasks familiar to laborers on railroads. The animation seemed fun and true to life.

Then the pace of innovation slowed during the first half of the 1950s. As though designers and their superiors felt ready to redirect their energy and ideas elsewhere. Only a few more operating cars made their debut, usually cast in a supporting role with a brand-new accessory meant to shift coal or blocks of ice.

Looking to the future, however, fascination with what rolling stock could be made to do would soon erupt again. The finest days of entertaining and highly ingenious freight cars were on the horizon, soon to completely revamp the line.

Novelties and exotics

The ingenious group of men in the Engineering Department must have been a fidgety bunch. Never, or so it seemed, were they content to relax or let up in the campaign to expand the roster of freight cars Lionel introduced as components of sets or as items to be sold separately.

Proof of how designers and model makers refused to sit back emerged in the final years of the 1950s. Lionel had made a

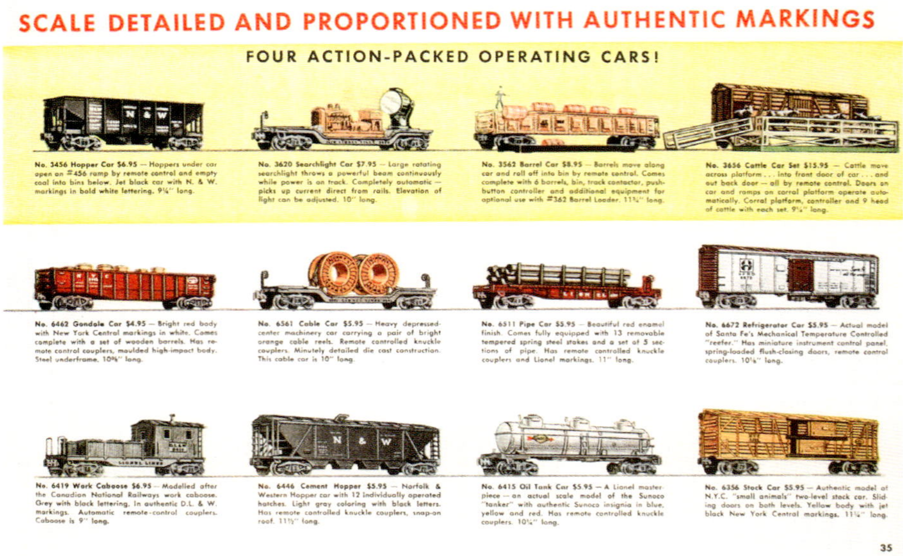

strong transition from smaller and fanciful toys to bigger and more detailed replicas. Every general type of freight car had been transformed; in fact, competing models had made their debut. Just check out the two cabooses (porthole and bay window) or the tank cars.

As though freed from the burden of updating all the basic models, the individuals working under Chief Engineer Joseph Bonanno blazed new trails. They delved deeply into railway industry publications, cyclopedias of rolling stock, public relations releases from car manufacturers, and literature distributed by railroads around the country. All as part of their hunt for new and exotic items.

The search bore exciting and appealing fruit. The roster of O gauge cars grew after 1954 to include longer and specialized flatcars, stock cars ferrying wild animals and sea creatures, automobile carriers, generator boxcars, and the initial cement hoppers and chemical tank cars. Children never quite knew what to expect when paging for the first time through the annual full-color Consumer Catalogs.

Fascinating loads

A second method of adding to the list of rolling stock involved less risk and research. It was so obvious we can only wonder why executives apparently did not consider it and attempt to capitalize on it until the last years of the 1950s.

An emphasis on the loads carried by miniature flatcars permitted Lionel to again capture the interest of youngsters, while giving them more to do with their trains. Additionally, as executives such as Alan Ginsburg and Ronald Saypol realized, loads represented a simple and effective way to garner financial assistance from outside businesses eager to see their corporate names and logos on Lionel trains.

Flatcars, produced quickly and efficiently, held trailers emblazoned with the names of trucking companies. Boxcars advertised different consumer goods, some of which would have been familiar to children (above all, Bosco Chocolate Syrup) and others that would surely have been unknown (Timken rail trucks).

Loads purchased from minor players in the toy field helped Lionel alter its image, particularly as decision-makers saw the advantages in reaching youngsters hypnotized by the armed forces as well as space exploration. A variety of military vehicles now rode on Lionel flatcars as did miniature rockets and helicopters.

The tendency to depend on loads to generate interest and variety in basic freight cars while experimenting with models of novel and even exotic rolling stock helped Lionel multiply its offerings. Designers and sales personnel who investigated what was happening on contemporary railroads laid the groundwork for the classics, whimsical albeit realistic, characterizing the third trend of the era.

Lapsing backward

Releases dating from the early 1960s corroborate the view that Lionel had promoted realism as far as it could with three-rail trains. Further advances in that direction would need to take place amid its growing roster of HO scale models.

Commercial demands and cultural leanings prodded a return to what had succeeded before. Lionel lapsed backward, reviving its tradition of manufacturing and merchandising ingenious playthings. Toward the close of the era, the firm recalled its roots to the point of renaming itself the Lionel Toy Corporation.

Before shutting down the Engineering Department after 1963, determined leaders brought out remarkable operating cars. No piece of rolling stock should be allowed to stand alone; it must offer impatient and bored kids much more to do.

Designers responded to corporate requests in a frenzied yet brilliant way. They equipped freight cars with mechanisms to launch satellites into orbit or send missiles upward to attack enemy posts. They relied on gears and cams to animate figures simulating sheriffs and outlaws, giraffes and horses, and cops and robbers.

> **Throughout the opening decade of the postwar period, Lionel had made headlines, revolutionized the toy industry, and boosted sales with its animated freight cars.**

Almost every new freight car introduced promised action or hilarity. How logical to see the models as tiny motion picture sets, where comedians and daredevils repeated their roles endlessly to delight and captivate youngsters watching.

Perhaps referring to the fourth phase in the development of rolling stock as a return to what had worked in the past downplays its significance. Lionel was not retreating to a time when merely a rudimentary grouping of small freight cars was enough to gratify customers. Rather, it believed innovative playthings designed to guarantee more thrills and spills stood as the final means of snagging picky kids.

2454 Baby Ruth Boxcar

Toy trains produced in the years right after World War II reflect the assumptions and goals pulling marketing leaders and engineers in different directions. An honest evaluation and appreciation of what Lionel was cataloging during the second half of the 1940s therefore demands understanding those competing views and ends.

The wish to develop more realistic models, which translated to putting out miniatures faithful to full-size locomotives and rolling stock, served as the goal at Lionel. Yet decision-makers hesitated to abide by the doctrine of realism when promoting their trains to kids. They knew youngsters, as well as parents and grandparents, represented their meal ticket for gathering new consumers into the Lionel fold.

Leaders compromised. They enhanced the realism of deluxe engines and railcars, while they made sure toys remained on the roster. Among the favorites blending toy-like qualities with touches of realism was the no. 2454 Baby Ruth Boxcar.

1946

Not quite Pennsy

Boxcars returned with fanfare to Lionel Lines in 1946. The Consumer Catalog delighted folks with dollars they couldn't wait to spend. Pictured in its pages, they discovered single-door and double-door boxcars, along with operating models.

Eagle-eyed readers noticed two different single-door boxcars. More difficult to locate was the no. 2454 shown as brown with white Pennsylvania RR markings. Only in the rear of the catalog, with O-27 separate-sale items, did it show up.

A second version of the 2454 proved easier to see. The Advertising Department elected to show an orange boxcar with Baby Ruth graphics on the left side and a circle-L Lionel logo on the right when depicting the single-door boxcar in one O gauge and two O-27 outfits.

Why Baby Ruth?

In retrospect, we realize the mistake in the illustration. The 2454 as made and cataloged in 1946 and 1947 had a Pennsylvania RR herald on the right. An element of realism to balance the whimsy in the candy name.

Lionel had been capitalizing on the sweet tooth of boys and girls since 1936. The 2454 was the latest in a series of short boxcars emblazoned with the name of one of America's most popular candy bars.

An agreement with Curtiss Candy Co. of Chicago made it possible for Lionel to make O-27 models promoting Baby Ruth. That chocolate-covered treat, with peanuts, caramel, and nougat, had first hit candy counters in 1921.

Tinplated boxcars with enticing lithographed images of a sliced Baby Ruth bar atop a plate had offered something tasty for kids settling for low-end trains. Lionel had churned out hundreds of thousands of 1514, 1679, and 2679 cars before World War II erupted. Issues of the firm's *Model Builder* magazine released during the war had then advertised Baby Ruth.

New treat

The deal with Curtiss must still have been in effect after the war because Lionel moved to hot-stamp the name of its candy bar on the orange-painted plastic body shell made for the new single-door boxcar. Brown-painted doors slid open or shut, giving kids more to do with a 2454.

Lionel brought back the Baby Ruth boxcar unchanged for a second year as a set component and as a separate-sale item. With a new type of knuckle coupler, it went into the line for 1948 as no. 6454.

A year after resuming electric train production, Lionel was back to promoting candy. Gone was the mouth-watering picture of a Baby Ruth bar. Instead, only its name appeared across from a Pennsylvania RR herald on X2454, X4454, and X6454 boxcars cataloged between 1946 and 1949.

That was true on cars with non-opening double doors put in Scout sets between 1948 and 1952. Similar Baby Ruth boxcars molded in white, red, or orange plastic became the rule through 1958.

More information

- $4.50 ($55.71)
- 9¼" long
- Metal frame had steps at four corners
- Version fitted with receiver as no. 4454 for Electronic Control Set

3454 Operating Merchandise Car

In 1946—long before boxcars learned how to launch helicopters or explode when being struck by missiles—Lionelers found it astounding that a model could deliver packages. Not merely transport miniature boxes and crates, but fling them out an open door into a waiting tray or station platform.

The no. 3454 Operating Merchandise Car honestly did represent a breakthrough for Lionel enthusiasts in the two years right after World War II. Only by thinking back 70 years can we appreciate it.

With pride

Everyone must have been bursting with joy because the O gauge and O-27 lines for 1946 were large and varied. Maybe more than the diversity of the lines, men and women gushed about what some of the railcars and freight loaders could do.

1946

The 3454 joined a handful of other newcomers equipped with electromagnets and solenoids so that, once positioned over an uncoupling/unloading section, a modeler could activate them via remote control. Action of some kind then resulted.

With the 3454 Operating Merchandise Car, pressing the correct button caused the sliding door on one side to spring open. All but simultaneously a tiny packing case was ejected. Pushing the button again repeated the activity until all six of the cubes manually loaded into a metal chute through a hatch door on the roof were out.

Far from spectacular from a current vantage but plenty amazing back in 1946. Enough that planners upgraded four O-27 outfits cataloged then by including a 3454 in them (two of those sets featured the same items with or without a whistle tender). They also offered the Operating Merchandise Car as a separate-sale item.

Older still

There was much to acknowledge about the 3454 as a key part of the O-27 line for 1946. Its striking appearance stood out as well. Unlike the cars illustrated in the Consumer Catalog as brown with white lettering, the actual models featured plastic shells (identical to those being used for single-door boxcars) painted bright silver.

The graphics, highlighted by a Pennsylvania RR keystone herald, were hot-stamped blue. Be aware, approximately a dozen early versions were stamped red.

Delighted as Lionel workers and modelers were with the Operating Merchandise Car, individuals with good memories had to concede the 3454 represented an updated version of an older car.

The era of remote-controlled operating cars and accessories had opened in 1938. A year later, Lionel had announced the no. 3814 Electrically Operated Merchandise Car. Designers had modified a regular-production O gauge boxcar to accommodate the apparatus necessary to slide open the door and flip out a crate. The 3814 stayed in the catalog through 1942.

What made the 3814 and later operating cars possible was the invention by Frank Pettit of a box coupler capable of being opened via remote control. Once he had refined that part, the "amateur mechanic" (as Pettit called himself) transformed the world of toy trains by equipping rolling stock with similar features.

Up to date

The 3454 represented a prewar item Lionel brought up to date for 1946 more aesthetically and less technically. Put simply, the mechanism inside the car owed more to what Pettit had devised before the war than anything engineers had done after.

Characteristic of the new times were the injection-molded plastic shell and the electromagnetic knuckle couplers with steel wheels attached to die-cast metal trucks. The six crates (black, burgundy, or red) had been altered, too. Postwar versions came imprinted with "Baby Ruth."

More information

- $5.95 ($73.67)
- 9¼" long
- Cataloged in 1946 and 1947
- Included nos. 160-1 unloading bin and 3854-53 miniature packing crates (envelope contained six)

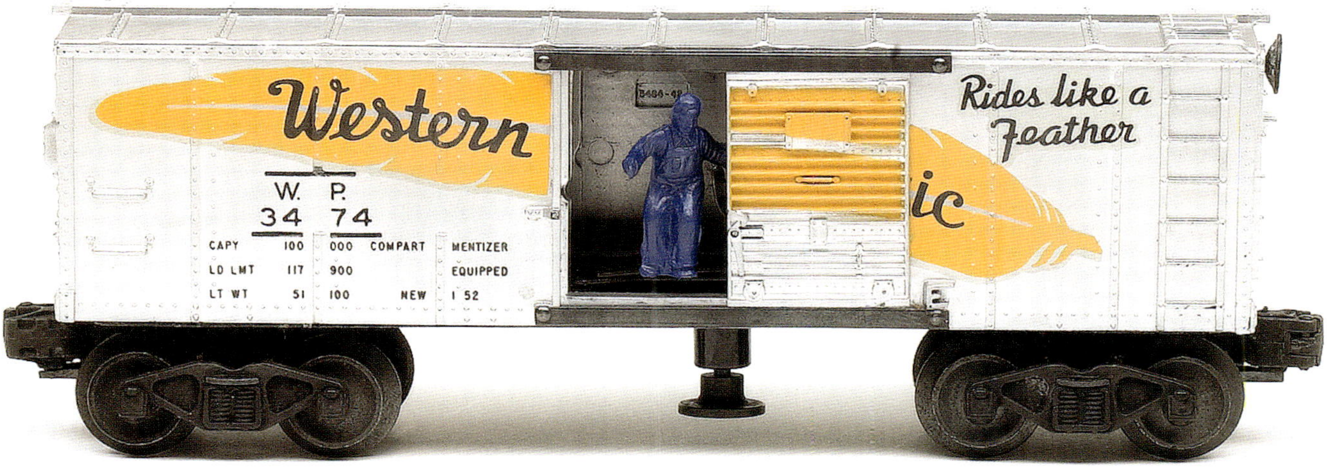

3474 Western Pacific Operating Boxcar

Lionel introduced F3 diesels and an operating boxcar with Western Pacific graphics in 1952. No documentation has surfaced to explain whether that railroad reached out to the toy train maker or vice versa. Passenger cars from American Model Toys had bothered the bosses at Lionel, so they envisioned streamliners with *California Zephyr* lettering.

But why did Lionel add another road name to the two operating boxcars rostered? The WP couldn't compete in recognition with the New York Central or the Santa Fe. Nonetheless, the no. 3474 Western Pacific model did make its debut.

1952

Real feathers

Until 1950, the Western Pacific had painted boxcars a familiar reddish brown. It had decorated those cars with a small herald highlighted by a silver feather against a black background. The feather alluded to its eastern route through the Feather River into the Sierra Nevadas.

For 1952, the WP joined the railroads then painting their boxcars in hues that caused them to stand out. It ordered 20 aluminum cars from Pullman-Standard equipped with steel gates inside to separate the interior into sections to protect partial loads as well as fragile freight.

Known as "Compartmentizer Cars," those boxcars were delivered wearing silver paint and an orange feather decorating each long side. To the right and above the feather was the slogan, "Rides like a Feather," to remind shippers of Western Pacific's commitment to careful handling.

Railway Age and *Trains & Travel* magazines announced the Western Pacific's unveiling of its 20 special boxcars in December of 1951. To Lionel's credit, it managed to have a replica within months. The model came painted silver and finished with decals.

Improved model

Lionel's fleet of boxcars might have been growing by 1952, but no one could say its looks were improving. Brown and orange remained the rule. A silver car with yellow graphics (and not orange) would be good.

Since the number of regular boxcars exceeded the two operating ones, planners opted to fit inside the Western Pacific shell what it needed to provide remote-control action. The 3474 relied on a plunger mechanism (enclosing a solenoid) attached to the underside of the sheet-metal frame.

The 3474 depended on the electromagnet put in a special track section for its animation. An operator stopped the car at just the right spot and then pressed a button on a remote controller. That energized the magnet, which pulled down the plunger to open a sliding door and bring a figure mounted on a metal rod forward.

The sequence devised by Development Engineer Frank Pettit (with assistance from Chief Engineer Joseph Bonanno, who received a patent for the operating boxcar in 1959) had worked wonders for the two 3464s. Now Lionel would rely on it to make the Western Pacific car a hit.

Trial and error

Perhaps because Lionel was debating how to mass-produce and then use the 3474 operating boxcar, errors about it weakened the description in the Advance Catalog for 1952. It was depicted as part of three outfits: one O-27 (no. 1483WS) and two O gauge (nos. 2179WS and 2183WS). Black-and-white images showed it as a dark model with a darker feather across each side—almost an orange or yellow boxcar with a red feather and white letters.

The WP car was mistakenly referred to as "3464" in the listings of the outfits and separate-sale cars. Doing so suggested the New York Central and Santa Fe boxcars with that number would not be returning to the line (neither of those models was shown in the Advance Catalog for 1952).

The Consumer Catalog corrected these inaccuracies. The WP car was labeled "3474" and shown as a silver model with an orange feather and black lettering. Now, though, it was a part of only the O-27 set.

More information

- $5.50 ($50.11)
- Cataloged in 1952 and 1953
- Separate sale only in 1953
- No. 3464-17 figure reduced in size for 1953

6464-25 Great Northern Boxcar

Who would have believed an inch (really 1¼") could redefine the identity of a manufacturer. Yet contemplating what was happening at Lionel in 1953 leads to no other conclusion. The inch or so added to the length of the boxcars being made advanced the trend of marketing electric trains steeped in realism. A little extra plastic proved those trains were less toys and more near-scale replicas.

To be sure, a few previous models had launched that trend. Regarding rolling stock, the tide turned when Lionel heralded three near-scale streamlined passenger cars for 1952. That trio laid the groundwork for the four boxcars inaugurating the no. 6464 series, a quartet that included the no. 6464-25 Great Northern.

Pushed to revive

Lionel, eager to convince model railroaders of its seriousness, had introduced O scale rolling stock in 1940. Advances in shaping metal and molding plastics had enabled Lionel to mass-produce those detailed models.

1953

Lionel might have intended to revive those classics after the war, but did nothing in 1946 except for adding a deluxe single-dome tank car. Engineers modified the boxcar to serve as an O gauge merchandise car. The hopper and caboose were buried by an avalanche of toy-like models.

American Model Toys set out in 1949 to steal dollars from Lionel with it streamlined coaches, diners, and observations. In 1952, AMT posed a second challenge by releasing more than a dozen near-scale boxcars and stock cars. Those models, most painted Tuscan red, had prototypically correct numbers and emblems for such railroads as the Erie, Southern, Santa Fe, and Canadian Pacific.

Irrespective of whether the Engineering Department had already begun to upgrade Lionel's roster with near-scale boxcars, the appearance of AMT's models pushed it into overdrive. The passion for realism again became paramount.

Inch to spare

Here's where that previously mentioned inch assumes importance. Engineers finished a new molding for the body shell of the near-scale boxcar executives requested. Since 1946, Lionel had been manufacturing toy-like boxcars 9¼" in length. The new ones would be 10½" long.

Increasing the dimensions of the boxcar transformed it. Longer by the O scale equivalent of 6 feet and wider, too, the car seemed far more realistic than its shorter predecessors. The die-cast metal trucks and knuckle couplers also helped, as did a metal brake wheel. Doors that slid open and closed increased the play value.

Even so, size mattered most in providing Lionel with a rugged and authentic replica of the ubiquitous boxcar. Now it remained to be seen how men in charge of marketing and art, not to mention factory workers, would decorate the new models.

Broad outlook

Lionel had been coordinating with major railroads beyond the Northeast to broaden their locomotive and car listings. They carried forward that key trend with the new 6464 boxcars.

Great Northern Ry. had a rich history as the northernmost transcontinental line. Founded in 1857, its tracks spanned 8,300 miles through 10 states and two Canadian provinces. Boxcars with its herald depicting a Rocky Mountain goat were familiar in postwar days. A good reason why AMT finished a Great Northern boxcar in 1952 and American Flyer added one in 1953.

And a great reason for Lionel to match its rivals with the 6464-25. That orange-painted beauty (flat or glossy) came hot-stamped white with the name, initials, and emblem of the railroad, along with the corporation's own circle-L logo.

More information

- $5.50 ($49.73)
- Incorrectly shown with black and not white lettering in Advance and Consumer Catalogs for 1953
- Used as component of O gauge outfit no. 2203WS in 1953 and O-27 outfit no. 1515WS in 1954

6468 Baltimore & Ohio Double-Door Boxcar

The trend toward designing and manufacturing larger, more realistic cars for the three-rail roster accelerated dramatically in 1953. Whatever impetus engineers felt to move from toy-like models to near-scale ones gained a sense of urgency from the items that competitors, notably American Model Toys, were rushing into the marketplace.

Lionel met that challenge. The line for 1953 included, along with single-door boxcars, a triple-dome tank car, a flatcar carrying pipes, and an automobile boxcar.

1953

The no. 6468 Baltimore & Ohio Double-Door Boxcar has much to show about Lionel's renewed commitment to realistic, accurate modeling. This O gauge model also sheds a good deal of light on the postwar relationship between America's principal railroads and the country's booming automotive industry.

The need for special boxcars

The idea of designing a boxcar with two sliding doors on each side was not a fanciful notion. Offering the deep blue 6468 model with Baltimore & Ohio lettering and graphics reflected Lionel's wish to present replicas of popular equipment.

The boxcar introduced in 1953 was not the first double-door model cataloged after World War II. From 1946 through 1948, the firm offered the no. X2458. That brown-painted double-door boxcar with Pennsylvania RR markings was listed as an automobile car.

Almost from the time automobiles were first mass-produced in the eastern and midwestern regions in the early 20th century, they were transported in railcars.

Railroads like the Pennsylvania, New York Central, and Grand Trunk Western used 40-foot boxcars to bring partially completed automobiles from plants in Michigan to dealers for final assembly. Double doors on the sides and/or a door at one end enabled unfinished autos to be loaded and then stacked inside.

By the 1930s, steel boxcars, often with rounded roofs, were becoming the rule. These accommodated finished automobiles. As many as four could be carried inside a boxcar, thanks to stronger rack systems. One set of automobiles was secured to a rack, which was raised so more autos could be loaded underneath.

Lionel creates a three-rail model

Lionel based its postwar models on those double-door boxcars. The A.C. Gilbert Co., which also sought to replicate the latest rolling stock, never added an auto boxcar to its American Flyer line.

Lionel burst ahead. When it started modifying the line in 1952, going from drab, compact models to larger, vividly colored items, a new double-door boxcar became a priority. The 6468 played an important role in this transition.

The 10½"-long model was touted in the consumer catalog as "longer" with a "modern design roof." The copywriter justified Lionel's returning to the type of double-door car it had dropped. The automobile boxcar came painted a flat or glossy blue, with white hot-stamped markings.

Besides being available for separate sale for $5.50, the 6468 showed up in two cataloged outfits. For O-27 enthusiasts, there was the no. 1507WS, a five-car train led by a no. 2046 small Hudson. O gaugers could opt for the no. 2205WS, a five-car train pulled by the great no. 736 Berkshire.

Something brown

The blue 6468 returned in 1954 and '55. In the latter year, Lionel also released a few B&O cars painted Tuscan and packed in boxes with an "X" stamped on each end. These scarce variations came only in the no. 1535W Santa Fe F3 set.

Unfortunately, how many brown automobile boxcars were produced and whether Lionel intended them for special customers still perplex collectors. Answers may not ever be forthcoming, but interest in those scarce models remains strong.

More information

- $5.50 ($49.73)
- Cataloged 1953 through 1955
- Doors unique to automobile boxcars (part nos. 6468-6 and -10)
- Priced raised to $5.95 in 1955

3424 Wabash Operating Brakeman Car

How much a toy entertains remains central when remembering the electric trains and accessories from postwar days. What Lionel described as "play value" still nurtures memories of those wonderful models that left us laughing and excited.

Animation and interaction increased the enjoyment children associated with particular items. They especially loved railcars equipped with figures that moved. From little rubberized men who shifted back and forth on a horizontal plane, engineers graduated to miniature laborers traveling vertically. They launched that trend with the no. 3424 Operating Brakeman Car.

Great minds

Something incredible must have been floating in the air over the Lionel factory in New Jersey and the Gilbert plant in Connecticut late in 1955 or early the next year. The creative minds at the rival companies started crafting boxcars with a figure that seemed to walk on the roof.

The Flyer line for 1956 introduced the no. 970 Seaboard Operating Boxcar. Designers sliced an opening into the roof of an S gauge boxcar A metal rod attached to a motor inside protruded. The fixture held a painted figure that, when activated, strolled from one end to the other.

Astonishing to observe a Lionel no. 6464-275 State of Maine boxcar with a long circular route cut into its route. Although that rare engineering mock-up had no figure or mechanism, the idea behind it was plain. A miniature brakeman would walk around the roof when the special car was being operated.

Was it sheer coincidence that designers at both major toy train manufacturers sought to develop similar animated boxcars? Why did Lionel abandon its endeavor?

1956

More exciting

When engineers conceived of what became the 3424 remains a mystery. What they had in mind was an operating boxcar more sophisticated and complex than the American Flyer model. Its animation would replicate a thrilling scene from the infancy of railroading. The Operating Brakeman Car lifted operating cars into a higher realm of magical illusions.

Until the 3424 made its debut in 1956, figures on accessories and cars moved laterally and were hidden in shacks or behind sliding doors. Solenoids, plungers, and coils were responsible for laborers tossing milk cans or safeguarding crossings.

The 3424 relied on similar technology to provide animation of another sort. Men had once needed to clamber from one freight car to the next turning brake wheels. An already dangerous job became more perilous because of low obstructions that could kill.

In the 19th and early 20th centuries, railroads erected poles with a section extending over the tracks from which hung thick strands of rope called "telltales." A brakeman standing on a freight car knew that after being "caressed" by these ropes he had better hit the deck—and fast.

Novel creation

Perhaps Chief Engineer Joseph Bonanno, who received a patent for an "Operating Brakeman" in 1961, thought telltales, though an anachronism, could serve as the premise behind a successful car.

The illusion—a brakeman reacted when he felt the telltales—made the 3424 a winner. In reality, a solenoid controlled the figure. A contact roller on one truck picked up power for the coil inside the solenoid. When the sliding shoe on the other truck made contact with a grounding blade in the base of the telltale assembly, the circuit was completed and the figure moved.

With this operating car, cataloged as a set component and separate-sale item through 1958, Lionel leaped into a new and entertaining phase of design.

More information

- $8.95 ($79.44)
- 10⅝" long
- Price raised to $9.95 in 1957
- Figure could be white or blue vinylite
- Advance Catalog showed 3424 with Baltimore & Ohio Sentinel markings

3494-150 Missouri Pacific Operating Boxcar

The push toward greater fidelity to O scale dimensions gained speed after 1952. The introduction of four near-scale boxcars turned the tide. With those entries in the no. 6464 series, Lionel announced a similarly realistic double-door auto boxcar and an operating boxcar.

1956

Between 1953 and 1958, the near-scale operating boxcars grew to encompass seven members. Interchangeable in terms of their technology, they differed in decoration. Collectors might find it difficult to avoid favoring one road name over another. Topping many lists would be the no. 3494-150 Missouri Pacific.

Mechanically the same

The steps necessary to develop a series of near-scale boxcars, principally creating a new body shell and the doors and door guides to go on it, facilitated the introduction of related cars. Namely, the double-door automobile boxcar and the operating single-door boxcar, both of which also made their debut in 1953.

Executives, accustomed to cataloging an operating boxcar, pressed designers to supplement the line for 1953 with an updated version. They wanted a 6464 boxcar to be equipped with a plunger mechanism.

The process involved merely modifying the sheet-metal frame being used on the new near-scale boxcars. Engineers did so to create the no. 3484 Operating Boxcar, decorated for the Pennsylvania RR.

The inaugural member was, in technical terms, just an oversized descendant of the operating boxcars offered since 1949. The 3484, like the 3464 and 3474 models, came with a metal plunger activated via remote control to open a sliding door on the car and permit the blue vinylite railroad worker to move forward.

Oddly overlooked

The parade of operating boxcars built to nearly scale proportions marched on at a steady pace. The monochromatic paint scheme of the Pennsy car yielded the next year to a similarly drab one painted orange with Santa Fe markings.

Meanwhile, something wonderful was happening with the second batch of 6464 boxcars. Lionel leaped beyond painting their entire body shell a single color to masking long sections while laborers sprayed on a new hue. Resulting in 1954 in a couple of exciting additions to the series, each of which showed two strong colors.

The 6464-125 New York Central and 6464-150 Missouri Pacific boxcars inspired the next operating models. Someone in sales or engineering thought it sensible to catalog animated versions of the two most colorful near-scale boxcars.

Only not for long! Which was where the approach to marketing the nos. 3494-1 New York Central and 3494-150 operating boxcars seemed baffling. The costs involved with making them must have been minimal. Production supervisors were going to use shells all but finished and fit them with parts and assemblies already in stock. Yet Lionel cataloged the New York Central operating boxcar for only 1955 and the Missouri Pacific car for only 1956.

So gorgeous

The Missouri Pacific reached out to Lionel in the early 1950s. That midwestern railroad, whose network of 10,000 miles of track over 10 states made it among the largest in the country, expressed its fervent wish to have an O gauge diesel locomotive or passenger equipment decorated with its name and herald.

Lionel answered by adding a Missouri Pacific boxcar to its 6464 series in 1954. It painted blue bands along the top and bottom of the sides of the gray plastic shell, with rubber-stamped lettering and car data.

An operating version of that boxcar entered the line in 1956, a year after Lionel dropped the regular model from its line. Yet planners acted as though they wanted little to do with the 3494-150. They omitted it from outfits and deleted it after one year. Curiously, they then revived the 6464-150 for the 1957 line.

More information

- $7.95 ($70.56)
- 10½" long
- Unpainted yellow multi-block doors
- Large no. 3562-62 figure with painted face and hands

3530 Operating Generator Car

The toy train market underwent significant shifts as the postwar era progressed. Consumers demanded more because the full-size lines they watched in action kept adding specialized rolling stock to handle large and unique loads or meet changing needs.

Don't think engineers at Lionel missed out. Their ongoing research and observant eyes taught them about the latest and most exotic cars. Pushed to proceed, they developed fascinating models. One with the traits of a boxcar and a searchlight car was the no. 3530 Operating Generator Car.

1956

Specialized cars

By the middle of the 1950s, Lionel had brought out more realistic models of commonplace freight cars. Those near-scale and detailed replicas could be multiplied with additional paint schemes and road names. No reason to allocate valuable time and resources into developing similar kinds of modern boxcars, gondolas, and flatcars.

So engineers hunted for odd railcars. Next, they sought to show how models of those railcars could attract customers while being economically made and decorated.

Prototype first

Let your imagination drift back more than 60 years, with someone flipping through a railway publication or opening an envelope sent by the Electro-Motive Division of General Motors with photographs and descriptions of its latest equipment, including "Motive Power Units."

The first units had reached customers in 1954. They were, in essence, plain boxcars housing a standard 567 motor as well as a generator usually made by EMD. The mobile units served to supply electric power for carnivals and other businesses that traveled or areas crippled by a natural disaster and therefore in need of electricity.

Lionel replicated the 1,000-kilowatt mobile power station as a boxcar with a floodlight. Designers created a new body shell similar to the one for 6464 boxcars. Workers molded the shell of blue polystyrene and painted a white lightning-bolt stripe across each side. They painted the doors a matching shade of blue. White graphics were hot-stamped on blue plastic; blue graphics were hot-stamped on white.

The orange generator came from Lionel searchlight cars. The floodlight was a new type held by a magnet to the base of the no. 3650 Searchlight Extension Car, which also made its debut in 1956.

More to come

The instruction sheet packed with each Operating Generator Car explained how the model could be parked on a siding or moved wherever it was needed. It picked up current via a contact roller, which directed it from the active rails to the power pole and then to the searchlight through a pair of green wires ("cables") an operator clipped to the two terminals mounted on the roof of the generator car.

Manipulating a switch attached to the left-hand door activated the light inside the car and set off a humming intended to simulate usage. Further suggesting that the generator was tirelessly creating energy, the floodlight beamed brightly.

Late arrival

The 3530 was a separate-sale item only in 1956. That fact, coupled with the inaccurate depictions of the Operating Generator Car in the Advance and Accessory Catalogs, left the impression final development took longer than anticipated.

Not until the Consumer Catalog was finished for autumn 1956 did Lionel present a correct illustration of the 3530.

More information

- $12.95 ($114.94)
- Component of O gauge outfits no. 2291W and 2295WS in 1957 and no. 2519W in 1958
- Earliest examples had "EMD 3530" underlined in white and a full-length white stripe

6024 Shredded Wheat Boxcar

A mundane piece of rolling stock made its debut in 1948. That simple and inexpensive boxcar went unnoticed by many customers, whose focus was on the deluxe outfits and locomotives with broad shoulders filling the Consumer Catalog released for that key year.

In the dark about what item could seem so plain and unimpressive and yet have a significant impact? The piece of rolling stock suddenly pushed into the limelight was the short, unpainted plastic boxcar with double non-opening doors on each side. Every year from 1948 until the era closed 21 years later, Lionel cataloged at least one such model. The no. 6024 Shredded Wheat Boxcar illuminates its history.

1957

Fundamentals

The tale began with the decision to battle Louis Marx & Co. for the low end of the market. A simple steam engine and tender pulling a few unadorned plastic cars would break ground as the Scout set.

Included in the better of the two Scout sets for 1948 was a no. 1004 boxcar. It served as the prototype for the minimally decorated models that followed through 1961. Designers created a new tool to use when injection-molding the plastic bodies secured to sheet-metal frames with a screw at one end and a slot at the other.

Shells were 8½" long. Molded into each side were six vertical rows of simulated rivets, two shut doors, and two grab irons at the left and seven on the right. The roof had a catwalk; one end had a brake wheel.

Lionel used and reused the type I body shell for a wide array of boxcars assigned product numbers 1004, 6004, 6014, 6024, 6034, and 6044. Unpainted shells came in orange, red, or white polystyrene plastic. They typically were hot-stamped on the left side with a Pennsylvania RR keystone and the same rudimentary car data.

Lettering on the right side differentiated the short boxcars. Wording on some of the models released between 1948 and 1957 mentioned Baby Ruth candy, Bosco chocolate flavored syrup, Chun King Chinese food, Nabisco Shredded Wheat cereal, and Whirlpool washers and dryers. Others advertised fishing gear from Airex (a subsidiary of Lionel). Those boxcars omitted the Pennsy herald.

Sales opportunities

Did the brief list of consumer goods promoted on the different boxcars come as a surprise? Why, other than the Pennsy emblem and a few models decorated for the Frisco railroad, did the vast majority of low-end cars advertised household wares?

The answer, or so it would appear, was that the companies producing those foods, appliances, and more had shown a willingness to pay Lionel for what amounted to advertising space.

In 1957, the National Biscuit Co. worked out an agreement with the toy train giant to have various Lionel locomotives illustrated on boxes of its popular Shredded Wheat brand. Either as part of that contract or independently emerged a short boxcar hot-stamped black with the name of that breakfast cereal and the Nabisco corporate logo.

Lionel Executive Vice President Alan Ginsburg recognized the marketing opportunities awakened by the public's association of their toys as wholesome and meaningful. They sought to capitalize on it by inviting a range of outside businesses to invest in the inexpensive boxcars.

How exciting to study correspondence, diagrams, and prototypes to learn how Lionel made a pitch to many companies. Some bought in, notably RCA Whirlpool and Wix Corp. Others did not, including Coast to Coast grocery stores, Coca Cola, Hot Point appliances, Lipton Tea, Pillsbury flour, and Willard Batteries.

The actual boxcars and the failed proposals shed much light on how Lionel's sales philosophy was changing. Replicating the practices and cars on full-size railroads to amuse children no longer seemed the sole reason purpose of their trains.

More information

- Component of O-27 outfit no. 737/1589WS
- Incorrectly illustrated as red with white graphics in Consumer Catalog for 1957
- Equipped with bar-end or AAR trucks with operating couplers

6464-650 Denver & Rio Grande Western Boxcar

The popular and influential series of near-scale boxcars modestly launched with four monochromatic pieces in 1953 mushroomed into a group of postwar icons. Few models captured the attention—and wallets—of Lionel collectors as ferociously.

Every member of the no. 6464 fraternity earns a place of honor on a display or layout. If beauty, as defined by striking colors, becomes the criterion by which to judge them, the queen may well be no. 6464-650 Denver & Rio Grande Western.

Rainbow emerged

The development of the series of near-scale boxcars progressed at a slow pace. The drab models offered in 1953 gave way to the first entries with a second color the next year. The no. 6464-275 State of Maine smashed that barrier in 1955. It had painted bands of white and red over its blue shell.

Most likely, the dramatic change in decoration occurred because Lionel had adopted new devices capable of covering designated areas on a plastic body shell, so a laborer could spray them with different shades of paint quickly and accurately.

General Foreman Romualdo Camuso had fabricated crude masks for that task in his home workshop. Supervisors utilized them for diesel shells and rolling stock, beginning in 1955. Never again would complicated paint schemes defeat them.

A stunning assortment of 6464 boxcars injected the cataloged train line with amazing color over the next few years. Of course, what Lionel was making merely reflected the rainbow of eye-catching designs full-size railroads were then developing. Shields on the Rutland, elongated ovals on the Central of Georgia, and stripes on the Baltimore & Ohio and the Great Northern beautified Lionel's roster.

1957

Mountain time

Besides beefing up the list of near-scale boxcars to attract more customers, executives capitalized on their ability to duplicate more paint schemes in order to broaden the railroads represented in Lionelville.

More major as well as regional lines appeared, which satisfied customers living outside the Northeast.

Many lines joined the three-rail association in the 1950s. The Western Pacific stepped through the door in 1952. The Minneapolis & St. Louis entered the next year. Then came the Southern, followed by the Wabash. The New Haven stole the spotlight in 1956. A year later arrived the Denver & Rio Grande Western.

The D&RGW spanned territory between the Rocky Mountains and the Sierra Nevada range. It was also known for handling the famous *California Zephyr* streamlined passenger through picturesque gorges in the Rockies.

One of Camuso's paint masks helped crews decorate F3 A and B unit shells for splendid Denver & Rio Grande Western diesels cataloged in 1957 and 1958. A different one led to the creation of the 6464-650 Rio Grande boxcar. A Southern Pacific-type caboose decorated to match the F3s and the boxcar joined in 1958.

Handsome boxcar

Lionel specified taking an unpainted yellow plastic shell and spraying it silver to cover the roof and obtain a lower band along each side of a 6464-650. A black stripe applied with hot stamping separated the silver band. The scheme was extended across the sliding yellow side door.

Even though the D&RGW locomotive, boxcar, and caboose departed the cataloged line after 1958, their legacy was not forgotten. Maybe that explained the decision to bring back the 6464-650 for 1966, the last memorable year.

The style of shell and type of trucks used for Rio Grande boxcars changed for 1966. Rare examples came painted yellow and silver. They also boasted a roof spray-painted yellow rather than silver.

More information

- $5.95 ($51.12)
- Component of O-27 outfit no. 732/1581 in 1957
- Priced raised to $6.00 in 1966
- Factory errors lack thin black stripes
- Used in promotional outfit no. 19590 in 1966

3428 Operating Mail Car

Models, even the most popular and best loved, run their course in the product line. Their design gets old and outdated, or their animation dulls and becomes lackluster. Marketing executives evaluate sales and, disappointed in the results, ask engineers to create something new and improved to take their place to please customers.

Developing innovations to supersede formerly novel items characterized operating boxcars as the 1950s wound down. The near-scale models had lost their sheen, motivating designers to devise a replacement: no. 3428 Operating Mail Car.

Trusted mechanism

Chief Engineer Joseph Bonanno and Development Engineer Frank Pettit had avidly studied the no. 3462 Automatic Milk Car. After watching people fall in love with it in 1947, they vowed to build on its renown.

Pettit lit the match. He had learned through trial and error how to simulate activities done on full-size railcars. From creating remote-controlled models that dumped their contents, he had progressed to seeing what a charged plunger mechanism could accomplish.

Thanks to the solenoid lodged inside that assembly, an electromagnet in an uncoupling track section could activate the plunger. The force of that part being pulled down would cause motion on an operating car situated above the magnet.

In the case of the rudimentary operating boxcar, the force would open a sliding door and cause a figure mounted on a metal rod to move forward. The animation suggested a railroad laborer toiling inside the car.

1959

Small and big

What Pettit had tinkered and Bonanno refined became a mainstay. The short boxcars introduced in 1946 were mechanized for the first time three years later. Operating models numbered 3464 and 3474 lasted through 1953.

When near-scale boxcars overshadowed their smaller brethren in 1953 and after, Lionel developed operating versions. One by one, the nos. 3484 and 3494 made their debuts. Besides being longer, they soon featured more colorful paint schemes as well as regional road names.

The same plunger mechanism was installed on the big cars, which still depended on remote-controlled track sections. As before, a blue figure dashed forward into the opened doorway to say hi.

Mail time

The near-scale operating boxcars found a place in the line starting in 1953. Lionel largely repeated schemes used on non-operating models. Then a pair of road names never seen previously arrived in 1957 and lasted in the cataloged roster for a second year. Nos. 3494-550 Monon and 3494-625 Soo Line grabbed suffixes intended for the series of 6464 boxcars, suggesting planners considered making them non-operating.

Designers realized they could do more with the forward motion created when the solenoid was yanked down and the rod thrust ahead. If they modified the figure and crammed a tiny magnet right below his clenched hands, he would be able to clutch an object. When pushed forward with enough momentum and then abruptly stopped, that object should lose its grip and fly out of the open door.

Excited by the prospect of making something new, engineers decided a mailbag would be the perfect thing to fling. The mask developed for nos. 6464-275 and 3494-275 State of Maine boxcar let them visualize red, white, and blue cars on which to hot-stamp United State Mail and Railway Post Office lettering.

The 3428 Operating Mail Car broke new ground when it reached retailers in 1959, vanquishing earlier operating boxcars. Lionel assigned it to one cataloged O-27 outfit that year and another in 1960.

Meanwhile, a non-operating version (no. 6428) joined the team that year, cataloged through 1961 and again in 1965 and 1966. First time Lionel replaced an operating car with a simpler double.

More information

- $7.95 ($65.96)
- 10½" long
- Cataloged in 1959 and 1960
- Vinylite figure could be blue (holding gray mailbag) or gray (holding blue mailbag)

6470 Explosives Boxcar

Something significant and ominous happened to the train line after 1958. No longer were logs and coal big business in Lionelville. Rockets, military vehicles, and missiles replaced those materials as flatcar loads. That was because kids once devoted to electric trains seemed increasingly passionate about the armed forces and space exploration.

Engineering and sales executives paid attention to changing attitudes and set out to capitalize on them, always with an eye on what other toymakers were doing. Outside firms influenced an item symbolizing the ongoing shifts in taste and inclination—the no. 6470 Explosives Boxcar.

Changing times

A trend exploding in 1959 with the 6470 and other cars promising action had gained traction the year before. Lionel released flatcars bearing antiaircraft trucks, radar vehicles, and so forth. Those military loads, purchased from Pyro Plastics in Union, N.J., had featured U.S. Marine Corps or U.S. Navy insignia. Slick choices compared with the typical logs, trailers, and boats.

Yet change was hardly the rule in 1958. Gondolas still had canisters or culverts rather than anything novel or dangerous. As for boxcars, the series of near-scale models did not grow. Carryovers were business as usual in terms of road names and paint schemes (the pastel-colored duo in the Lady Lionel set being exceptions).

What a difference a year makes! Engineers took up the challenge of adding animation and excitement to the line in 1959. Already, they were scrutinizing the innovative military-oriented and space-themed locomotives and cars made by Kusan.

Lionel rolled out flatcars with radar-scanning scopes, firefighting equipment, and artillery-type as well as intercontinental missiles. They carried helicopters that had a mechanism to launch them into the sky.

At first glance, the near-scale boxcar inserted into the roster resembled one of the earlier 6464 types. But looks can deceive. Having little in common with the older Great Northern or Boston & Maine types, it led Lionel into a new era, when a boxcar could be the target of enemies.

1959

Going bang!

The no. 6470 Explosives Boxcar shared traits with various near-scale models. Same sheet-metal frame, now equipped with AAR trucks and operating couplers. The unpainted red plastic body shell had white hot-stamped lettering announcing danger and warning of explosives on board.

Lionel might have released a similar boxcar in 1958 to compete with Kusan. Such a model would have consisted of spellbinding graphics only.

Designers might have laughed in a sinister tone next, when they described what they had made possible with the 6470. Unlike other near-scale boxcars, its sides, ends, and roof were not a single molded part. Nope, each was a separate piece. Molded hooks and a lock-pin that slid through the roof held them together.

Inside the shell was a spring and trigger mechanism. It caused the car to collapse into pieces whenever its trigger side, as the instruction sheet named it, was bumped.

Engineers likely had known about Torpedo Attack and other toys equipped with springs so their loose-fitting plastic pieces scattered when struck. They applied that design concept to create the 6470.

Lionel created new items for blowing up Explosives Boxcars. A projectile fired by the new 44 U.S. Army Mobile Missile Launcher, 470 IRBM Missile Launching Platform, or 6650 IRBM Missile Launching Car was all it took to detonate the spring-loaded side.

Rough love

The 6470 endured three long years of destruction in the cataloged line, starting in 1959. Lionel sold the Explosives Boxcar separately then and in 1960.

One O-27 and two Super O sets used a 6470 in 1959; then one O-27 and one Super O outfit did in 1960. The run ended in 1961 with one O-27 set. That year, the no. 6448 Target Range Car stepped in for the 6470 to take its licks through 1964.

More information

- $5.95 ($49.36)
- 10½" long
- Cataloged from 1959 through 1961
- Component of 46 promotional outfits between 1960 and 1965

6445 Fort Knox Gold Reserve Car

Toymakers in the late 1950s and early 1960s, searching for something special that might hook kids, exploited their curiosity about what goes on "inside stuff." But as long as toys were made out of wood, cardstock, or pressed or die-cast metal, there was no way to enable a child to gaze through its opaque surface and study the interior workings.

The introduction of thermoplastics during the 1940s shattered that barrier. A toymaker could create transparent shells that were durable and safe to use.

1961

Engineers at Lionel became familiar with clear, "see-through" body shells after the war. Not until more than a decade had passed did they acknowledge the appeal of models with transparent assemblies. The breakthrough came in 1961 with the no. 6445 Fort Knox Gold Reserve Car, offered in outfits and individually.

Clear and invisible

Lionel had first capitalized on the capacity of transparent shells to unveil the inner mechanics of an electric train in 1948. Eager to show off the two motors put in the new no. 2333 replica of an Electro-Motive F3 diesel, the firm created a few dozen Santa Fe units with clear bodies and shipped them to its regional showrooms and major dealers for display.

Using the transparent diesels only for demonstration might have been a missed opportunity for Lionel. In 1959, a novel plaything exploded onto the market. Renwal announced its Visible Man, a 16"-tall model kit of the male body. Inside a clear-plastic exterior (the skin) were assembled tiny veins, bones, and organs.

This easy-to-build kit, which could be taken apart and put together again, took the toy field by storm. Orders flooded in from all over the country. Soon a Visible Woman had joined her male counterpart. In time, there were even clear-plastic models that showed the "innards" of a horse, a dog, and a V-8 automobile motor.

Lionel acts

If kids were intrigued by what went on inside a human being, perhaps they were curious about what was carried inside an enclosed railcar. That line of reasoning likely sparked Tony Rocco, part of the Engineering Department, to design something that the corporation could have nicknamed the Visible Boxcar.

Tony pushed things when he came up with the idea behind the no. 3435 Traveling Aquarium Car in 1959. Two years later, he modified the plastic shell of the "fish car" to create the 10½"-long 6445 Fort Knox Gold Reserve Car, which stayed in the line through 1963. Kids could at last see what a boxcar supposedly carried.

The 6445 was no ordinary boxcar with soda crackers, refrigerators, or other goods. Instead, Tony imagined a special car with clear plastic sides (windows, really) behind which were piles of dazzling gold bullion.

The silver-painted model had black hot-stamped lettering, a brake wheel, and AAR trucks with operating couplers. Lionel altered the mold to put a slot in the roof in which kids could insert coins.

Good uses

Men handling the development of outfits designated the Fort Knox Gold Reserve Car as appropriate for both O-27 and Super O trains in 1961. A year later, however, they restricted the 6445 to only a single Super O Old West set.

Deleted after 1963, when it was separate sale only, the car with "see-thru sides" influenced thinking at Lionel for years. General Mills, which leased the rights to make Lionel trains after 1969, offered at least a half dozen reissues between 1979 and 1986.

Those models, led by a duplicate of the postwar car (no. 9320), were painted blue, gold, maroon, orange, or silver. Their lettering celebrated past or present U.S. mints in Denver, New Orleans, and Philadelphia.

Over the past 25 years, Lionel has entranced consumers with novel loads. Behind the windows have sat scale vehicles, aliens, mummies, and more.

More information

- $5.95 ($48.04)
- Incorrectly shown in Consumer Catalog for 1962 with orange body as part of outfit no. 13036
- Component of 15 promotional sets between 1961 and 1964

3619 Helicopter Reconnaissance Car

Members of the Engineering Department during the late 1950s and early 1960s needed, along with familiarity with electrical motors and magnetism, a vivid imagination. They had to be capable of surpassing what full-size railroads operated in order to envision amazing novelties—and then be able to develop those novelties.

Evidence of how engineers succeeded was the no. 3619 Helicopter Reconnaissance Car. After imagining a boxcar that launched a helicopter, they figured out which parts and assemblies on hand they could use to make an unprecedented operating car.

Unlimited ideas

Visitors to Lionel's archives have described a few unbelievable operating cars that ended up being too difficult or costly to mass-produce. A flatcar with caged gorillas never entered the catalog. Neither did a boxcar that dispensed candy or a car with equipment to simulate spraying weeds.

Designers win acclaim for conceiving of such unique models and then making progress on operating prototypes. Chief Engineer Bonanno must have been pleased with the efforts of his department and then felt disappointment when innovative projects had to be scrapped or delayed.

A boxcar that transported a concealed helicopter and then, by remote control, launched that aircraft through a retractable roof would have struck Lionel's engineers as preposterous had it been suggested early in the postwar era. They might have scorned the idea as something out of a science fiction magazine and unlikely to become a reality until the 21st century.

Yet the 3619 reveals how, later in postwar days, designers and model makers could conceive of something once unbelievable and, thanks to their expertise and cooperation, develop an O gauge version that production teams at the plant could efficiently and inexpensively manufacture.

Space breakthrough

The Helicopter Reconnaissance Car represents one of the space- and military-oriented items offered during the late postwar years. Some seemed silly and proved ineffective in operation. Others turned out to be authentic in look and reliable on tracks.

1962

Deserving of praise were the operating flatcars. By hand or remote control, they sent a small satellite up toward a ceiling or a missile across a bedroom. Definitely entertaining, even though larger and faster models, including the 175 Rocket Launcher and 44 Mobile Missile Launcher, overshadowed them.

In 1962 came what the catalog declared was "The secret weapon of tomorrow." The Helicopter Reconnaissance Car had cool looks and operated dependably. Its unpainted light or dark yellow plastic body (reworked from the 3665 Minuteman Missile Launching Car, itself reworked from the 3530 Electro Mobile Power Car) had black and red hot-stamped graphics.

Bond-like operation

The car's operation suggested the unbelievable machines in James Bond movies Traveling on a freight train, the 3619 seemed "innocent looking," as the catalog put it.

Ah, but stop the boxcar over an uncoupling track section and press the button on a remote-control device. The unpainted black roof of the Helicopter Reconnaissance Car separated as two long halves opened, revealing a small red plastic helicopter. That model (originally developed as a flatcar load for Lionel's line of HO scale trains) was secured to the "spring spool" mounted inside. Once catapulted into the sky automatically, its rotor spun wildly to begin aerial surveillance of enemy territory.

The effect was dazzling. The 11"-long 3619 demonstrated how engineers were reacting to the space race with innovative and action-packed models.

More information

- $10.95 ($87.54)
- Part of five O-27 and Super O outfits in 1962 and 1963
- Cataloged as separate-sale item between 1962 and 1964
- Component of 24 promotional outfits between 1962 and 1965

3666 Minuteman Car

Do you know about everything Lionel offered during the postwar era? Plenty of collectors and operators insist they have memorized the roster of O gauge locomotives, rolling stock, accessories, and transformers. Then something appears most of them have missed.

Envision an operating car guaranteed to provide thrills and action. See if you can conceive of a model fairly described as an accessory on eight-wheel trucks. It's a freight car never placed in Lionel's consumer catalogs. Get ready to learn about the no. 3666 Minuteman Car, a desirable piece of rolling stock found only in promotional outfits released in 1964 and 1965.

1964

Not the first Minuteman

Are you focusing on the Minuteman?

Lionel introduced a different yet similar model in 1961. For the no. 3665 Minuteman Missile Launching Car, designers had brilliantly used parts and assemblies associated with a handful of previous additions to the roster of cars.

Among the items borrowed were the frame from no. 6464 near-scale boxcars and the body shell from the no. 6530 Fire and Safety Training Car (new in 1960). The latter, of course, was derived from the shell of the no. 3530 Operating Generator Car, which had entered the line in 1956.

Most importantly, designers adapted the firing mechanism initially used on the no. 6650 Missile Launching Flatcar, which made its debut in 1959. For the Minuteman Missile Launching Car, however, they fastened the launcher on top of the frame while devising a new roof whose two long halves opened via remote control so an operator could fire the missile at any target.

The 3665 car appeared in cataloged outfits every year between 1961 and 1963. When Lionel decided to pull the plug on the Minuteman Missile Launching Car, it made the model available for separate sale only. The listed retail price in 1964, as it had been since the operating car had arrived in 1961, was only $9.95.

Something a little different

Lionel executives, eager to increase sales of promotional sets, offered two retail giants in 1964 a new version of the Minuteman Car known as a "cannon boxcar." The newcomer had the unpainted white plastic body with blue and red hot-stamped lettering of its comrade. Instead of a mechanism firing missiles, the 3666 had a plastic "cannon" able to shoot silver-painted wood shells.

Designers had come up with a plunger-operated cannon-firing mechanism not just for the 3666 but also for another O gauge car used solely in promotional sets in 1964, the no. 6651 U.S. Marine Corps Cannon Firing Car. The olive drab plastic cannon shot shells for both cars slightly varying in length and diameter.

The 3666 showed up in 1964 in outfit no. 19326 (Sears, Roebuck and Co. no. 9820), a four-car O-27 train headed by a no. 240 steam engine. The same year it was included in a five-car set offered through Western Auto Stores (no. 19332).

The cannon boxcar returned in 1965 in two sets sold exclusively through Sears. Outfit no. 19326 included the same models as found in its set box the year before. The motive power now consisted of a no. 238 steam engine and tender.

Meanwhile, promotional outfit no. 19434 coupled a no. 221 Marine Corps or no. 221 Santa Fe Alco diesel A unit to the four freight cars. Rounding out that neat set was a no. 347 Rocket Launching Platform (also packed in outfit 19326).

Sort of scarce

The relative scarcity of the 3666 Minuteman Car should appeal. If that doesn't motivate you to get one, thinking about it having weaponry sure to enliven any O gauge layout might do the trick. A car never added to the cataloged line is cool.

Before commencing your search, keep in mind that as a set component only, the item called a Cannon Firing Boxcar never had a component box. Finally, beware of the reproductions of the wood shells that have flooded the marketplace.

More information

- Measured 11" long
- Never a part of the cataloged line
- Came with four wood shells
- Correct product number is 3666-25

2460 Bucyrus Erie Operating Crane Car

The more miniature trains enabled youngsters to do, the more popular those toys would be. Popularity naturally translated into profits for the manufacturers. It became a priority, then, for companies to develop items, especially locomotives and accessories, with additional features sure to keep children busy and happy.

Rolling stock occupied a separate field. Designers struggled to broaden the appeal of boxcars, gondolas, and so forth. Doors that slid open or shut and loads lifted on or off manually all but exhausted what was possible before the late 1930s, when remote-controlled animation transformed the world of toy trains.

An exception was a flatcar equipped with some sort of boom or derrick. In 1946, folks wanted a no. 2460 Operating Crane Car.

Prewar heritage

The 2460, pictured on the cover of the Consumer Catalog for 1946, represented the latest and most realistic rendition of an item that had been a hallmark of Lionel's line from its beginning. Joshua Cowen had filled out his 2⅞" gauge roster with the no. 500 Derrick Car in 1903.

1946

Yet the subsequent Standard gauge line did not boast a crane until the no. 219 in 1926. The first O gauge model appeared only in 1930 with the no. 810.

No other domestic manufacturer countered with a crane car during the 1920s or well into the next decade. Ives never had one, although after that firm declared bankruptcy in 1928 and Lionel gained control, it issued a 219 under the Ives name. The American Flyer Manufacturing Co. did not broaden either its Wide or O gauge model lines with a crane car.

Not until 1939, after A.C. Gilbert Co. bought the assets of American Flyer, did someone challenge Lionel. The no. 514 wrecker car, which Gilbert developed for its budding O gauge list, paved the way with its die-cast metal frame and vividly painted sheet-metal parts. In 1941, Gilbert announced the no. 481 wrecker crane, which substituted a sheet-metal frame.

Postwar excitement

The situation changed dramatically—and beneficially, as far as modelers were concerned—once federal restrictions on the production of toys were lifted in 1945. Then it was merely a matter of time and planning before Lionel took action. The advantages of selling a crane car were too great to let the opportunity slip by.

For the less-prestigious O-27 roster, Lionel relied on a prewar carryover, now equipped with realistic knuckle couplers. The colorful and toy-like no. 2560 Operating Crane Car seemed the correct choice.

For the upscale O gauge roster, designers finished a magnificent model of a hefty car distinguished by its large cab and rugged boom assembly with a pulley, block, and hook. The 2460 looked as modern and powerful as anything!

The big and strong 2460 Crane Car flexed its muscles over an 8⅜"-long die-cast metal frame and deluxe six-wheel trucks like those used on Lionel's top-of-the-line heavyweight passenger cars and tenders. Those features made it sturdier and better able to handle loads than could the delicate 7½"-long 2560.

Lionel's growing reliance on injection-molded plastics raised the 2460 to a high level of realism. The neatly detailed cab, painted light or dark gray in 1946 to stand out from the black-painted frame, had black hot-stamped markings. As impressive was the long boom, which Lionel based on a Bucyrus Erie prototype.

Superb operation

No debate that the 2460 Operating Crane Car earned applause for its appearance and innovation. But what mattered most was its performance. That baby could do it all, thanks to a rotating cab, a functioning boom and hook, and die-cast metal cranks inserted into the end and side of the cab.

Lionel switched to a black-painted cab with white hot-stamped graphics, starting later in 1946 (that version is worth much less than a model with a gray cab). Other than minor changes to the markings, the 2460 stayed the same through 1950.

More information

- $9.75 ($120.71)
- Cataloged from 1946 through 1950
- Component of work train outfits through 1949
- Added to O-27 line after 1947

2560 Lionel Lines Operating Crane Car

The finest locomotives and rolling stock cataloged immediately after World War II reflected Lionel's commitment to developing realistic models. Near-scale dimensions enhanced by extensive details impressed and delighted consumers then and continue to gratify collectors.

All the same, progress in transforming the train line, failed to occur immediately. Executives had no alternative to marketing a few items considered toys. That point applied in particular to members of the O-27 roster, which generally cost less to make and sold at lower prices.

1946

Certain pieces hearkened back to the marvels of the late prewar era. They dazzled with their colors and shapes, pleasing kids who loved to have fun with their trains. No wonder youngsters in 1946 and 1947 asked for a no. 2560 Operating Crane Car.

Prewar pleasure

The pleasures children could cultivate with a toy derrick and its pulley and hook could never be limited. They enjoyed snagging a small object before turning a hand crank on the crane to move, raise, or lower it.

Lionel cataloged crane cars long before the start of the postwar era. But it did not introduce such models until fairly late. The Standard gauge roster got its first crane car in 1926. O gauge enthusiasts had to wait another four years for theirs.

The no. 810 Work Crane Car, which left modelers breathless in 1930, kept at its job of lifting derailed rolling stock and vehicles for the next dozen years. Its rainbow of colors for the cab, roof, and boom made the Lionel Lines model a real crowd-pleaser. Executives updated it with the remote-controlled electric couplers introduced in 1938, christening the new model no. 2810 (cataloged through 1942).

Also in 1938, a shorter model with a smaller cab and less-detailed boom made its debut. The no. 2660 Work Crane Car provided the firm with a similar piece at a lower price level through 1942. It featured the new couplers, too.

Happy returns

Individuals at the helm when World War II came to a close, fervently debated how Lionel might assemble the most complete groups of rolling stock for its O-27 and O gauge lines. Among other areas, they switched a spotlight on crane cars for 1946. They adopted a smart approach, one deftly blending the wisdom of reviving something older and trusted while developing something entirely new.

The pressure to act increased once executives realized A.C. Gilbert Co. intended to challenge Lionel with a full complement of S gauge models in its American Flyer line. The pair of wrecker cars Gilbert brought out before the war would unquestionably sire a newcomer. For Lionel to delay an operating crane car would cede a noteworthy segment to its newest competitor.

Garnering publicity and accolades was Lionel's completely new and impressive no. 2460 Bucyrus Erie Operating Crane Car assigned to the O gauge roster. The Consumer Catalog showed the replica of a modern maintenance-of-way car as an exclusive part of two work train outfits and a separate-sale item.

Meanwhile, designers revived the frame, cab, boom, and other parts used to assemble 2660 cars for the all-but-identical 7½"-long 2560 Crane Car. The latter, of course, came with the new remote-controlled knuckle couplers.

Major distinguishing marks associated with the 2560 included a sheet-metal frame with steps at all four corners; it was painted flat or glossy black. The cab again came painted light yellow with the roof in red. Lionel compression-molded the boom, as it did the one used on the 2460, out of unpainted Bakelite.

Two die-cast metal hand cranks enabled a modeler to maneuver the boom and guide the solid hook attached with white cord. Lionel Lines and the product number were rubber-stamped black at the rear of the cab, with a circle-L nearby.

More information

- $5.50 ($68.10)
- Unpainted Bakelite boom could be black, brown, or green
- Consumer Catalogs incorrectly showed brown cab (frame had Pennsylvania RR marking in 1947)

6561 Lionel Lines Flatcar with Cable Reels

Many important trends in Lionel's post-World War II development took off and gathered speed during the 1950s. One shift involved enhancing the appeal of toy trains by creating models sure to capitalize on the public's growing fascination with international military competition and space exploration. Another, very different trend related to the use of paint masks to expand the list of diesels sold.

Other trends touched on design and decoration, selection of trains, and marketing and advertising strategies. How about, too, the imaginative use of flatcar loads?

As soon as the conversation focuses on distinctive loads, the assortment of flatcars dominates the discussion. A key player in the emergence of novel items being transported is no. 6561 Lionel Lines Flatcar with Cable Reels.

Trend begins

By the end of the 1950s, annual catalogs illustrated car after car with different loads. Miniature military vehicles gained attention, as did automobiles and girders. Helicopters and rockets were popular choices, along with trailers.

1953

The trend began after the war with the introduction of the no. 2411 "Big Inch" Flatcar in 1946. That die-cast metal model painted gray came loaded with metal pipes and then wood logs. The next year saw a die-cast metal flatcar whose center section was depressed so it could accommodate taller loads. A plastic transformer rode on the brand-new no. 2461 in 1947.

That flatcar remained in the cataloged line as the 2461 and later as no. 6461 through 1950. Engineers decided the depressed-center car would complement the plastic generator they wanted to use with a floodlight on the no. 6520 Searchlight Car (new in 1949).

Cable reels worked fine

Executives, likely believing the flatcar with a transformer had exhausted its appeal, deleted it from the cataloged roster after 1950. Nothing replaced the 6461.

The Gilbert Company was bolstering its flatcars by adding unique loads. The S gauge no. 636 Erie depressed-center car with a single cable reel entered the American Flyer line in 1948.

But the trend at Lionel of using flatcars to hold different loads did not leap ahead until 1953. Then the momentum launched accelerated every year for at least the next decade. The 6561 set things in motion.

The 10"-long die-cast metal car with a depressed center was painted gray. The product number and Lionel Lines markings were rubber-stamped black. A metal brake stand at each end added realism.

The load capturing attention was a pair of unpainted plastic reels, both wound with a single layer of aluminum wire. An elastic band stretched over the reels to secure them; the crimped eyelet at each end of the cord was tucked into the hole and slot added to each end of the body (the sole alteration made to it).

Left out in 1953

Lionel failed to designate the 6561 as a component of any O-27 or O gauge outfit in 1953. Yet the illustration of the new Lionel Lines Flatcar with Cable Reels in the Advance Catalog matched what was later produced. That fact countered any argument that Lionel made the 6561 too late in 1953 to include it in cataloged sets.

Executives remedied the situation a year later, adding the 6561 to top O-27 and O gauge F3 freight trains. They acted similarly in 1955, making the Lionel Lines Flatcar with Cable Reels a component of high-end outfits in both lines.

But in 1956, the final year Lionel cataloged the 6561, planners relegated it to the items sold separately. Evidently, they believed the commercial appeal of cable reels as a flatcar load had diminished.

More information

- $5.95 ($53.80)
- Two unpainted gray or orange reels were the standard load; gray reels are worth a bit more
- Gray reels shown in Consumer Catalog for 1953; orange reels shown in 1954 through 1956

3620 Lionel Lines Rotating Searchlight Car

Sometimes with Lionel, the best ideas yielding the most popular kinds of rolling stock had to wait. Yes, for reasons never quite clear, the men at the top might hesitate to proceed. Or they would deliberately choose to delay certain projects.

An outstanding and puzzling example of such inaction after the war was an operating searchlight car. Instead of reviving a prewar model right after the war, Lionel waited to release a new type in 1949.

Then the firm moved ahead with more sophisticated searchlight cars over a 12-year span. The first three of those five models were basic in appearance, but their operation went from mainly manual with the no. 6520 to wholly automatic with the no. 3620 Rotating Searchlight Car.

1954

Prewar invention

The idea of mounting one or two floodlights on a toy railcar was not new. Lionel had introduced searchlight cars for both its Standard and O gauge lines in 1931.

Throughout the 1930s, operating floodlight cars occupied spots of prominence. In fact, two models—nos. 2620 and 2820—remained in the O gauge catalog until production was suspended in 1942.

Surprisingly, then, engineers and executives held back after the war. The only item in 1946 with anything close to a searchlight was the deluxe model of the brand-new wrecker caboose. The no. 2420 was it. Lionel appeared content to let the Gilbert Company dazzle consumers with a true searchlight car for its American Flyer line.

1949 arrival

We'll never know why the largest toy train maker did not herald its first searchlight car of the postwar era until 1949. In that year, the no. 6520 made its debut as a set component and a separate-sale item.

That car boasted a look unlike any searchlight car seen before the war. The design departed from a flatcar with a light mounted on a pressed steel frame.

Lionel's model makers took the die-cast metal depressed-center chassis they had created for the no. 2461 Transformer Car (new in 1947) and adapted it to hold a modern-looking metal searchlight. With the 6520 the light could be switched on by remote control but rotated strictly by hand.

Designers did something beyond just substituting a heavy depressed-center flatcar for a plain model. They came up with a small generator, to be molded out of plastic and mounted at the end of the 6520 opposite from the floodlight. That generator came in green, maroon, or orange.

Besides creating a model that looked up to date and felt hefty to a child, Lionel improved its searchlight car by developing a brand-new floodlight that, like the generator, seemed to be in the right proportion to the car. Now, the firm had a new operating model that looked right on an O gauge or an O-27 work train.

Getting better

The only drawback with the 6520 related to its operation. Owners could maneuver the floodlight only by hand.

Leave it to Development Engineer Frank Pettit to correct the shortcoming. He adapted a vibrating mechanism he had been tinkering with for the searchlight car. Once the floodlight was illuminated, rubber "fingers" on its base rubbed against the round platform beneath it so the light could rotate automatically.

The improved searchlight car, designated no. 3520 and introduced in 1952, promised more control over how the light went on and off and where it shined.

Designers went on fine-tuning the model until they had one whose operation had nothing to do with remote control.

The 10"-long 3620, introduced in 1954 and cataloged for two more years, depended entirely on track power to illuminate and swivel around a darkened room. Hands-off operation had finally arrived, and kids loved watching the bright light rotate while their favorite locomotive pulled the searchlight car over main lines.

More information

- $7.95 ($71.35)
- Cataloged from 1954 through 1956 as both set component (O-27 and O gauge) and separate-sale item
- Searchlight housings (part 3520-12) were unpainted gray or painted gray over orange plastic

6414 Evans Auto Loader

Squeezing into just one page a proper history and appreciation of any of the iconic engines and railcars Lionel cataloged during the postwar era can feel impossible. Telling newcomers or experts about Lionel's F3s or 6464-series boxcars taxes the imagination to the limit, much the way the Lovin' Spoonful lamented in 1965 the impossible task of "trying to tell a stranger 'bout rock and roll." Can't be done!

One classic deserving a more comprehensive treatment is the no. 6414 Evans Auto Loader. With that novel use of a flatcar, Lionel showed how its vision had grown in response to what consumers demanded. It heralded in 1955 a great model that remained in the line through 1966.

New phase

The Engineering Department devoted hours learning about what was happening on railroads. The goal was to discover the latest locomotives and rolling stock that Lionel might replicate in hopes of outdistancing any rivals.

1955

By the mid-1950s, Lionel, like Gilbert and Marx, had released models of every kind of freight car. Getting an edge in the market meant creating something brand new, perhaps slightly exotic or unexpected, and enticing to consumers.

Success arrived when Lionel brought out the 6414. That model, like nos. 6418 Machinery Car and 6517 Bay Window Caboose also new in 1955, inaugurated a new phase for the Lionel line.

Key innovation

The history of the 6414 began in February 1954, when Lionel heard that the Evans Products Co. demonstrated for the New York Central a new loader capable of transporting six cars. A press release explaining that Evans had built its auto loader on a standard 54-foot flatcar would influence Lionel's designers.

Automobiles weren't strangers to Lionel, which had cataloged double-door boxcars identified as automobile cars. That was how railroads brought Fords and Chryslers to dealers until flatcars fitted with special frames became the norm. Evans, based near Detroit, led in that area and sent blueprints and pictures to Lionel.

For the 6414, designers began with a no. 6511-2 red-plastic frame made for the near-scale flatcar introduced in 1953. They used tabs at four stake holes on the frame to attach a two-piece stamped-steel superstructure meant to be painted black. White rubber-stamped graphics included "Auto-Loader" and Evans logos (not the General Motors markings shown on the mock-up depicted in the Advance Catalog).

Packed with each 11"-long 6414 (originally in cardboard sleeves) were four plastic cars based on Ford two-door sedans. The early autos were the finest—maroon (red), blue, yellow, and white molded bodies (4$\frac{5}{16}$" long), with chrome bumpers, clear window inserts, and rubber tires. Now the owner of an Evans Auto Loader also had a fleet of miniature cars to play with anywhere.

Ongoing changes

The Evans Auto Loader underwent minor changes during its 12-year tenure. Lionel also used no. 6424-11 frames at least as early as 1958, when it began hot-stamping "6414" to the left and not the right of "Lionel." Plastic trucks replaced metal ones that year, and different types of couplers were installed.

In 1962, Lionel shifted to gray bumpers on the automobiles. Two years later, decision-makers ordered those features eliminated. They decreed in 1964 open windows and molded-in wheels to save pennies.

The resulting "cheapie" autos are prized by collectors. They also hunt for scarce autos Lionel molded in bright green and brown (and shades of blue, white, and yellow).

Consequently, unauthorized reproductions of the scarce autos have inundated the market. Buyers should measure the autos (reproductions tended to be $\frac{1}{16}$" shorter) and check for details and lettering stamped inside the bodies and frames.

More information

- $8.95 ($80.63)
- Used in O-27 and O gauge outfits
- Price reduced to $7.95 in 1957 and increased to $8.00 in 1965
- Models for 1965 and 1966 included maroon autos with gray bumpers

6418 Machinery Car

The need for Lionel to offer models of contemporary, often specialized freight cars had assumed urgency by the middle 1950s. Right after the war, consumers were more than satisfied to be able to purchase fundamental items. All the company had to catalog were a boxcar, flatcar, gondola, tank car, and so forth.

Before long, however, modelers began asking for more realistic cars. With American Model Toys expanding the O gauge market, and Gilbert answering with scale replicas running on S gauge track, Lionel had to modify its roster. It responded with near-scale examples of those basic freight cars, including a flatcar. The no. 6511 with a load of pipes made its debut in 1953.

The next stage witnessed the development of O gauge models of the sort of freight cars railroads had built to handle unique tasks and larger loads. Lionel broke into that area in 1955 with the no. 6362 Rail Truck Car. Also in that year arrived the no. 6418 Machinery Car.

1955

New needs

Railroads had been buying from car manufacturers and occasionally constructing in their own shops "heavy-capacity flatcars" at least since the early 1910s. Among those newly designed pieces were flatcars with a depressed center.

Those freight cars, with their low center of gravity, handled heavier and bulkier loads throughout the prewar era and right into the postwar. Loads stood out, such as immense electrical transformers, generators, turbines, and boilers.

Lionel engineers seized on the opportunity of putting out a replica in 1947. They designed a die-cast metal flatcar with a depressed center. Using information from the November 1940 issue of *Model Builder* magazine, they featured a plastic transformer molded in two pieces and painted black or red as the load of the no. 2461. Lionel cataloged the same model with magnetic couplers as no. 6461 in 1949 and 1950.

Longer still

Change never stopped on full-size railroads after the war, so there was no reason to imagine it would at Lionel or its competitors. Indeed, Gilbert responded with a long depressed-center flatcar carrying a miniature reel of wire in 1948.

It took five years, but Lionel released its no. 6561 Flatcar with Cable Reels. The slightly modified depressed-center flatcar transported two reels and not one.

Even after pausing for a year following the debut of the near-scale flatcar carrying miniature pipes, designers had not lost their taste for innovation. Instead, they dug deeper into industry publications and encyclopedias of railcars to learn what Lionel could replicate to entice consumers fascinated with the current scene.

Research, along with keen observation of freight trains passing through communities in New Jersey and New York, impressed engineers and other Lionel employees with the sight of modern rolling stock. The enormous depressed-center cars the Pennsylvania RR had been building since 1951 left them amazed.

The Pennsy had constructed nine FD1 depressed-center flatcars. Not only were they much longer, exceeding 72 feet in length, but also their capacity hit 150 tons. The midsection was 30 feet long and rode 2½ feet above the rails. Integral cast-steel span bolsters supported the body, which needed eight sets of trucks.

One look at that monster probably sufficed to motivate the engineers. They developed a die-cast metal car with a depressed center, suggesting they had stretched the 10"-long body formerly used by the 2461 and 6461 Transformer Cars until it had nearly doubled in size. Now they had a model 16" long.

First use

Designers equipped the elongated flatcar with two sets of O gauge trucks at each end. The Machinery Car, while a challenge to place on track because of its 16 wheels, sure looked good. Now the only question was what to do with it.

For 1955, Lionel decided to strap onto the eye-catching depressed-center flatcar a pair of injection-molded girders like those being used for the no. 214 Plate Girder Bridge. Those plastic components initially came as black or orange with Lionel in raised lettering (the top surface of the letters hot-stamped white). Later the markings were switched to U.S. Steel with that firm's logo at one end.

Finally, designers elected to update the old transformer car for 1956. They installed a similar load molded out of black plastic right in the middle of the 16-wheel depressed-central flatcar. Though neat, the transformer looked too small.

More information

- $7.95 ($ 71.62)
- Cataloged from 1955 through 1957
- Blank plaque on underside first had number on it
- Component of one O gauge outfit in 1956 and 1957

6430 Flatcar with Cooper-Jarrett Vans

1956

The need to broaden the appeal of what Lionel made influenced what it developed and marketed as the 1950s wore on. Youngsters were becoming pickier, with new and intriguing toys introduced to shift their interest from what Lionel produced. Holding its share of the expanding market proved challenging for the toy train giant.

What Lionel did with flatcars reveals how its sales and engineering personnel reacted to a changing market. Not only did they depend on an array of loads to infuse rolling stock with play value, they also explored ways of using what was put on cars to bring in more revenue. Both angles shaped the background of the no. 6430 Flatcar with Cooper-Jarrett Vans.

Trailers travel

The notion of railroads carrying trailers on flatcars both before and after tractors hauled them to and from points of transshipment had been tried since the late 1920s. It gained popularity during the prewar era and picked up speed afterward. Typically, railroads outfitted older flatcars or constructed specially equipped new ones to handle one trailer (average length was 20 feet). Longer cars, usually 53 feet in length, were able to handle two trailers.

Innovations made during the early 1950s, above all, a trailer hitch from American Car & Foundry in 1955, facilitated both loading and unloading.

New equipment installed on railcars increased trailer-on-flatcar traffic for the rest of the 1950s. That trend, in turn, provided incentives for railroads to build new flatcars intended for hauling trailers.

Accessory first

What was happening on full-size railroads inspired the designers of toy trains. The process involved in transferring trailers on and off special flatcars captured the imagination of Lionel's engineers in 1955.

Consequently, the firm broke ground with an accessory promising plenty of action even if manual and not remote-controlled operation defined it. The no. 460 Piggyback Transportation Set depended on fine motors skills as well as the patient manipulation of a hand crank and lever to maneuver trailers between a railcar and the gray plastic platform. Central to the animation was a big red plastic lift truck.

Inside the box of a 460 was a no. 3460 flatcar, along with two green plastic trailers. On their sides were thin metal tags identifying the trailers as Lionel Trains. On the front of each trailer was a smaller tag with the name of a manufacturer (Fruehauf) and its model (Duravan).

Making money

Ronald Saypol, who had risen from a sales position in New York City to assisting Executive Vice-President Alan Ginsburg, believed opportunities to earn extra dollars existed by persuading businesses to pay Lionel to put their names on cars. Responsible for having engineered the switch on tank cars from Sunoco to Gulf, he looked for places to advertise other businesses.

Saypol fastened on the trailers in every Piggyback Transportation Set. Why stick with Lionel Trains markings on them when a potential customer, specifically a trucking firm, might pay to affix its name?

Saypol's wish for sponsors intensified after planners decided to release the 6430 flatcar with a pair of trailers as a separate-sale item and a set component in 1956. But an illustration of the new model in the Accessory Catalog showed the two trailers again lettered for Lionel Trains.

Bothered by what was shown, Saypol pushed himself to find a sponsor. By the time the 6430 appeared in the Consumer Catalog, it featured trailers decorated for Cooper-Jarrett Inc., a long-distance trucking company based in Morristown, N.J., not too far from the Lionel factory.

That was it! A flatcar load ripe for promotion never came with the name of another business during postwar days.

More information

- $6.95 ($61.69)
- Cataloged from 1956 through 1958
- Price reduced to $5.95 for 1958
- Frame went from part no. 6511-2 to no. 6424-11
- Color of trailers varied from light gray to white

6826 Flatcar with Christmas Trees

Every autumn for the past several years, Lionel has distributed a special catalog dedicated to its trains and accessories that have a link to Christmas. Recent catalogs have showcased Polar Express passenger sets for O gauge as well as Large scale enthusiasts. Also receiving attention have been outfits decorated for the Nutcracker Route and the beloved motion picture, *A Christmas Story*.

These items are the tip of the snow-capped iceberg! Add in cars painted red and green and lettered for the North Pole Central, annual holiday-themed Lionel and American Flyer rolling stock, and accessories with candy canes, wreathes, wrapped gifts, snow globes, and Santa and his elves.

1959

What a contrast with life in Lionelville during the postwar era. During a time characterized by a booming growth in the number of children and remembered for songs about Rudolph the Red-Nosed Reindeer and Frosty the Snowman, Lionel did nothing to capitalize on Christmas. Not until after changes in leadership in 1958 and 1959 did Lionel introduce the no. 6826 Flatcar with Christmas Trees.

No stranger to December 25

When did men in charge become aware of the association of toy trains with Christmas? Common sense suggests they knew it almost from the start, certainly by the 1910s. Vintage photos indicate families were placing three-rail track around their Christmas trees by the second decade of the 20th century and arranging structures and other holiday paraphernalia near it.

Advertisements celebrating Lionel trains as the perfect gift at the holidays appeared in mass-circulation publications as early as 1923 and never disappeared. After Lionel launched a magazine in 1930 to promote its products and the hobby of model railroading, illustrations and articles connected trains with Christmas. Yet the firm had yet to create a train with a holiday link.

Not until the mid-1930s, when Lionel made handcars, did it have something tied to December 25. In 1935, a year after making history with the no. 1100 with Mickey and Minnie Mouse, designers created the no. 1105 handcar with a Christmas tree at one end and a figure of Santa Claus with Mickey Mouse peeking out of his sack at the other end.

How well the 1105 sold remains a mystery. Evidently, Lionel offered the Santa Claus handcar for a second year, suggesting it got a positive response. All the same, it remained an anomaly amid a line of electric trains soon to be shaped by a big push for scale realism.

Waiting and waiting

Children or adults hoping after World War II for Lionel to insert into its cataloged line a piece of rolling stock or an accessory reminiscent of Christmas were going to be disappointed for many years. They might enjoy displays of O gauge sets erected in the windows of department stores and on the floors of toy shops, but that was the extent of what Lionel intended to do in the 1940s and '50s.

Not until 1959 did Lionel announce a freight car tied to Christmas. About all that can be written about the story behind the 6826 was it carried forward the strategy of developing items that amounted to adding a novel load to a flatcar. In the case of the 6826, a no. 6511-2 red-plastic frame transported weeds intended to be replicas of Christmas trees.

That was it! No Santa and sleigh or elves building toys. Just a flatcar equipped with a brake wheel and two operating couplers and only "Lionel" and "6826" hot-stamped white on each side. The vegetation might well have been plucked from the woods surrounding the Lionel factory in northern New Jersey.

Lionel cataloged the 6826 in a single O-27 steam freight outfit in both 1959 (no. 1613S) and 1960 (no. 1635WS). Only during the first year did it make the 11"-long red flatcar with Christmas trees available for separate sale at $5.95.

Amazing to think no one in a leadership role wanted to expand on the Christmas offerings in the 1960s, especially in light of how much it does today. Perhaps the Grinch or Scrooge managed to get on the payroll.
Bah Humbug!

More information

- $5.95 ($49.36)
- Cataloged in 1959 and 1960
- Four metal stakes added, according to *Lionel Service Manual*
- Equipped with AAR trucks with operating couplers

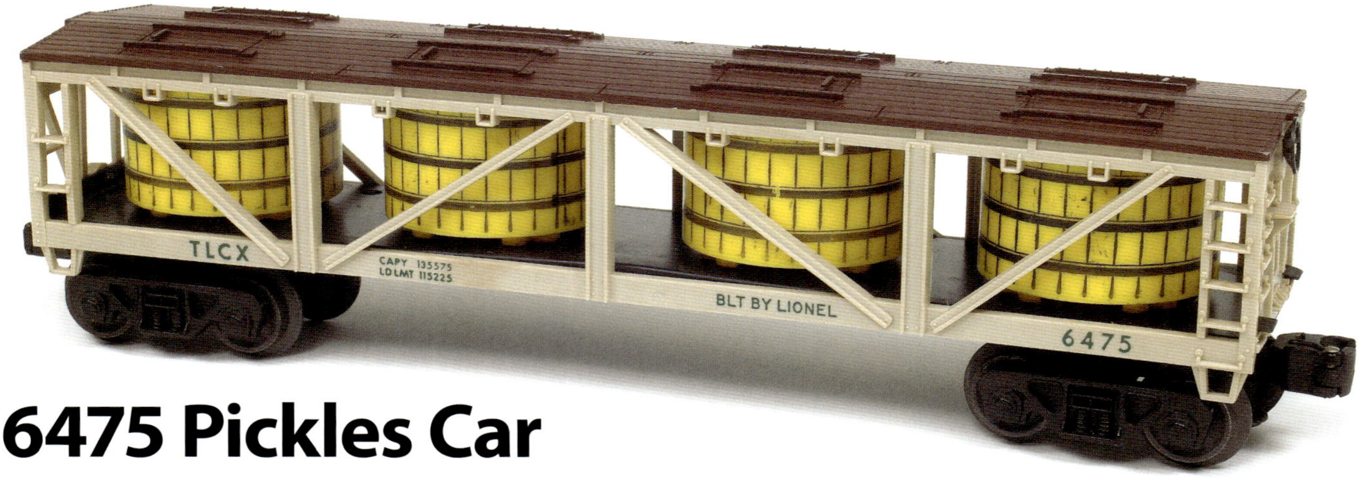

6475 Pickles Car

Anyone assembling a representative collection of electric trains developed by one manufacturer ends up acquiring a diverse assortment of individual pieces that help observers understand more about that firm. Locomotives may be values according to their improved performance while rolling stock can show advances in detailing.

Regardless of the trains collected, their owners and any visitors likely come away having learned about how a business strived to leave a mark in the marketplace. They acknowledge success and innovation as well as failure and shortsightedness. Greater appreciation of what was being done by designers and sales personnel, factory laborers and advertising executives, typically results.

These perspectives shape any discussion of Lionel toward the end of the postwar era, when profitability was on the downswing and the market for trains kept shrinking. During the 1960s, individuals stepped up and augmented the line with clever and entertaining additions. A noteworthy example of their effort and imagination was the no. 6475 Pickles Car, which was cataloged from 1960 through 1962.

1960

Different sources

As the 1950s wound down, the pressure to come up with novel ideas for the roster of freight cars heated up. Members of the Engineering Department were accustomed to researching the latest cars used on American railroads to haul raw materials and finished goods. They also tried to envision unique models with only tangential connections to what was authentic.

Which approach explained the background behind the railcar purported to be transporting pickles in its four vats? Did any manufacturers of processed foods really depend on such specialized cars to haul sweet and dill pickles? Or was the 6475 merely the product of a designer with a whimsical sense of imagination?

The Pickles Car, which earned praise as the final breakthrough in freight cars produced by Lionel during the postwar era, really did have a basis in reality.

The Engineering Department developed the 6475 after members studied specialized railcars, some going back as far as the first quarter of the 20th century. H.J. Heinz and other businesses had used them to ship pickles in brine.

The history of railcars carrying pickles began in the 1890s with cut-down boxcars nicknamed "coffin cars." Joining them a generation later were flatcars on which vats or tubs made of Cyprus wood were secured with metal supports.

Lionel first demonstrated interest in an O gauge model of the Heinz vat cars in the late prewar era. Robert Sherman, famed for the work he later did on Lionel's catalogs, wrote an article in *Model Builder* (the company's magazine for hobbyists) in which he showed readers how to build a pickle car from scratch.

Pickles to pineapples

Designers consulted the instructions Sherman shared in *Model Builder* about making a model of a pickle car while they scrutinized the accompanying illustration of the O gauge model his friend Walter J. Hill had built from scratch. Meanwhile, Chief Engineer Joseph Bonanno was in contact with the H.J. Heinz Co. in 1959, requesting blueprints and historic pictures of its vat cars.

Every bit of work culminated in the release of the 6475. The Consumer Catalog for 1960 gushed about the 11"-long newcomer, "Here is a delightful, entertaining car that will add flavor to your freight.... New in every respect."

Buyers of a Pickle Car discovered they owned a model consisting of an unpainted tan plastic body with step at each of the four corners. Lionel markings and car data were hot-stamped green on the lower portion of the shell.

A plastic roof painted light or dark brown covered four unpainted yellow vats. Each of the short cylinders had the word "Pickles" hot-stamped red on their exterior. Completing the decoration were black rubber-stamped hoops and staves.

What the Consumer Catalog for 1962 promised was going to "spice up" any layout yielded the next year to a far more fanciful freight car. Seeking to improve a promotional outfit offered to Libby, McNeill & Libby, which marketed canned foods, Lionel conceived of a vat car supposedly packed with the Libby brand of crushed pineapple. Anything to make a sale, right?

More information

- $5.95 ($48.53)
- Component of both O-27 outfits (1960 and 1961) and Super O sets (1960-1962)
- Part of eight promotional outfits between 1960 and 1962

3470 Aerial Target Launching Car

Innovations and breakthroughs galore solidified the proud reputation of the Lionel Corporation as the premier manufacturer of electric trains during the postwar era. Read that statement and then picture the classics: Santa Fe F3 diesels, milk cars, Pennsylvania GG1 electrics, and so many extraordinary animated accessories.

Honesty demands acknowledging the achievements of other firms. Not only did they produce outstanding models, but they also put on the market items Lionel felt compelled to emulate and try to surpass.

1962

Kusan, a toy business in Nashville, entered the train field almost a decade after the war. Yet thanks to Design Engineer George Dunbar, it developed several cars with exciting operating features. Engineers and sales executives at Lionel studied what the newcomer had done when creating its line. Consider what led in 1962 to the introduction of the no. 3470 Aerial Target Launching Car (cataloged through 1964).

Fun for all!

Making a mark in the crowded toy train marketplace demanded Kusan up the ante when it came to enjoyment and entertainment. Dunbar proved worthy of the task when he developed a military-oriented O gauge train set whose components thrilled with their many operating features.

Then in 1958, Kusan surpassed itself by unveiling the no. KF-119 Satellite Train. A yellow-and-gray diesel unit pulled four freight cars plus a matching caboose. The animation and special effects found on the best three cars attested to Dunbar's imagination and design skills.

A floodlight distinguished one of the gray flatcars with yellow bases. A radar scanner served as the attraction of a second one. Red highlights and a figure left those two models looking ominous and slick.

The true star of the Satellite Train was the no. K-901 USAX Dynamic Injection Compressortron. That depressed-center flatcar transported a massive gray plastic contraption whose motor generated a steady stream of air through its red opening. The exhaust caused a lightweight satellite (resembling a Ping-Pong ball with red toothpicks sticking out of it) to remain suspended an inch or two above the car.

Lionel saw

Kusan demonstrated that the day when a train maker could offer sets with few special visual and aural effects had vanished. Youngsters in the late 1950s expected every item in a set to promise more fun.

Perusing sets cataloged by Lionel after 1959 showed how it was learning that lesson. Traditional rolling stock had been forgotten, and ingenious cars designed as operating playthings had arrived.

While aspects of the Satellite Train followed what Lionel had pioneered—a searchlight car and canisters loaded into the gondola—the Dynamic Injection Compressortron represented something unprecedented. Like the near-scale cars American Model Toys had made, it threw down a gauntlet Lionel couldn't ignore.

Match made

The Engineering Department worked overtime to meet demands for novel cars. Chief Engineer Joseph Bonanno should have been thrilled with their effort because, thanks to his men, the Consumer Catalog for 1962 could proclaim, "Six New and Exciting Lionel 'Space Age' Action Cars."

Drawing plenty of applause was the 3470. Atop an unpainted dark blue frame (no. 6511-2), designers secured a one-piece white molded shell housing the battery-driven mechanism. Like the Kusan model, it used a blower that generated air upward through a plastic nozzle and a basket.

Lionel packed four yellow balloons with red Lionel data printed on them. An operator inflated one balloon, laid it in the basket, and switched on the air compressor. Aerodynamic principles explained why the balloon hovered in place while elevated above the slowly moving railcar.

More information

- $9.95 ($79.54)
- Used in 19 promotional outfits between 1962 and 1965
- Scarce version (no. 3470-100) had light blue frame with one operating and one fixed coupler

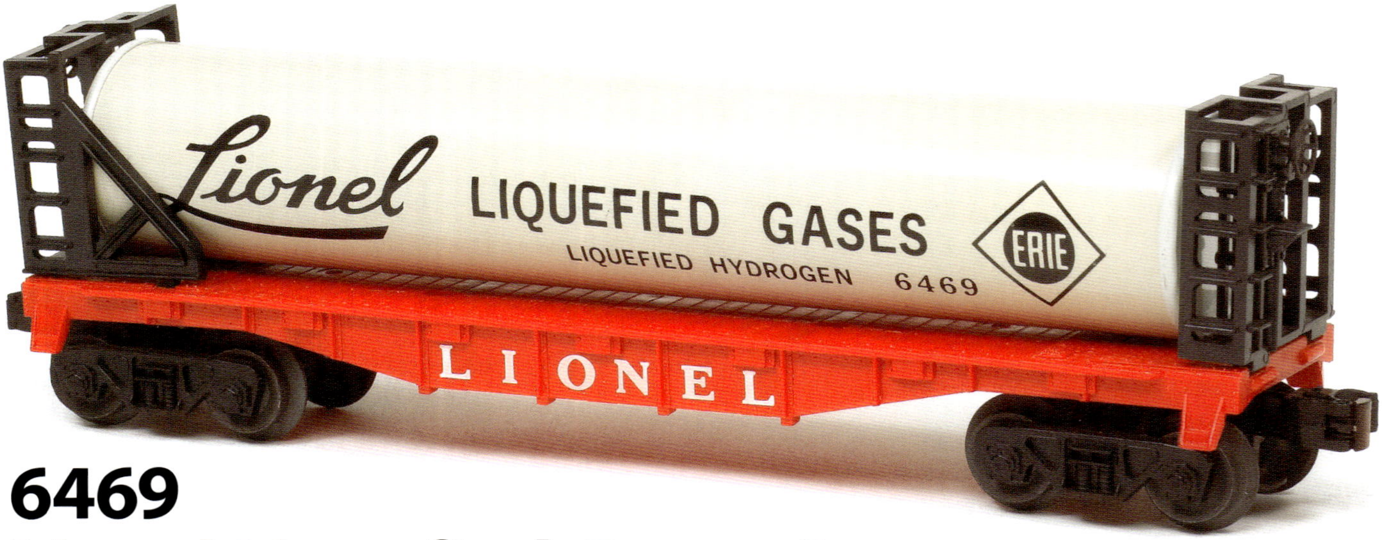

6469 Lionel Liquefied Gases Car

Knowing in retrospect that corporate heads shuttered the Engineering Department after 1963 drives a reappraisal of any of the pieces of rolling stock making their debut in that year. They provide a snapshot of how designers were struggling to complete projects, still hoping to expand the train line at a critical moment.

Best to view new rolling stock as evidence of how designers developed products without undermining quality and feasibility. Innovation was encouraged, as long as it didn't cost too much. An example of how engineers walked a much thinner tightrope was the no. 6469 Liquefied Gases Car.

New tankers

Starting in the 1930s, products beyond oil and gasoline depended on tank cars to get to markets. Liquefied types of petroleum gas, in particular butane and propane used for heating residential structures, took on importance. Demand for high-pressure cars skyrocketed in the 1940s and 1950s. Insulated tankers handled anhydrous ammonia, chlorine, and methyl chloride.

Manufacturers of toy trains thus had a powerful incentive to add models of that new breed of tank car. Lionel wanted to do so, but the prospect of having to develop new tooling and molds for a novel single-dome tanker required allocating limited resources.

Therefore, if designers hoped to add a tank car transporting liquefied gases to the Lionel roster, they would have to chart a simple and inexpensive course.

1963

Familiar start

Pressure to save money by eliminating steps in the design and production never abated for the Engineering Department. They hunted for shortcuts and cost-saving measures when finishing work on railcars.

Often, flatcars illustrated the ingenuity of designers. For example, in 1956, they fitted the common no. 6511-2 red-plastic frame with a black-plastic bulkhead at each end so Lionel might announce another contemporary flatcar—the oddly named no. 6467 Miscellaneous Car, cataloged for one year only.

The same model returned in 1957, only now it had a load. The no. 6477 Miscellaneous Car, cataloged through 1958, came with the five silver-gray plastic pipes previously packed with each no. 6511 Pipe Car, which Lionel had dropped.

Good thing someone remembered the Miscellaneous Car. Indeed, that flatcar was about to live up to its name, as clever designers embellished it with a new part.

New identity

A single part! That was all designers found necessary to expand the roster with a cool model mimicking the sort of tank car used to transport liquefied gases.

Riding neatly between the black bulkheads attached to a frame molded of red plastic was a cardboard tube. Glossy white paper wrapped around the open cylinder filled at each end with a steel cap painted to match. The white surface had minimal graphics, such as the Erie Railroad diamond herald and "Lionel" in cursive letters.

As produced in mass, the 6469 used a different frame from the one picked for the various Miscellaneous Cars. Instead of a 6511-2, factory supervisors opted for the no. 6424-11, which designers had modified in 1963 by opening the stake holes and removing the truck-mounting plates. As a result, the rear of the bulkheads on the model—closer to a flatcar than a tank car—could be secured only by glue.

False advertising

Judged on its appearance, the Liquefied Gases Car could not claim to be a high-pressure tanker. Corporate heads might name the 6469 anything they wanted, but what they offered resembled nothing seen on the Erie or other lines.

Not the first time Lionel had departed from reality. Yet what had seemed cute with stock cars described as carrying giraffes or fish looked with the 6469 like a desperate attempt to mislead consumers.

More information

- $4.95 ($39.05)
- Measured 11" long
- Used in one O-27 set and one Super O outfit in 1963
- Beware of reproductions of tank

2452 Pennsylvania Railroad Gondola

The question of when the postwar era began, at least for American toy train enthusiasts, should be open and shut. Simple as pie! What is there to argue about? By strict definition, the post-World War II period began when the global conflict concluded. Which means when the Japanese surrendered in August of 1945.

Want to be more technical? Then the postwar era began at the holiday season of 1945. Lionel showed a public starving for new electric trains a complete outfit.

Scrutinizing the single new Lionel set leads to a surprising realization. The steam engine and tender and every car resembled what had been available before the war. Except for one humble and plain model. The no. 2452 Pennsylvania RR gondola in set no. 463W launched the era.

Forget symbols

Arguments about when the postwar era began focus on symbolic breakthroughs occurring after events attributed to 1945. Toy train historians have made the case for 1946 or 1947 or even 1948.

For example, some contend the era began in 1946. Lionel announced a line of O-27 and O gauge trains, and Gilbert jumped in with American Flyer scale models produced for the S gauge market.

Votes for 1947 relate to Lionel's replica of the GG1 electric zipping over Pennsy main lines. Not since the scale model of a New York Central 4-6-4 Hudson made headlines in 1937 had Lionel dared allocate resources to develop a contemporary engine lauded for its power and beauty.

As for 1948, well, that was the year Lionel cast its fortunes with the diesel locomotives modernizing rosters everywhere. The firm joined forces with General Motors and two rail systems to create highly detailed replicas out of injection-molded plastic and then magnificently decorated in a pair of road names.

Plastic future

Yet what made the F3 diesels significant and innovative as symbols of the postwar toy industry and thus symbolically kicked off the era emerged right after the war ended. Something novel and notable characterized the set offered in 1945.

The 2452 Pennsylvania RR Gondola deserves far more acclaim than hobbyists customarily give it because how it was produced foreshadowed what was rapidly transforming life, including but not limited to, the domestic toy field.

1945

Lionel manufactured the realistic if shortened model of a common freight car by capitalizing on a revolutionary process and material. Plastics that could be liquefied and then injected into sturdy and intricately detailed molds promised to yield durable parts.

Engineers and production supervisors had experimented with different plastics before the war. Then compression-molded types, especially one with the Bakelite name, had enabled factory laborers to make tough parts added to die-cast metal assemblies as well as shells secured to sheet-metal frames.

Advances in plastics technology made during the war years wouldn't be abandoned afterward. Industries adopted them. Lionel in 1945 and its rivals thereafter, sought to make components for locomotives, railcars, and accessories out of injection-molded plastics. The 2452 led the way.

Sweetly short

The 2452 looked realistic when compared with the gondolas Lionel cataloged before the war, all of which it made out of pressed steel components. The plastic shell featured integrally molded grab irons and ribs. Better, designers mounted the body on a metal frame with a step at each corner.

Specifications instructed workers to paint the shell black and then hot-stamp on both sides the Pennsylvania name, number, and keystone herald white. Accurate car data as well as relevant Lionel information finished the decoration. A separately attached and somewhat delicate metal brake wheel sealed the deal.

Admittedly less than prototypical in terms of dimensions, the 8"-long O gauge model still impressed. The 2452 guided people into the future, showing consumers as well as corporate leaders the amazing possibilities of new plastics.

More information

- $3.95 ($48.90)
- Cataloged from 1945 through 1947 (separate sale in 1946 and 1947)
- Model lacking brake wheels added to O-27 line in 1946 as no. 2452X
- Included four wood barrels in 1945

6462-25 New York Central Gondola

Change was always afoot at Lionel during the postwar decades. Experiments were made that, once deemed successful, launched trends advancing the entire product line. Kids clamoring for trains and accessories more than half a century ago may not have been aware of how the line was evolving, but one studying Lionel during that critical and glorious era acknowledges its intelligent and informed shifts.

1954

Standing out among key trends was the movement from small and whimsical toys offered in the late 1940s to near-scale and realistic models introduced during the middle and late 1950s. Even a cursory look at the catalogs revealed how less serious pieces kept losing their place to more authentic replicas.

Just as a gondola represented the first step toward detailed cars formed out of injection-molded plastics, so did a gondola do much to push Lionel into revamping its list of rolling stock. The no. 6462 New York Central foretold a new devotion to longer models with more faithful proportions. One variation, no. 6462-25, shed light on a different trend, one involving color.

Longer gondola

The Pennsy gondola became a key member of the O-27 and O gauge rosters after 1945. The no. 2452, whether it had an "X" suffix or not, filled some sets over the next two years. Lionel updated it in 1948 with magnetic knuckle couplers. Otherwise, the no. 6452 duplicated its predecessor.

A year later, however, when leaders remained content with short boxcars, hoppers, and cabooses while removing near-scale tank cars, they decided to retire the compact gondola. Once leftover stock of the 8"-long 6452 was exhausted, the supply was not going to be replenished.

In place of the Pennsy gondola, designers put a longer model. The no. 6462 also had an injection-molded shell with extensive detailing. Its length (just under 10½") and other dimensions approximated those of a scale replica.

Additionally, factory workers attached a metal step to each corner of the frame and secured a metal brake wheel to the upper right side of each 6462. Too bad that efficiency dictated removing first the steps and later the brake wheels.

The near-scale gondola made its debut as a black-painted model with New York Central lettering and graphics hot-stamped white. Three lines of car data appeared initially, but shortly thereafter two lines became the rule on all 6462s.

Colorful stage

Expanding the roster occasionally put Lionel in a quandary. Royalty agreements with Sun Oil Co., for example, ensured that all its tank cars were decorated for that refiner. With boxcars, however, designers had the freedom to increase the group with the names of more railroads.

Executives took a different approach with the 6462. The fact that it came lettered for only one road suggested Lionel had finalized an arrangement with the New York Central. In exchange for exclusivity, the railroad almost surely paid the toy train maker.

As a consequence, Lionel likely was restricted from expanding its roster of long gondolas with more road names. The avenue opened to it was reduced to color. So long as New York Central graphics were stamped on the side, designers and others were permitted to create 6462 gondolas in any and all color schemes.

Red-painted versions soon joined their black-painted peers. Why, red gondolas might have appeared in the same year—1949—black ones debuted. At the least, red cars arrived a year later. They also had steps at each corner of their frames and metal brake wheels, plus six wood barrels.

Green performer

Four years later, the Consumer Catalog revealed something new. After long emphasizing the black version in full-color illustrations, the Advertising Department showcased a green-painted New York Central gondola. Lionel thus increased its list of near-scale gondolas by introducing a third color scheme.

The no. 6462-25 duplicated what had been standard since 1949. It had New York Central graphics and car data hot-stamped white. Long gone by 1954 were the metal steps, and brake wheels were no longer offered on the gondolas.

More information

- $4.75 ($42.63)
- Cataloged from 1954 through 1957
- Included in both O-27 and O gauge outfits in 1954
- Shown only in Consumer Catalog for 1954

3562-50 Santa Fe Operating Barrel Car

Logs and coal were big business in Lionelville during the postwar era. So were cattle, piggyback trailers, scrap meal, milk containers, and culverts, as proved by the operating cars and accessories cataloged. So many exciting and innovative items made it possible for youngsters to load and transport those commodities.

Sometimes overlooked when assessing the bills of lading of the Lionel Lines was a different good—wood barrels. But they set Lionel apart from competitors that never offered O gauge cars with barrels.

During the middle of the 1950s, the corporation ascended new heights, first with an accessory to handle barrels and then with versions of the no. 3562 Santa Fe Operating Barrel Car.

Prewar pioneer

Engineers in 1939 opened a brand new era when it came to replicas of wood barrels. Until then, Standard and O gauge cars had merely transported them after children deftly picked them up and placed them in gondolas or in boxcars.

A year after Lionel had announced a remote-controlled freight car capable of dumping chunks of what was claimed to be coal, designers relied on the same solenoids and electromagnets to develop a gondola that could empty little barrels.

The no. 3652 Operating Gondola tipped 12 wood barrels out a swinging door into a tray next to a special track section. The car, which featured a yellow-painted sheet-metal body on a black frame, appeared in the line through 1942.

1955

More animation

Executives revised for 1946 the prewar log and coal dumping cars as well as the merchandise car. They did not, however, bring back the operating gondola, not as it originally looked or in a modified fashion. Lionel, except for placing a few barrels in its nos. 2452, 6452, and 6462 gondolas, had gotten out of the trade.

Or so it must have seemed. Behind the scenes in the early 1950s, members of the Engineering Department, led on this project by Frank Pettit, were exploring new methods for creating an operating freight car that could move around barrels.

The key for Pettit was figuring out how to capitalize on the vibrating mechanism he had developed in the late 1940s for the 3656 Operating Cattle Car and Corral. The more he fine-tuned it, the more ways he envisioned using it to generate movement—circular, lateral, or horizontal.

The last idea paved the way for the development of a novel and popular car that joined the Lionel roster in 1954. The 3562 Operating Barrel Car served as a component of four O-27 and O gauge outfits that year while being made available for separate sale, too. The number of sets containing a barrel car increased in 1955, but then fell to three in 1956, two in 1957, and none in 1958.

As designed by Pettit and his clever colleagues, the 3562 operated in a simple yet interesting manner. A modeler removed the six barrels packed in a small box and laid them in the metal trough in the middle of the car. By pushing a button on the controller, he activated the vibrating mechanism installed below the trough.

Shaking the barrels directed them toward the uppermost end of the trough. Once there and unencumbered by gates, they rolled off the open end. A solid blue Vinylite figure stood nearby, ready it appeared to push each falling barrel off the gondola and into a no. 160 Bakelite Tray.

Colors galore

Between 1954 and 1958, the barrel car remained a notable part of the O-27 and O gauge lines. Lionel altered its color, going from a black body with a black tray to a yellow tray whose paint matched the shade used on the barrel loader.

Next came the gray-painted 3562-25 and yellow-painted 3562-50. Lionel then quit painting the car and offered a version in yellow plastic followed by one in orange plastic (no. 3562-75). The Santa Fe name and car data never changed.

More information

- $8.95 ($80.63)
- Cataloged from 1955 through 1957
- Component of O-27 and O gauge outfits in 1955 and 1956
- Sold separately all three years
- Price raised to $9.95 for 1957

6562 New York Central Canister Car

Engineers and sales personnel at Lionel had assimilated a fundamental tenet of the toy train industry by the 1950s, one co-founder Joshua Lionel Cowen had shaped more than half a century earlier. They all understood that the gondola was the perfect railcar to reduce in size and put in a toy train, regardless of size or gauge.

An open car with four raised sides meant a child could pop objects—Lincoln logs, spools, vehicles, Erector Set parts, pebbles, die-cast metal figures, and twigs— into a gondola and later pluck them out with ease. No load was likely to roll off, as on a flatcar, or prove tough to remove, as with a boxcar.

The corollary to that point, designers had comprehended as well, was the need for them to offer more sophisticated loads than what children might gather from their toy chests or scavenge from backyards. Providing novel, interesting items for gondolas would boost sales, as turned out to be the case when Lionel introduced the no. 6562 New York Central Canister Car in 1956.

1956

Upgrade needed

Since 1945, Lionel had recognized the wisdom of packing a gondola in most of its freight outfits. Fortunately for planners, the same models, whether short 2452 Pennsy Gondolas or long 6462 New York Central Gondolas worked nicely.

Four to six small wood barrels often served as the load for the gondolas. Problems emerged only when consumers complained about the nature of those loads. Increasingly, barrels seemed old-fashioned and boring when bumping along in a moving gondola. Upgrading the car load seemed logical and efficient.

Gilbert's lead

Changing from wood barrels to a more modern and appealing load might enable Lionel to sell additional gondolas, a task held back by inherent limitations. Either because of contract specifications or financial concerns, the company never quit stamping New York Central graphics on its gondolas. Other than changing the colors, was there any way to make the models more attractive?

Individuals at A.C. Gilbert Co. had devised a solution in 1955. They cataloged American Flyer gondolas with two new loads: plastic pipes and canisters.

Black lettering on one side of a canister "Air Activated Container") informed S gauge modelers it originated from The LCL Corp. and weighed 4,430 pounds with a capacity of 22,000 pounds.

Gondolas on the Delaware & Hudson, Lehigh Valley, New York Central, and a few other eastern railroads actually carried such canisters. American Car & Foundry manufactured full-size less-than-carload containers that used compressed air to transfer powdered cement from the canister to a silo or similar storage site.

Lionel reacted

Men at Lionel, always on the lookout for something to improve the line, must have acknowledged how their chief competitor had taught them a lesson. They transformed the basic New York Central gondola by placing within it four unpainted red plastic canisters. Some came with white lettering and others with black.

Between 1956 and 1958, the unpainted plastic body shell used for the Canister Car might be gray with maroon or red graphics (no. 6562-1), red with white graphics (no. 6562-25), or black with white graphics (no. 6562-50). The lettering of all cars was consistently hot-stamped.

The 6562 led a strange life because it immediately had a smaller sibling. For in 1956, Lionel took its short gondola, packed in four of the LCL canisters, and introduced the no. 6112 model. While the 6562 filled two midrange O-27 sets in that year, the 6112 occupied a spot of prominence in two low-end O-27 outfits.

Then in 1957, Lionel upgraded the 6562 to an O gauge outfit while relying heavily on the 6112 for as a component of O-27 freight trains. Meanwhile, a long gondola painted pink and transporting four white canisters went into the no. 1587S Lady Lionel as the no. 6462-500. It was the only 6462 to come with canisters.

More information

- $4.95 ($43.94)
- Measured 10⅜" long
- Cataloged from 1956 through 1958
- Available for separate sale only in 1958

3444 Erie Railroad Animated Gondola

The designers, draftsmen, model makers, and electrical engineers in the Engineering Department created dependable mechanisms and then found ways of using the motion and other special effects generated to develop locomotives, cars and more.

Those individuals also expressed their ingenuity and brilliance when they shifted from trying to replicate activities connected with full-size railroading to coming up with entertaining animation unlike anything seen on main lines or yards.

An assortment of gears, pulleys, solenoids, and electromagnets served to generate reliable and enjoyable animation. Among the first and most memorable of the new style car was the no. 3444 Erie Railroad Animated Gondola, which began delighting audiences in 1957.

1957

Entertainment value

In addition to accessories, notably the automatic gateman, whimsical animation underwrote the success of several of Lionel's operating pieces of rolling stock. Remote-controlled cars able to unload led to the milk and cattle carriers in the 1940s.

Designers fine-tuning better and more entertaining operating cars concluded they need not rely on human figures to get folks chuckling. Animals worked as well. Lionel hit a home run on the whimsical front with stock cars that had the heads of giraffes ducking inside and out.

Operating gondolas

Boxcars, modified to deliver miniature crates or shift laborers, often served as the stages for the little movie designers assembled. Similar kinds of freight cars, namely refrigerator cars and stock cars, served a similar purpose.

Cleverly, members of Bonanno's staff (occasionally influenced by outside contributions) sought to develop entertaining animation for other types of rolling stock. Their campaign started with the long gondola added to the line in 1949, and they would succeed in giving Lionel models unlike anything on the market.

First was the operating barrel car, which made its debut in 1954. A cool model yet one whose animation revolved around work. The figure on the no. 3562 appeared to do nothing but slave away at pushing wood barrels off the gondola.

For 1957, designers came up with something different. They took the basic injection-molded plastic gondola that had carried canisters and changed its look, going with white Erie Railroad graphics. Filling the center of the car were wood packing crates simulated with tan plastic.

Slapstick animation

One of the vibrating motors devised by Frank Pettit went inside the 10¾"-long gondola, along with a pair of "pulley drums." Around the two rollers designers fitted a spool of DuPont polyester film that could, thanks to holes punched in its edges, be turned by sprockets on the rollers.

An open track in the gondola's bed let the upper edge of the 16mm film poke through. Anything clipped to the edge would zip around the base of the car.

Someone who loved slapstick humor attached a painted plastic figure of a hobo to one part of the loop and near it, a police officer. When the mechanism and its pulley drums were activated and the film moved, it looked just like the cop was chasing—but never catching—the tramp.

Another trend

The release of the 3444 Animated Gondola and other operating cars also utilizing figures to perform humorous activities shed light on another trend at Lionel. Designers remembered they were in the business of creating illusions. Electricity let them to generate motion and animation.

Like magicians or movie producers, engineers wanted their audience to suspend its belief and abandon its demand for realism. Then consumers might enjoy seeing something go on their rational faculties insisted could not happen.

More information

- $9.95 ($85.49)
- Cataloged from 1957 through 1959
- Used in five outfits
- Shown in Advance Catalog for 1960 priced at $10.95

3459 Automatic Dumping Ore Car

What color should a manufacturer producing and marketing models of freight cars make them? The question, while on the surface a bit frivolous, assumed greater meaning at Lionel and its rivals because they needed to maximize the appeal of their rolling stock if they hoped to maximize their profits and continue to expand.

The vacillation between dull if authentic schemes at one extreme and eye-catching if whimsical colors at the other surfaced after the war. Railcars, notably boxcars, crane cars, and tank cars, reflected a debate initiated many years before. That discussion influenced the decoration of the no. 3459 Automatic Dumping Ore Car, in particular, the desirable green-painted variation from 1948.

Improved look

About a decade before Lionel thought of painting the 3459 green, members of its Engineering Department put the finishing touches on the first remote-controlled operating cars. Frank Pettit, part of the Sales Department and later named to the post of development engineer, devised a preliminary model of a car able to empty a bin filled with coal.

What the Engineering Department fine-tuned entered the line in 1938 as the nos. 3659 and 3859 dump cars in 1938. They remained there through 1942.

Partnering a slightly revised version of a prewar car with a newly designed model—as Lionel did with its crane car—summarized what occurred with operating dump cars, starting in 1946. The toy-like revision, now numbered 3559, shared space in the product line with the 3459.

Real inspiration

The mechanism developed for the dump car underwent improvements after the war. At the same time, engineers saw the advantages of updating the car's appearance, creating a rugged and modern-looking one to go with the 3559.

In 1940, the November issue of *Model Builder* magazine had shown a dump car owned by the Delaware, Lackawanna & Western Railroad. Designers studied that prototype and made it the basis of the 3459 Automatic Dumping Car for 1946.

1946

The Consumer Catalog for that year revealed that Lionel planned to release a silver car lettered for the Baltimore & Ohio. Only B&O graphics never became the rule. Blue Lionel Lines markings were hot-stamped on the sheet-metal aluminum-finished bin secured to the black-painted die-cast metal frame on a relatively small number of 3459s in 1946.

From then through 1948, the majority of operating coal dump cars had a black-painted bin with white hot-stamped Lionel Lines markings. Did the Automatic Dumping Ore Car have to appear so mean and rough? Someone must have raised that question because two paint samples indicate yellow (shown on the December 1948 cover of *Science Illustrated* magazine) and red were considered though ultimately rejected.

Finally in green

A color variation of the 3459 recognized as legitimate yet not uncommon was painted dark green. Like the silver- or black-painted Automatic Dumping Ore Cars, it had the solenoid and plunger (activated by sliding shoes on the trucks) perfected during the late prewar years.

After offering silver and black cars in 1946, Lionel produced only black ones the next year. Those variations were available in two cataloged sets and as a separate-sale item for $7. For 1948, the model came in five outfits, and the price for a 3459 (including a no. 160 Bin and a no. 207 Bag of Artificial Coal) was raised to $7.75.

What about the green version of the familiar ore dumping car? Nothing in the Consumer Catalog for 1948 (or 1947) indicated Lionel had dump cars painted that shade. Every illustration depicted the black car; none of the descriptions suggested the 3459 came in green.

Yet Lionel experts who have observed a number of original examples of outfit no. 2137WS, an O gauge four-car freight train led by a no. 675 steamer, believe the green dump car often appeared there. Presumably, it could also be obtained separately.

More information

- $7.00 ($86.67)
- Measured 9½" long
- Black brake stand at each end
- Used in O gauge and O-27 sets
- Tray could be sheet metal and not Bakelite in 1946

6456 Lehigh Valley Short Hopper

It's easy to forget when viewing the postwar era how many years it spanned. The boy who begged his parents for a Lionel outfit in the late 1940s might have grown up and become a father of a child begging for a set in the late 1960s. The trains enticing them would, largely, have been worlds apart.

With a few exceptions: Kids delighted to see Lionel introduce a short hopper in 1948 would have recognized the ones cataloged two decades later. Still lettered for the Lehigh Valley, hoppers went from black to assorted colors. Perhaps the quintessential model, one that in various hues found a home on three-rail layouts from coast to coast, was no. 6456.

1948

Plain style

Hopper cars—the type left open to the elements and built with slanted bays on the bottom to facilitate unloading of raw materials using gravity—had been staples of the O gauge roster since the 1920s.

Simple hoppers never left the line for the remainder of the prewar era. Joining them in 1940 was a replica of a Baltimore & Ohio four-bay hopper. Crafted to scale proportions, it boasted a die-cast metal body painted black that came with four manually operated double doors below.

That classic reappeared in the Consumer Catalog for 1946 as no. 2856. Yet Lionel chose not to make it or even offer anything like it for 1946 and 1947.

The next year, the no. 2456 hopper fell short of the B&O model. Yet with an 8$\frac{9}{16}$"-long injection-molded shell and metal brake wheel, it was a step forward for a toy firm striving to flush out the array of railcars.

Plain and stolid—a succinct description of the hopper painted black and hot-stamped white. The markings on each 2456 included data about the capacity, maximum load, and year of construction. Lionel added its product number.

More meaningful to children dreaming their hoppers brimmed over with coal were the name and diamond-shaped herald of the Lehigh Valley Railroad. That regional line handled a spur reaching the Lionel factory in northern New Jersey.

Rising high

The 2456 lasted for merely a year. For the short hopper planners designated for only the O gauge roster (as a set component and a separate-sale item) came equipped with the coil type of remote-controlled knuckle couplers Lionel was rapidly replacing with magnetic ones.

Indeed, a short hopper whose staple-end trucks had been updated with the improved couplers also arrived in 1948. (How often did Lionel ever catalog in the same year what were conflicting versions of the identical piece of rolling stock?)

The 6456 served as a double of the 2456 during their year together. Same shell, same paint, same hot-stamping, same brake wheel. For reasons known internally, men in charge assigned the 6456 to the O-27 area.

Then, a second variation of the 6456 hit the market. Lionel added Lehigh Valley hoppers painted a rich shade of maroon. Still using the white hot-stamped graphics, the car seemed slicker and more appealing.

More colors

Minor alterations to the body shell represented the major variations of the 6456 during its seven-year tenure. During 1952, the hopper went through the transition from staple-end trucks to bar-end trucks affecting all other models.

More noticeable were the additional colors used on the Lehigh Valley short hopper. Gray-painted and red-painted 6456 cars (white or yellow hot-stamped graphics) were associated with 1954 production. Undated experiments were sprayed coral, mint green, pink, or yellow.

Later models—given different product numbers but generally decorated for the Lehigh Valley—featured unpainted or painted shells in more hues. What black and maroon had launched eventually included gray and yellow plus more reds.

More information

- $4.25 ($42.58)
- Cataloged from 1948 through 1955
- Price dropped to $3.95 in 1950 and then raised to $4.75 in 1951
- Maroon version first shown in Consumer Catalog for 1951
- Shell modified for no. 3456 Norfolk & Western Operating Hopper (1950)

3359 Lionel Lines Twin-Bin Dump Car

The postwar era was a golden age for more than electric trains. Year after year, a landmark musical opened on Broadway, from *South Pacific* to *My Fair Lady* to *West Side Story*. Among the best of them was *Annie Get Your Gun*, a delightful account of the life of famed sharpshooter, Annie Oakley, who was played by a legendary performer, Mary Martin. A highlight was the duet, sung by Annie and the male lead in which they trade boast, "Anything you can do I can do better."

1955

Did engineers at Gilbert and Lionel belt out that tune? Reviewing what each firm released during the postwar era, it seems as though "Anything you can do I can do better" was their motto.

Locomotives, boxcars, accessories, and even operating dump cars epitomized the competition between the two companies. Seen from that angle, the innovative qualities of otherwise run-of-the-mill models assume new meaning, including the no. 3359 Lionel Lines Twin-Bin Dump Car.

Constant upgrades

The idea of a car with a bin secured to its frame that could be tilted to release its load didn't originate after the war. Lionel, among others, had introduced manually run dumping cars in the 1920s. A breakthrough occurred with the nos. 3659 and 3859 dump cars in 1938. A solenoid on those cars made it possible to dump pellets of coal by remote control. The coal could be emptied into a tray by the track or the hopper of a new coal elevator (nos. 96 manual and 97 remote-controlled types).

Lionel did more after the war than just catalog an old dump car it had sold up to 1942 (renumbered 3559). With constant improvement the theme of the firm's efforts, it designed the no. 3459, a small and rugged dump car and refined its mechanism to operate consistently.

Gilbert had no intention of conceding the fun of unloading coal to Lionel. The American Flyer no. 719 dump car beat the competition, when judged on appearance, operation, and markings (it was lettered for the Chicago, Burlington & Quincy rather than a fictitious railroad). Still, the updated Lionel no. 3469 was no slouch and lasted in the catalog from 1949 through 1955.

Another song

The saga of competing dump cars might have concluded, except designers seemed determined to keep singing, "Anything you can do I can do better." Especially, the Engineering Department at Lionel. They must have seen how much the Flyer dump car had going in its favor, above all, scale dimensions. It was a faithful, if small, replica of what railroads used.

The 3469 seemed out of place, notably after 1953, when the campaign to replace older, toy-like models with near-scale ones sped up. With longer boxcars, flatcars, and more filling the line, time was running out on a coal dump car that dated to 1946.

Lionel's designers went to work and developed the best model ever. The 3359 handed them victory and was never countered by Gilbert.

Slow action

The Twin-Bin Dump Car was longer and sleeker than its predecessors. Its unpainted gray plastic body, red motor housing, and black hot-stamped details made it look more realistic than the 3469.

The 3359 had two bins that unloaded slowly and individually, all due to refinements in the car's mechanism. The principles behind dumping by remote control had not changed, but after studying a twin-bin car used to maintain track on New York City's subways, engineers discovered ways to replicate the action.

This evolution didn't get much attention in the Lionel catalog for 1955, although it was a component of three O gauge outfits in that year and the next, followed by one Super O set in 1957 and 1958. After 1958, when atomic energy enthralled and coal seemed old-fashioned, Lionel abandoned dump cars and loaders.

More information

- $8.95 ($80.63)
- 11½" long
- Cataloged from 1955 through 1958
- Packed with nos. 160 Tray and 207 Bag of Artificial Coal
- Price increased to $10.95 in 1958

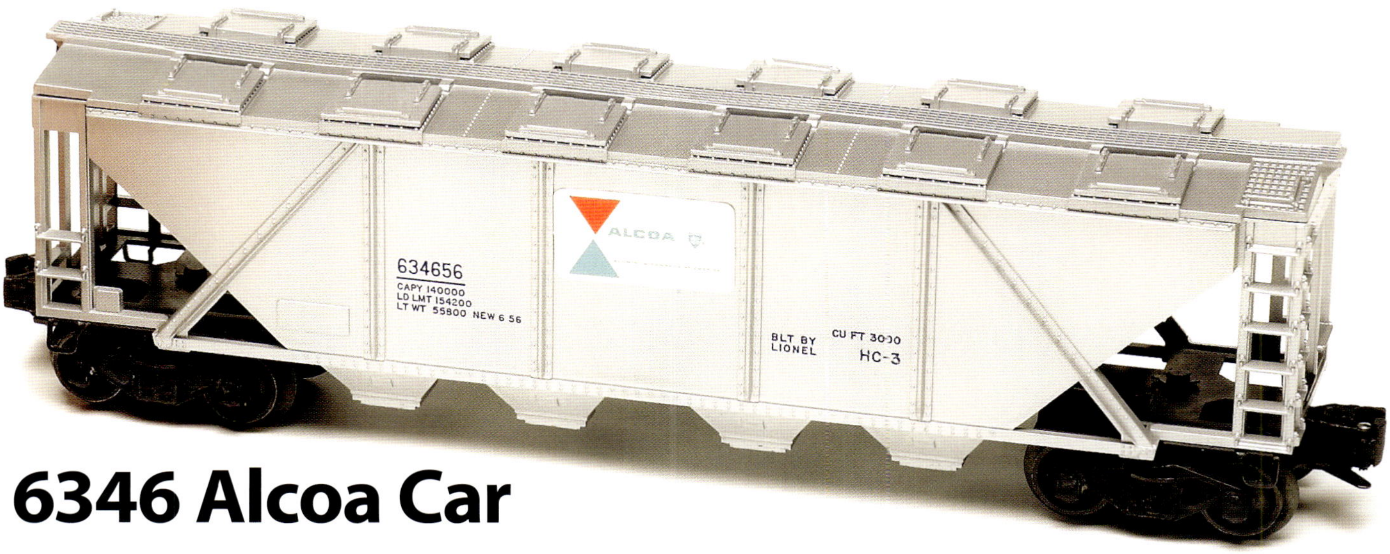

6346 Alcoa Car

Every piece of rolling stock Lionel manufactured in quantity and marketed during the postwar era had a purpose. Executives overseeing the cataloged line added and deleted railcars from it for clearly defined reasons. There was nothing done in a haphazard or arbitrary fashion. Further, the overriding principle informing what planners at the corporation did related to finances: What was likely to sell best while enabling engineers and supervisors to manage production costs efficiently?

Shifting from a generalization that can fit every model to probe particular pieces leads to difficulties. Surely, planners had reasons for every railroad they selected for boxcars and every scheme used on gondolas. Yet documentation setting forth their reasoning hardly exists.

Unfortunately, therefore, certain items from the era remained draped in mystery. Why did planners decide on names or decoration that in retrospect seem so far from typical? An example of an odd pick for what to add to the line at the height of postwar days was the no. 6346 Alcoa Car.

1956

Covered hoppers

The process of moving from short, toy-like freight cars to longer and more detailed ones reached a peak in 1954. Designers made a near-scale replica of a covered hopper a priority for two reasons.

First, their competitors at the Gilbert Company had introduced a similar car for the American Flyer line the previous year. Second, domestic rail industry had given a lot of publicity to the PS-2 type brought out by Pullman-Standard in 1952.

The Engineering Department thus created a new 11½"-long hopper body (almost 3" longer than the short one introduced as the no. 2456 in 1948). According to the *Lionel Service Manual*, it was a scale reproduction of a 70-ton covered hopper currently being used by the Norfolk & Western Railway.

Keep in mind that Lionel elected to progress from a short open hopper to a large covered hopper. It referred to the newcomer as a cement hopper, as Gilbert had done. In reality, the N&W transported coal and not cement in its hoppers, which typically came with two bays and not four as with the Lionel.

The no. 6446 Cement Car, cataloged through 1955, featured a removable top, unlike the Gilbert model. The cover of Lionel's car had two rows of six hatches; eight hatches were hinged and could be lifted up. Too bad the "four simulated double hoppers underneath" didn't open.

Not expected

The sequence of events that unfolded in 1955 made solid financial sense.

Lionel again cataloged the 6446 N&W Cement Cars (black with white graphics or gray with black graphics) as components of O-27 and O gauge outfits. It also used the longer body shells to broaden the roster with near-scale open quad hoppers attractively painted black or maroon with white Lehigh Valley markings.

A slightly confused situation characterized 1956. Lionel did keep updated N&W covered hoppers (identified as no. 6446-25) while dropping the older ones.

Joining those railcars was the 6346, described in the Consumer Catalog as "Equipped with 12 opening roof hatches," a claim suggesting Lionel had altered the tooling for the cover. That modification, like the model's silver scheme, might have been justified by the wish to provide customers with an attractive hopper.

But why complement the blue hot-stamped car data on the sides with adhesive labels showcasing the name and logo of Alcoa (Aluminum Co. of America)? Lionel enjoyed a solid relationship with Alcoa, purchasing aluminum from it for parts used on streamlined passenger cars. So this might have been an attempt by Lionel to show gratitude to Alcoa.

Or, the 6346 could have represented the result of a deal made with Alcoa for it to underwrite the expense of decorating a freight car.

Key executives, in particular Executive Vice-President Alan Ginsburg and his top assistant, Ronald Saypol, aimed to reach out to businesses to earn dollars for Lionel by getting them to pay for having their name or products emblazoned across the sides of boxcars, tank cars, and specialized models.

More information

- Catalogs never specified retail price
- Used in one O gauge and two O-27 outfits
- Rare variation has red lettering

6636 Alaska Railroad Open Quad Hopper

Not once during the first half-century of its history had Lionel created a train set in response to a current event. Contemporary American history, whether touching on elections, foreign affairs, or domestic celebrations had not influenced the development or the decoration of an outfit, a locomotive, or even a freight car.

So the decision to offer a special O-27 set in honor of the admission of Alaska as the 49th state in the Union in 1959 represented a landmark. But Lionel did more with the marketing potentialities of the event. It also brought out two near-scale models to entice O gauge modelers. While the no. 6464-825 Alaska Railroad boxcar received attention, its companion was neglected. No need to ignore the no. 6636 Alaska Railroad Open Quad Hopper.

Watching the headlines

By the middle 1950s, a younger generation of decision-makers had assumed principal positions at Lionel. Starting with President Lawrence Cowen and Executive Vice-President Alan Ginsburg, those middle-aged men included Advertising Manager Jacques Zuccaire and Ginsburg's top aide, Ronald Saypol.

1959

That coterie intended to broaden the market. They negotiated deals with producers of consumer goods to subsidize the decoration of models and worked with regional railroads for financial assistance in return for developing and painting a host of diesel and electric locomotives.

Saypol, Ginsburg, and others paid attention to what was happening around them. Reading the headlines and watching news programs on television impressed upon them the interest in the anticipated admission of Alaska and Hawaii to the Union. The fact that railroads played a notable part in the economy of Alaska suggested making replicas would be wise.

Trying to benefit

Several months before Alaska officially entered on January 3, 1959, Lionel's leaders had discussed how to benefit from that event. In preparation, members of the Engineering Department had requested blueprints of locomotives and freight cars on the Alaska Railroad.

The preliminary work culminated in the introduction of a four-car outfit for the O-27 line cataloged in 1959. The no. 1611 Alaskan retailed for only $25, which put it at low segment of the roster. Nervous that the train might generate minimal interest, executives perhaps were hedging their bets by keeping the set short and cheap.

Two freight cars decorated for the Alaska Railroad joined another pair to fill out the set led by an NW2 diesel switcher. The no. 6162-60 long gondola had an unpainted yellow body with blue hot-stamped lettering. It typically came with three red plastic canisters. The no. 6027 Southern Pacific-type caboose reversed the gondola's scheme, having a dark blue shell and yellow hot-stamped graphics.

Quality models

Incidentally, correspondence between Lionel executives and the U.S. Department of the Interior and the Alaska Railroad from 1958, plus engineering mock-ups and inter-office memos, indicated they had more in mind, including diesels.

Only a boxcar and a quad hopper made it to production, however. Those cars, pushed forward in a memorandum from Saypol to Chief Engineer Joseph Bonanno dated September 2, 1958, attracted notice.

The 6636 Open Quad Hopper came painted black with yellow hot-stamped markings, a brake wheel, and spreader-brace holes and a brace. Besides being sold for $4.95, it was part of two steam freight outfits in 1959: the O-27 no. 1625WS and the Super O no. 2531WS.

The large Alaska hopper and boxcar, maybe more than the inexpensive O-27 train set, fed the public's hunger to identify with the newest state in the Union. Thanks to Lionel, model railroaders could own a tiny piece of the rugged Alaska Railroad.

More information

- $4.95 ($41.07)
- Measured 11½" long
- Component of O-27 outfit no. 1635WS in 1960
- HO scale version (no. 0836) cataloged in 1959 and 1960

3472 Automatic Refrigerated Milk Car

Amid the changes that took place in the ownership and management of Lionel during the quarter century after peace returned to the world in 1945, the Engineering Department remained remarkably stable. From the end of the war until the department was shut down after 1963, it functioned smoothly under Chief Engineer Joseph Bonanno.

The contributions made by Bonanno, along with his principal associates (John DiGirolamo, Frank Pettit, John Salles, and Morris Zion), boggle the mind. Also during the 1940s and 1950s, outsiders contacted Lionel with ideas for items or mailed prototypes they thought worth adding to the line.

Some of those concepts and mock-ups did result in additions after Bonanno and his team made adjustments and refined them for efficient and economical mass-production. The greatest was the Automatic Refrigerated Milk Car—improved to be the no. 3472.

1949

Meet Mr. Smith

The impetus for that operating car, which was used with an ancillary piece, came from beyond the Lionel plant in northern New Jersey. Richard G. Smith, of whom next to nothing is known, developed the Automatic Refrigerated Milk Car, which made its debut as the no. 3462 in 1947.

Smith, aware of how designers relied on electromagnets and plungers, invented what his 1944 patent application titled "Toy Railroad Accessories." Influenced by the ejection mechanism Pettit had used on the no. 3814 Operating Merchandise Car, Smith devised an operating car that threw out silver cans—the foundation of the 3462.

However, Joseph Bonanno and Abram Gash (another member of the engineering team) received a patent in 1954 for what is plainly the Operating Milk Car. They refined Smith's basic design so Lionel could mass-produce this car.

Little man

The key to the charm and wonder of the 3462 was the figure. He appeared to be shoving cans out of the 9¼"-long reefer onto the sheet-metal platform. Without the wee guy, the 3462 would have been as lifeless as the merchandise cars cataloged in 1946 and 1947.

The sequence of animation began when an operator parked an Automatic Refrigerated Milk Car over an uncoupling track section. Next, he or she pressed the button on the remote controller sold with it. That caused the plunger inside the solenoid installed on the model to be pulled down.

Activating the mechanism moved the figure secured to a metal rod inside the refrigerator car, creating the magical illusion he was working. An arm on that mechanism pushed the cans (already loaded through a roof hatch) out the door and onto the painted a metal platform.

From the moment the Automatic Refrigerated Milk Car arrived, it was a terrific seller. The animation was entertaining and reliable. Best of all, modelers were in charge of what occurred; they had to take control to get the cans out of the car.

Getting better

The development of magnetic couplers secured to staple-end trucks caused Lionel to update its roster in 1948 and 1949. The milk car took its turn in being fitted with the improved parts. Thus in 1949 appeared the 3472, which resembled in appearance and operation its historic predecessor.

The car initially had a plastic body shell painted white. After the first production run of the 3472, Lionel switched to molding the shell out of white polystyrene, which reduced costs of labor and materials.

The graphics, which included the product number, name, and circle-L corporate herald, were hot-stamped black, as they had been on the 3462. Shiny aluminum doors eventually gave way to white plastic.

Also packed inside the 3472's box were a no. 3462-70 Box of Magnetic Milk Cans and a no. 3462P-1 Platform. That ancillary piece, which was formed out of stainless steel, came with its base painted green and the railings painted white.

More information

- $9.50 ($96.37)
- Cataloged from 1949 through 1953
- Price raised to $11.50 in 1951 and then lowered to $10.50 in 1952
- Seven milk cans cut to five in 1952

6356 New York Central Stock Car

The postwar freight car roster, while picayune when compared against the enormous assortment of models Lionel currently releases each year, still leaves you a bit awestruck. Particularly by the middle of the 1950s, the different types of railcars cataloged and the variety of railroad names, colors, and dimensions of those items amazed.

The near-scale boxcars in the no. 6464 series have captivated and mystified Lionel experts for almost half a century. Same is true with operating freight cars. All the while, hobbyists seem to have closed their eyes to the finest models of stock cars, a short parade that began in 1954 with the no. 6356 New York Central.

Long history

On American and Canadian railroads, specially designed freight cars had been carrying live animals to market since the middle of the 19th century. That trend continued into the first half of the next century, although livestock traffic declined after World War II as more shippers used trucks.

1954

Railroads had proved reluctant to upgrade their stock cars by switching from wood to steel construction as they had with other types of freight cars after the 1920s. They stuck with older, often shorter single-deck railcars, recognized by their open slats and unique bracing patterns.

Lionel had been cataloging stock cars since the 1910s. From the time it introduced locomotives and rolling stock promoted as O gauge in 1915, the company had offered miniature versions of the familiar car used to transport cattle. Sliding doors distinguished even the earliest and most primitive stock cars.

Postwar addition

Knowing Lionel had cataloged O-27 and O gauge stock cars from the day it entered that segment of the field made the absence of such models in the years immediately after the war astonishing. Compounding the mystery was the fact that the American Flyer line developed by Gilbert included a stock car with sliding doors.

Youngsters enthralled by stock cars had to wait until 1949 to get one for their three-rail layouts. That pioneering model was the no. 3656 Lionel Lines Stock car, which operated. Used in conjunction with the Operating Stockyard with Cattle Set, the short, orange-painted model moved specially designed tiny cows in and out of its opening side doors through vibrating action.

A year later, designers removed the doors and mechanism from the 3656 to create a non-operating stock car. They painted what was numbered 6656 bright yellow and added hot-stamped Lionel Lines information and a circle-L herald.

Stopgap car

Sales and engineering personnel must have taken a breath of relief after the 6656 entered the line. Yet another gap had been filled, they knew, giving Lionel virtually every basic kind of freight car for its completely updated roster of freight cars.

Yet the debut of near-scale O gauge rolling stock from American Model Toys, a group that included a trio of realistic stock cars, forced Lionel to take action.

The talented crew laboring under Chief Engineer Joseph Bonanno responded with an outstanding stock car in 1954. The 6356 matched in appearance, if it did not surpass, its three rivals from AMT.

Boldly yellow

Lionel painted the 6356 a bold shade of yellow, like the one used previously for the 6656 (no longer cataloged after 1953). Black lettering, typically hot-stamped but occasionally rubber-stamped, completed the decoration. Designers left the newcomer nearly identical to the Missouri-Kansas-Texas stock car being marketed by AMT (now Auburn Model Trains).

Surprisingly, Lionel added New York Central graphics to the near-scale stock car. Why was that surprising? Because at the time 10 North American railroads owned more stock cars than the 1,600 listed by the New York Central. A Union Pacific, Northern Pacific, or Milwaukee Road car might have sold better.

More information

- $5.95 ($53.40)
- Measured 11¼" long
- Cataloged in 1954 and 1955
- Component of O-27 and O gauge outfits in 1954 only

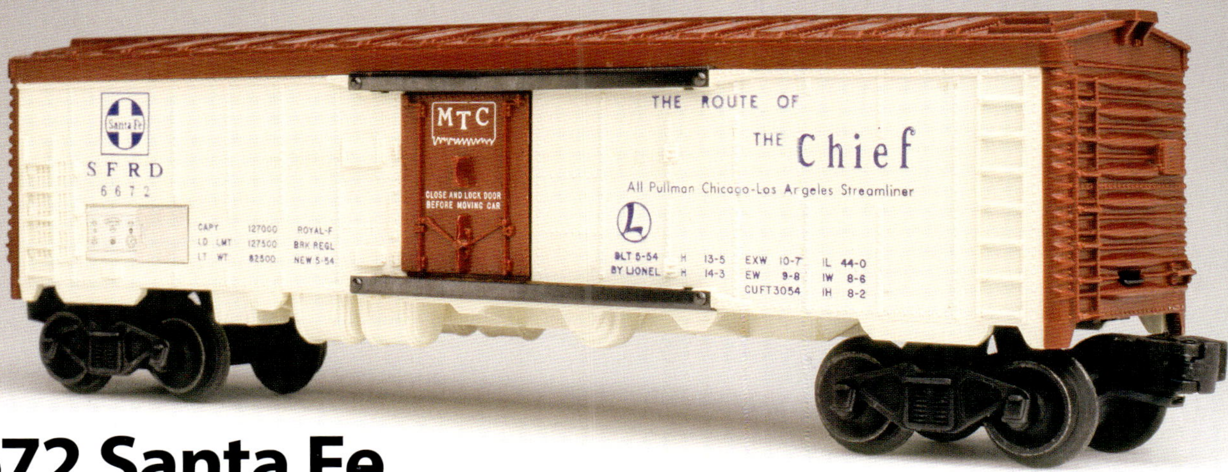

6672 Santa Fe Refrigerator Car

The pathway followed during the first part of the postwar era assumed familiarity. Lionel went from bringing out newly created, toy-like freight cars to modifying those fundamental railcars to give them larger dimensions, scale-like proportions, and many realistic details.

1954

The course taken by refrigerator cars differed from that of boxcars or gondolas. The latter types went directly from the toys introduced after the war to the bigger and more authentic replicas consumers demanded, especially once American Model Toys brought out near-scale boxcars and more in O gauge.

Refrigerator cars progressed differently because, as with stock cars, Lionel did not rush out a basic model. It waited until heralding an operating type. Only when the 3462 Automatic Refrigerated Milk Car made history did a non-operating version arrive. It gave way to a striking near-scale modern refrigerator car, the no. 6672 Santa Fe, in 1954.

Better to wait

From 1929 through 1942, Lionel had been able to brag about offering refrigerator cars in its train lines. The process was simple—merely a matter of suggesting the models transported frozen goods. Put different doors on boxcars and splash different paints on them. Then announce the white railcars with blue roofs looking like boxcars actually were refrigerator cars.

The ploy that had persuaded youngsters before the war appealed to executives at Gilbert after the war. Not their counterparts at Lionel. They revolutionized the toy train field with the operating milk car.

The concept proved ingenious, and the 3462 outshone the plain Flyer reefer. Not until 1950, when Lionel celebrated its 50th year, did it release a non-operating version of the milk car, christening it the no. 6472 Refrigerator Car. That model was lackluster in comparison to its operating cousin, just as the new no. 6656 Stock Car fell behind its operating twin.

Industry changes

Refrigerator cars probably demanded the highest concentration of imagination from children. Unlike boxcars or gondolas, which could be loaded with small items, O or S gauge reefers were never going to be transporting frozen vegetables or meat.

Toy train manufacturers, then, relied on different doors and paint colors to suggest their models were actually keeping cargoes at frigid temperatures. When in the early 1950s, designers at Lionel focused on updating the short and plain-looking 6472, they still had to exploit that underlying illusion.

Maintaining the facade must have been difficult because people could see laborers push blocks of ice into hatches on the top of "ice-bunker refrigerator cars." Those reefers ruled the rails throughout the first half of the 20th century. Lionel put out a convincing one in 1955 with its no. 6352.

By then, the market for frozen foods and juices had motivated railroads to abandon older reefers in favor of new mechanical types. Those longer refrigerator cars, with smooth steel sides and plug doors, promised the subzero temperatures essential for safely transporting frozen foods.

Faithful replica

The 10⅛"-long 6672 joined several other near-scale, replicas of contemporary rolling stock in the line cataloged for 1954. The Consumer Catalog declared it "a new type [of] refrigerator car being used by the Santa Fe Railroad." The copywriter underscored the lack of ice hatches on the detailed model "because the car is cooled by mechanical temperature control."

Engineers devised a new technique for molding the major plastic parts used for the Santa Fe refrigerator car. The brown roof and ends (left unpainted) were one piece, and the white bottom and sides (also left unpainted) were another.

Curiously, Lionel did not assign the 6672 to an outfit until 1955. Perhaps the model was not ready until so late in 1954 it could be listed only for separate sale.

More information

- $5.95 ($53.40)
- Cataloged from 1954 through 1956
- Variations relate to color of lettering (black or blue), lines of car data (two or three), and presence of Lionel circle-L herald

6434 Illuminated Poultry Car

Study the immense variety of freight cars cataloged during the postwar era and interesting changes become apparent. Designers worked daily to improve the roster. They searched for little ways to make models more appealing to the public and less costly to produce in quantity.

1958

Perhaps one employee had a brainstorm about how to transform the humble near-scale stock car. Introduced with fanfare in 1954, that model had been languishing ever since. Nothing helped, even a new paint scheme that was part of its transformation in identity two years later.

Missing from the two-level stock car, someone in engineering must have declared, were animals. Kids needed to see the cargo it carried. Willing to try anything, designers finished artwork showing the small livestock typically transported in stock cars with two levels. From their fertile minds burst forth in 1958 the no. 6434 Illuminated Poultry Car.

Slow going

Confidence in the appeal of a stock car seemed to wax and wane at Lionel. The company had dragged its feet after the war, not cataloging a model until 1949, when it broke into the market with an operating car that worked in conjunction with a corral to simulate the movement of tiny cattle.

Lionel followed with a non-operating stock car in 1950. Then, pushed by the near-scale versions from American Model Toys, they had abandoned the short stock car in favor of a longer model in 1954.

The inaugural 11¼"-long stock car differed slightly from the railcar typically envisioned. People usually associated stock cars with the transport of cows. The Consumer Catalog for 1954 clarified, however, that the pairs of short sliding doors on each side indicated it was used to ship "pigs, sheep, or goats."

No big deal! Lionel announced the yellow-painted stock car with black New York Central markings with excitement. It put no. 6356 in one O-27 and three O gauge outfits in 1954. The next year, though, the model was not a component of a single outfit, with its inventory being sold separately.

Planners dropped the 6356 after 1955 and invested their hope in a novel car. They recommended painting the plastic shell white and calling it the no. 6376 Circus Car. Cautiously assigning the updated stock car to only one O gauge set for 1956, they must have been disappointed by the response. The 6376 ended up as a separate-sale item in 1957, leftover stock likely being sold off.

Timely change

The line for 1958 saw the individuals in charge adopting two approaches with stock cars. For some reason, they imagined another basic car might appeal if given the right road name. Out came the no. 6556 Missouri-Kansas-Texas model.

Collectors now prize the red-painted car with white hot-stamped markings, which Lionel produced in low numbers. Yet knowing the 6556 did not return for even a second year in the catalog suggests it failed to captivate many consumers.

Enthusiasts did take more of a liking to the 6434, which shared several traits with the M-K-T stock car, right down to the plastic body shell painted red. Setting the Illuminated Poultry Car apart were, of course, the four translucent panels fabricated out of polystyrene on which were printed rows of chickens and turkeys. Interior illumination made it easier for onlookers to see all the poultry.

Louis Melchionne, who handled various artistic tasks for Engineering, created the illustrations of hens, roosters, and so forth that were reproduced on polystyrene panels, held in place with eight small gussets.

Laying eggs

Five Super O outfits cataloged for 1958 featured an Illuminated Poultry Car, including the sole set containing a 6556 M-K-T stock car. Safe to say, therefore, corporate leaders believed the 6434 would impress potential customers.

Unfortunately, after seeing the upgraded stock car offered for separate sale only a year later, the conclusion it missed the mark was unavoidable. All Lionel could do for 1959 was exhaust whatever inventory of 6434s was left while hoping to do better with an operating version—the new no. 3434 Chicken Sweeper Car.

More information

- $6.95 ($58.06)
- Cataloged in 1958 and 1959
- Component of no. 2543WS Super O Berkshire Freight Outfit in 1959

3366 Operating Circus Car and Corral

The mark of a great business in any field is the ability of its leaders to continue to innovate and develop new products while at the same time constantly improving its current line. Achieving both goals should enable it to withstand challenges in the marketplace because it succeeds at exceeding the expectations of customers.

The no. 3366 Operating Circus Car and Corral, an animated car that came with its own accessory, epitomizes much of what was best about Lionel. For this model represented, not the first incarnation of an operating stock car with an unloading and loading mechanized platform, but an ongoing improvement of something that had already proved to be popular.

1959

Starting small

The story of the animated circus-oriented car and its platform introduced by Lionel in 1959 went back a decade. The big news in 1949, besides the first diesel switcher and operating boxcars in the line, was a new operating car that used an accessory to replicate the shipment of cattle.

Driving the development of the no. 3656 remote-controlled cattle car and platform was the success of the no. 3462 milk car. That revolutionary model had been selling in amazing quantities since entering the line in 1947. Lionel's leaders pressed their designers to duplicate it.

Frank Pettit, named the "development engineer," proved to be up to that task. He developed an operating car that made fuller use of its platform than did the milk car to enable kids to imitate an activity found on railroads throughout the West.

Vibration generated by electricity could, Pettit saw, cause figures placed on top of a special surface to shake and move. Specifically, he installed a remote-controlled solenoid on the underside of both a special stock car and the base of the platform of the metal corral used with it. By activating these solenoids, an operator started the runway inside the car and the floor of platform buzzing and vibrating.

Once everything was vibrating, rubberized cows would move, thanks to "fingers" glued to the underside of their bases. Pettit aimed for the beasts loaded inside the car to move ahead, through the opened door, and down a ramp. Cows would shuttle around the confines of the stockyard and be directed to climb up the other ramp.

Trying horses

Too bad the cattle fell down or meandered in circles once in the stockyard. So Lionel kept modifying the platform in hopes of eliminating those frustrating problems.

A better idea arrived in 1956. Having dropped the 3656, Lionel released a superior item. The no. 3356 Operating Horse Car and Corral looked better, and its newly designed metal and plastic platform worked more consistently and reliably.

The improved design of the platform, with its narrow, curved channel, pleased modelers. The mechanics of that operating car and accessory had not changed from Pettit's original design. But the sleek horses (a step above the pudgy cows) almost pranced around the yard.

Circus time

Lionel kept the 3356 in its line through 1959, offering it for separate sale and as a component of five outfits. Then it replaced that car and its corral with all-but-identical ones molded in white and gray polystyrene, respectively. The 3366 Operating Circus Car had a red-painted roofwalk and red hot-stamped graphics.

Smart—or desperate?—to attempt to boost sales of an item that might have worn out its welcome by changing its identity. Lionel had sought to exploit the popularity of the circus with a Mickey Mouse train in the middle 1930s. It hoped an operating car and corral with a similar theme would again win applause.

More information

- $17.95 ($148.92)
- Came with no. 3366-100 box with nine white vinylite horses
- Cataloged from 1959 through 1961
- Part of only one outfit: no. 2555W for 1960

3435 Traveling Aquarium Car

The longer the postwar era went on, the wider engineers stretched the definition of a boxcar. From a simple rendition of what everybody could see on a train, they progressed to operating types. Soon, they had broadened their visions to include specialized boxcars intended to generate electrical power, assist firefighters, and even serve as targets.

The unexpected additions to the roster often originated in unique rolling stock actually developed for railroads and industries. Other innovative boxcars represented fanciful creations by engineers.

Then there were the memorable models with some basis in reality that a designer had fine-tuned until they approached toy-like whimsy. The no. 3435 Traveling Aquarium Car epitomized that marvelous blend of actual and amazing.

They did exist

The 3435, which made its debut in 1959 as a set component and separate-sale item, showed how designers and other contributors remained on the lookout for highly specialized railcars.

1959

Full-size cars created to carry fish in a safe manner had existed since the 1880s. The Bureau of Fisheries used wood baggage and passenger coaches whose interiors had been converted to hold tanks of fresh water. Trout, carp, and a few other types intended to stock streams and rivers were transported in those huge tanks.

The New York Central developed special boxcars to bring live fish to metropolitan markets. Again, fitting the cars with big tanks was key.

During the 1950s, a stainless-steel sheathed lunch counter car belonging to the Chicago & Eastern Illinois Railroad changed hands, being purchased by the John G. Shedd Aquarium in Chicago. The Nautilus II arrived in 1957, prepared to hold and transport as many as 3,000 specimens of fish plus a crew.

Imagination helped

A member of the Engineering Department supposedly suggested what became the 3435. Anthony Rocco, a young man with a wicked sense of humor, came up with a prototype. He proposed a model that would look like a boxcar with open areas on each side. Miniature artwork showing sea life would be fitted in them.

A car with pictures of its cargo—fish and shellfish in the case of the 3435—had broadened the line for 1958, when the no. 6434 Poultry Dispatch Car had debuted. Rocco wanted to build on that concept.

To the rescue rode one of Tony's colleagues, Lou Melchionne who had painted the rows of chickens and turkeys that for the 6434 had been scaled down and reproduced on celluloid strips.

Chief Engineer Joseph Bonanno now told Lou to finish illustrations of sea life, including fish, kelp, and shellfish, for the 3435. Other men working with Bonanno wanted to add movement to the car.

Operating, too

Designers recommended doing more with the celluloid images of sea life. Just securing them along the side, as they had done with the 6434, no longer seemed adequate for boosting sales. They set out to get them to move, thereby creating the illusion living fish were swimming inside the tanks.

The answer lay with the no. 3444 Animated Gondola, which had made its debut in 1957. The same vibrating mechanism would add movement to the 3435.

Reels installed on the latter would automatically revolve the celluloid strips, which lightbulbs inside illuminated. The animation began when a switch was pushed and current traveling through metal wheelsets activated the two reels.

The reliable operation of the Traveling Aquarium Car never changed. However, Lionel did alter its appearance.

The earliest (and scarcest) version had gold hot-stamped lettering, a border around the circle-L logo, and tank designations. Next came cars without a gold border, followed by those 3435s that also lacked the two tank markings. Common models included only the name of the car and its number rubber-stamped yellow.

More information

- $12.95 ($107.44)
- Measured 10½" long
- Cataloged from 1959 through 1962
- Used in one O-27 and three Super O outfits in 1959 and one Super O set in 1960

3370 Sheriff and Outlaw Car

Exciting yet ominous developments engulfed Lionel after Joshua Cowen cut his ties and transferred leadership in 1959, not to his son, Lawrence, but to Roy Cohn, a distant member of his extended family. Over the next few years, the product line expanded into other areas while trains assumed new roles, especially as Lionel tried to retain its hold on kids.

1961

Designers and marketers, determined to boost the appeal of electric trains to a generation captured by other interests, gazed well beyond traditional railroading. They acknowledged the fascination Americans of all ages felt for both the nation's past and its future. Toy trains and accessories needed to reflect those passions.

Only from such a perspective does a novelty like the no. 3370 Sheriff and Outlaw Car make sense. It demonstrated the ability of ingenious engineers a to keep reinventing the identity and pleasures of toy trains.

Ongoing search

Reaching out to different audiences had challenged Lionel since the prewar era. In the 1930s alone, it had touted a miniature stove, two motorboats, and an operating airplane in hopes of expanding its base of customers. The 1940s saw chemistry outfits as well as construction kits broaden its line.

Limiting what Lionel sold to items for kids struck Lawrence Cowen as shortsighted. After the war he turned to fishing equipment and a stereoscopic camera.

Lionel's efforts to emulate the A.C. Gilbert Co. and sell "educational toys" to boys grew after Cohn took over. In the early 1960s, Lionel catalogs swelled with pictures of chemistry sets, microscopes, weather stations, and electronics kits.

Where did that leave trains? Sales and engineering supervisors never quit promoting realistic models. But they also said Lionel needed to return to making toys with animation and humor.

Heading west

In particular, Lionel had to reach the kids deserting their trains for TV. Lionel developed an old-time engine, freight cars, and coaches to entertain boys enthralled by westerns. That explained why Lionel introduced the Sheriff and Outlaw Car.

The 3370, whose unpainted green plastic shell was derived from the one designed in 1949 for the no. 3656 Operating Stock Car, put on a show as slick as any a boy might see on *Have Gun Will Travel* or at *Disneyland*. It proved how engineers could still inject a railcar with whimsy.

Easy operation

In 1961, two years after old-time General sets merged Lionelville with Tombstone, engineers rigged up what amounted to a gunfight on flanged wheels! For the 3370 they cut two slots in the roof of the shell and mounted an assembly inside, with a human figure attached at each end.

Designers secured a cam to one axle of the car and installed an actuator lever and pawl plus a ratchet wheel so the assembly would act like a seesaw. One end would rise while the other fell as the car moved.

Engineers had relied on a similar mechanism for the no. 3376 Operating Giraffe Car (new in 1960). For the 3370, they had model makers mold new figures, painting one to resemble an outlaw (dark clothes and a mask) and the other a sheriff (clean cut with tan duds). As the car moved, one guy stood to fire a six-shooter across the roof while his foe ducked.

The green car with yellow hot-stamped lettering came in two cataloged O-27 outfits in 1961 and a Super O set in 1962. Lionel also packed a 3370 in many promotional outfits, even after dropping it from the cataloged train line after 1964.

More information

- $7.95 ($64.19)
- 9¼" long
- Western & Atlantic lettering connected it to General trains
- Number 3370-1 is boxed version; 3370-25 is unboxed

2855 Sunoco Deluxe Single-Dome Oil Car

When, in 1940, Lionel introduced a quartet of brand-new freight cars with O scale dimensions and superb detailing, model railroaders had further proof that a new era had begun in the hobby. The four cars in the no. 700 series could take your breath away, as they were made of compression-molded plastic and stamped sheet metal and had immaculately printed car data, railroad names, and heralds.

Such a superb group of freight cars deserved additional life, and corporate heads anticipated reviving them after the war. Yet only the tank car enjoyed a successful return. In fact, Lionel cataloged different deluxe models from 1945 through 1950. The most desirable of them was the no. 2855 Sunoco Single-Dome Tank Car.

False start

Turning the calendar back to 1945, Lionel managed to release outfit no. 463W. The set included a slightly updated version of the tank car. No. 2755 had a sheet-metal body painted bright silver and decorated with decals for Sunoco, plus relevant car data.

1946

Men at the top looked forward to being able to produce a full line of O-27 and O gauge steam engines and rolling stock for 1946. Having updated the single-dome tank car, they expected to revive the entire series of scale-detailed freight cars. The tooling should have been ready to use, and the demand from the public for Lionel trains was booming.

Illustrations and descriptions of three models—Baltimore & Ohio open hopper, Sunoco tank car, and New York Central caboose—did surface in the Advance and the Consumer Catalogs for 1946. Printing images and references to those three models in the latter catalog would seem proof positive Lionel intended to produce those great cars for its first full postwar line.

The actual picture proved to be mixed. The hopper and caboose were never produced, perhaps because Lionel was overwhelmed in 1946 with orders for less-expensive O-27 outfits and rolling stock. Rather than devote resources and labor to making those top-of-the-line O gauge cars, leaders chose to abandon them in favor of small ones in high demand.

The scale boxcar had not been shown in the catalogs, though it did return in a different form. The old model went from a basic single-door boxcar to the deluxe no. 3854 Operating Merchandise Car.

More deluxe

Only the tank car boasted life after the war. Starting with the 2755 silver-painted Sunoco model in 1945, Lionel moved to a similar car offered between 1946 and 1948 as the no. 2555 and again in 1949 and 1950 as the no. 6555.

Those silver models with Sunoco emblems decaled on them were nice additions to the Lionel line, but they were commonplace and a bit ordinary. Just too many of them for kids then and collectors today to feel much excitement.

Not the 2855 Sunoco Single-Dome Tank Car. Lionel turned the spotlight on that beauty in 1946 and 1947, when it offered it painted a stark black and then a glossy gray. Both caught the attention of kids, especially since the red and yellow Sunoco heralds all but leaped off the car.

Lionel took pride in the 2855 Deluxe Single-Dome Tank Cars. It put them in its very top freight outfits, which outshone anything that had the silver tank cars in them. As for separate-sale availability, the black and gray cars were listed at $7.50, two dollars more than any of the silver sheet-metal Sunoco cars.

Cool heritage

The deluxe tank cars have a distinguished heritage from the late prewar era and show how superb a freight car Lionel was capable of manufacturing after the war. Too bad that the 2855 cars vanished from the line when Lionel was on the verge of transforming its line to showcase models with near-scale dimensions and realistic details and eye-catching paint schemes.

More information

- $7.50 ($92.86)
- Cataloged in 1946 and 1947
- Gray-painted model never shown in catalogs
- "2855" rubber-stamped white on bottom of frame

6315 Gulf Single-Dome Chemical Tank Car

Conversations with retired salesmen from Lionel and Gilbert inevitably touched on how heated competition between the two toy train manufacturers had been in the postwar era. Surprisingly, gentlemen from both companies minimized it. They spoke of the respect each business had felt for the other and even conceded the "other side" had put out decent trains. Still, they believed theirs had been superior.

Maybe circumstances had been peaceful during the 1940s and 1950s. Yet contesting for a bigger slice of the market must have ignited a few flames. Certainly among engineers, who tried to outdo what was out there and break new frontiers in realism, animation, play value, and innovation.

1956

Even an area as mundane as tank cars witnessed spirited jockeying back and forth. Lionel took a lead with oil cars after the war only to watch Gilbert create something known as a "chemical tank car" in the middle 1950s. A strong response was essential, which led designers at Lionel to bring out for 1956 the no. 6315 Gulf Single-Dome Chemical Tank Car.

More exotic

Many builders had constructed full-size tank cars, adapting their designs to meet the specifications of customers. Shippers dictated, to take key examples, the addition of ladders going up the side to the expansion dome and a platform with railings surrounding it. Those features made a tank car look important, maybe even hinting of the explosive nature of the liquid inside.

Executives at the Gilbert Company might have shared that feeling about certain modern tank cars when they decided to go beyond offering models presumably transporting oil or gasoline to something exotic and potentially dangerous. For 1954, they negotiated with Celanese Chemicals, hoping that firm would partially subsidize production of a green-and-yellow tank car for the American Flyer line. When the deal fell through, Gilbert slapped its name on the 910 Chemical Tank Car.

Better respond

Lionel's leaders must have realized they were in second place. Having suffered the indignity of seeing Gilbert add another chemical car with the no. 912 Koppers in 1955, Lionel countered in 1956 with the 6315 Single-Dome Chemical Tank Car.

That handsome chemical tanker sported plastic ladders and handrails, along with the all-important platform at the top of the dome. The tank was molded out of black plastic and then painted a burnt orange. The plastic ends were left solid black.

The distinctive combination of black and orange had not been selected haphazardly. Documents from the Engineering Department revealed the brand-new tank car was supposed to be decorated for Hooker Chemicals. When that deal fell through, Lionel kept the paint scheme associated with that manufacturer. (Ironically, it was Gilbert that offered a tanker with Hooker graphics, coming in 1959.)

With Lionel hammering out details of an arrangement with Gulf Oil to use its name and logo, individuals finishing the 6315 must have seen the single-dome chemical car as a perfect vehicle. The lettering rubber-stamped on the orange-painted tank promoted that prominent refiner.

Return performances

The Gulf Single-Dome Chemical Tank Car entered the line as a separate-sale item as well as the component of the top-of-the-line diesel freight outfit for 1956. It returned as part of a deluxe Super O set the next year. Troubling, then, to notice Lionel offered it only by itself for 1958 and at a price reduced from 1957.

Curiously, Lionel revived the 6315 for 1963, although the chemical tank car came with an unpainted orange plastic tank and ends. In place of the Gulf markings were rubber-stamped Lionel Lines graphics. Then for 1968, the same orange single-dome tank car returned with familiar Gulf lettering, just like the old 6315.

More information

- $6.95 ($61.69)
- Measured 10" long
- Cataloged from 1956 through 1958
- Price reduced to $5.95 in 1958
- Orange paint can vary in shade and finish

6425 Gulf Triple-Dome Tank Car

The trend toward larger, more detailed freight cars, which began with the no. 6462 Gondola in 1949, took off four years later. But tank cars presented a dilemma. Creating a realistic model meant going backwards. From 1945 through 1949, Lionel had cataloged single-dome oil cars (nos. 2555, 2755, 2855, and 6555) that neatly captured the look of the long, starkly decorated 8,000-gallon prototype.

Convinced a single-dome tank car would seem like a throwback, designers developed a triple-dome car. Its appearance naturally gave the impression of complexity and modernity. Three years later, when corporate heads needed to impress a new customer, Lionel updated it as the no. 6425 Gulf Triple-Dome Tank Car.

1956

Three was real

Car builders had been manufacturing three-dome cars since the pre-World War II era to meet the demands of shippers, typically petroleum refiners. Tank cars with three separate compartments might serve to send the same type of product to customers whose storage facilities were in three different locations. Or a refiner could rely on them to send three similar kinds of oil or gasoline to a single area.

Fairly common by the early 1950s, triple-dome tank cars hardly represented the latest advance in transportation of petroleum products. Even so, Lionel knew no replica had hit the O or S gauge market.

The answer to upgrading the basic tank car was the no. 6415. The 10¼"-long model of a 70-ton carrier of gasoline or oil made by Union Tank Car Co. had a silver-painted plastic shell with three expansion domes. The body came screwed to an unpainted black plastic frame.

Engineers developed new tooling for the 6415. The end pieces and dome caps were injection-molded plastic parts glued to the body. Details included metal handrails and ladders plus sleek brake stands—originally silver and later black. Bar-end couplers were the rule at that time.

The 6415 came with rubber-stamped lettering that ranged from medium blue to black. A three-color (black, red, and yellow) Sunoco herald was rubber-stamped on each side. Nearby was the trademark of the toy train company: the circle-L logo (a white "L" on a blue circular background).

For everybody

Lionel didn't envision the new Sunoco Triple-Dome Tank Car as exclusively an upper-end model. Instead, the 6415 showed up in O-27 and O gauge outfits in 1953 and 1954, as the no. 6465 Sunoco Double-Dome Tank Car did. However, only the former was available for separate sale during those two years—at $5.75.

Behind the scenes at Lionel, changes were brewing regarding rolling stock and its decoration. Tank cars had reflected an arrangement with Sun Oil dating back to the 1930s. Sun paid Lionel a royalty to advertise its Sunoco brands of gasoline and petroleum on tank cars and billboards.

Ronald Saypol, assisting Executive Vice-President Alan Ginsburg, worried that both Lionel and Sun had come to take the deal for granted. Hopeful a more lucrative agreement might be achieved, he reached out to Gulf Oil, which responded positively in 1956.

As a result, the silver-painted triple-dome tank car shed its Sunoco graphics in favor of Gulf's. The rubber-stamped orange-and-blue logo of that petroleum firm distinguished the 6425, not to mention the 6025 Single-Dome Tank Car and the 6315 Single-Dome Chemical Tank Car.

Not exclusive

Having a trio of tank cars decorated for Gulf ended up being an embarrassment of riches for Lionel. There was a model for every segment of the cataloged line for 1956, with the 6425 being the most versatile. It served first as a component of an O-27 outfit. Then it graduated to a pair of O gauge outfits a year later. The 6425 finished as part of a Super O freight in 1958.

More information

- $5.95 ($52.81)
- Cataloged from 1956 through 1958
- Rubber-stamped blue lettering
- Available for separate sale in 1956 and 1957
- Set component only in 1958

6465-110 Cities Service Double-Dome Tank Car

The financial benefits of bartering the rights to promote consumer goods on miniature freight cars became clear to executives during the 1930s. The scheme especially flourished with O and O-27 oil cars from the prewar era almost to the final years of the postwar period.

First came Sun Oil, followed by Shell before the war. Sunoco dominated for more than a decade after the war. Then Gulf pushed in at the end of the 1950s.

Yet another American petroleum refiner carved a spot for itself at the table during the early 1960s. The name Cities Service might not be familiar. Nevertheless, collectors should not overlook the eye-catching look of the no. 6465-110 Double-Dome Tank Car.

Twice as good

Single-dome tank cars had a monopoly when it came to the O and Standard gauge rosters Lionel cataloged from its earliest days through 1942. So modelers must have been pleasantly surprised with the addition of a double-dome model to 1946 O-27 roster.

1960

The no. 2465, whose body was made of injection-molded plastic, replicated a tanker built with separate storage capacities. Sunoco markings distinguished it, as they did the deluxe single-dome cars cataloged as O gauge entries.

The 9¼"-long no. 6465 replaced its otherwise identical twin once Lionel launched the transition from coil to magnetic knuckle couplers. The Sunoco car, described in the Consumer Catalog for 1949 as including air vents, outlets, handrails, and platforms, became a staple of the O-27 line at the middle of the 20th century. Even a few O gauge outfits came with a 6465 in 1951 and 1952.

What next?

The Sunoco Double-Dome Oil Car soldiered on through the 1950s. No longer part of the O gauge roster after the no. 6415 Sunoco Triple-Dome Tank Car arrived in 1953, the 6465 continued to be produced in the tens of thousands. A majority of O-27 sets were filled out with one of them.

Circumstances changed after an agreement with Gulf superseded the longtime deal with Sun. Single- and triple-dome cars decorated for Gulf or Lionel Lines squeezed out Sunoco models in 1957. The situation remained the same in 1958, when the 6465 returned with Gulf markings.

Few O-27 or Super O outfits had any sort of tank car in them by 1958. The next year, Lionel cataloged only one tank car. It assigned the 6465, now lettered for Lionel Lines, to only one low-end O-27 set.

Sales angle

The absence of tank cars reflected a changing market. Lionel could not afford to put in its outfits a model that did essentially nothing. Children demanded freight cars with animation or detachable loads.

Executives recognized the shortcomings of tank cars, particularly after the arrangement between Lionel and Gulf expired after 1958. For the first time since the Great Depression, no petroleum giant had signed on to sponsor three-rail cars.

That absence motivated Joe Kavanagh, who had joined Lionel in 1960 to direct the development of premiums and promotional outfits. He believed a Lionel train made the perfect premium and so aimed to win contracts from accounts to underwrite individual models and entire sets.

Kavanagh approached Cities Service about having its name and eye-catching green paint scheme used on a double-dome tank car. The firm, consisting of both oil and natural gas companies, would celebrate its 50th year in business in 1960.

The 6465-110 joined the line in 1960 as part of an O-27 set. It filled out two O-27 outfits a year later before retiring after being in one set in 1962.

More information

- $3.95 ($32.22)
- Price increased to $4.95 for 1962
- Equipped with AAR trucks and operating couplers
- Same car with archbar trucks and fixed couplers listed as 6045-50
- 6045-50 tank car used exclusively in promotional outfits between 1960 and 1963

2457 Pennsylvania Railroad N5 Caboose

Forget the fact that Lionel's brain trust had been afforded more than two years to lay the groundwork for the train line ushering in the next era of production. When federal restrictions on the manufacture of playthings were lifted once victory was in sight, designers and sales personnel would rush to fill the void in the market.

The result was the O gauge outfit and handful of accessories announced in a four-page brochure distributed prior to the 1945 holiday season. Nearly every item could trace its origin to prewar times, in particular the underestimated no. 2457 N5 Caboose.

Back to 1941

Cabooses differed in style, size, and color. Still, when toy train companies told engineers to construct miniature versions, they started with a few general visions.

A boxy model with a squat cupola in the center of the roof seemed right. Ladders at each end and outlined windows on the side added symmetry. Maybe there would be steps. Paint the caboose red to suggest whimsy or possibly deep brown for greater authenticity.

Lionel followed those guidelines in the 1930s. As its commitment to realism gained traction, pressure grew for better proportioned and more detailed models.

O scale models, including a replica of a New York Central caboose, left consumers dumbstruck in 1940. Far ahead of earlier pieces were the no. 717 New York Central Caboose and its twin with automatic box couplers and tinplate trucks (no. 2957).

A year later arrived a scale-detailed caboose based on a Pennsylvania RR prototype. Not as grand as the pair of scale models, the no. 2757 still surpassed older cabooses, due to a rugged design, extensive lettering, red window frames, smokestack, and lighting.

1945

Keep it going

Leaders, contemplating what to offer in 1945, focused almost exclusively on the two groups of top-of-the-line rolling stock. Few of the toy-like pieces formerly cataloged appealed anymore. They knew models would have the new remote-controlled knuckle couplers and die-cast trucks. From that perspective, nothing would match what Lionel had been used to fill the line in 1941 or 1942.

Aesthetically, the scale-detailed Pennsy caboose retained its advantages. The proportions and smokestack still impressed. So did the frosted celluloid inserts covering the windows. They glowed beautifully when the lightbulb inside burned brightly. The battery box and plastic air pump finished a superb rendition of an N5 caboose.

Sharp as ever

Therefore, decision-makers concluded, the 7"-long stamped-steel model would return as a component of set no. 463W in 1945. The brown-painted 2457 PRR caboose pleased with the red frames around each of its four windows.

Rubber-stamped white lettering heralded the railroad and car data. The graphics were not consistently applied in the middle of the caboose. Experts believed the off-center decoration represented rejected leftover inventory called into service to satisfy the demand for Lionel train sets on the eve of Christmas.

Not long after Lionel substituted bold red paint for the heavy brown. The later versions proved to be more plentiful, as reflected in their lower values. Red-painted 2457s came with red window frames and then more attractive black ones. Also, the neat "Eastern Div." stamped under the number was eventually removed.

Lionel had no intention of keeping a railcar with prewar traits around too long. For the 2457 and its non-illuminated comrade (no. 2472), the end was in sight in 1947 when engineers unveiled a model derived from a Southern Pacific caboose. The march toward realism left the N5s behind.

More information

- $4.50 ($55.71)
- Cataloged from 1945 through 1947
- Number "477618" taken from actual Pennsylvania RR N5 caboose
- Version fitted with receiver as no. 4457 for Electronic Control Set

6417 Pennsylvania Railroad N5c Porthole Caboose

Bold and determined described the mood at Lionel as 1952 rolled into 1953. No longer would shortages of materials caused by the Korean Conflict restrain manufacturing. Competition from newcomers, above all American Model Toys, stoked executives and engineers.

The line for 1953 earned acclaim then and should still be praised as one of the finest of the postwar era. Along with many classic steam and diesel locomotives, it showcased several kinds of rolling stock upgraded by designers. Near-scale dimensions and heightened detailing captured the renewed commitment at the corporation to marketing trains steeped in realism.

1953

Most respected of the newly introduced freight cars were the first four entries in the 6464 series of boxcars, along with an operating version and a double-door automobile car. To those models must be coupled the new flatcar and triple-dome tank car. Planners did not neglect the end of trains. They heralded the initial replica of a streamlined caboose, the no. 6417.

Pennsy beauty

At the middle of the 20th century, when Lionel celebrated its 50th year in business, the Pennsylvania RR ruled as the largest and wealthiest system in the United States. Indeed, the self-proclaimed "Standard Railroad of the World" had risen to become the richest and most powerful transportation company in the land.

For a manufacturer of toy trains to offer replicas of Pennsy equipment, or at least plaster its name on generic freight cars, made sense. Lionel had adopted that path at least since the final years of the prewar era. It was ready to begin again in 1945.

All-but-identical versions of the Pennsylvania RR's N5 caboose were mainstays in both the O-27 and O gauge lines from then through 1947. A Southern Pacific prototype inspired the caboose replacing them.

Yet the Pennsy, like Lionel, never stood still. After depending on the N5 "cabin car" (the railroad's first mass-produced steel caboose) for nearly three decades, officials pushed for something new in the 1940s.

Elements of streamlining, already influencing Pennsylvania locomotives, inspired the N5c cabin car unveiled in 1942. Pairs of portholes on the sides and ends looked much more modern than the rectangular windows typically found on cabooses.

One for Lionel

Publicity about porthole cabooses, likely supplemented by the willingness of the Pennsy to assist Lionel, led the toymaker to upgrade its roster with an O gauge model for 1953. Blueprints, painting diagrams, and other documentation sent to the Lionel factory facilitated the project.

Did Lionel need another caboose? The SP prototype yielded models whose varying degrees of detail made them perfect for every price point. The best of them—the no. 6457 with illumination, two brake wheels, and a coupler at each end—had gone with the premier outfits.

To distinguish the O gauge list from the O-27, planners endorsed a three-rail version of the aerodynamically advanced N5c. They limited porthole cabooses to the upper level and used SP-types for O-27.

The Advance Catalog for 1953 told retail accounts about the "New Streamline Caboose." Notice the "turret-type cupola and round windows." The 6417, used as a component of five of the seven cataloged freight sets as well as a separate-sale item, truly was "An excellent reproduction."

Illustrations in the Consumer Catalog correctly showed the illuminated 6417 as brown with the railroad, car data, and Lionel built information in white. But at least two images there, like those in the Advance Catalog, showed the number "477830," which the Pennsy had used on an actual porthole caboose. In reality, Lionel hot-stamped on the model "536417" (production year and product number).

More information

- $5.75 ($51.99)
- Measured 7⅛" long
- Cataloged from 1953 through 1957
- Price raised to $5.95 in 1955
- Scarce version lacked "New York Zone" under the number

6517 Lionel Lines Bay Window Caboose

Everything should have been set by the middle 1950s regarding a deluxe caboose for the O gauge line. In 1953, Engineering aided by the Pennsylvania RR completed a superb model of its N5c porthole caboose. That illuminated model crowned most freight sets that year.

So satisfied were planners with the no. 6417 Porthole Caboose they had deleted the finest Southern Pacific caboose (no. 6457). Then they made additional use of the porthole caboose in 1954, creating Lionel Lines versions for the O-27 and O gauge rosters and a Lehigh Valley version in gray to match the new Train Master.

1955

Time for Lionel to rest on its laurels? Not at all! Pushing to the peak in 1955 climbed another outstanding model derived from a unique prototype. The no. 6517 Lionel Lines Bay Window Caboose demonstrated how vigorously the firm could replicate actual equipment.

Ever enough?

Astonishing to realize a bay window model represented the fifth kind of caboose Lionel had cataloged in the decade since resuming production after the war. None of its rivals had come near that figure or ever would in postwar days.

Lionel had progressed from the tin-plated steel Pennsylvania RR N5 caboose, a prewar revival, to the ubiquitous plastic type based on a Southern Pacific prototype. The latter had made its debut in 1947 and, in some form or another, never departed until the era ended in 1969.

Instead of stopping with all the SP-type cabooses (painted or unpainted, detailed or plain, illuminated or not), Lionel had upped the ante in 1953 with a deluxe replica of a Pennsy porthole caboose. Meanwhile, from 1946 on, it offered fans of work trains a wrecking caboose with a squat house and long toolboxes (and sometimes a searchlight). Lionel usually paired it with a crane car.

Lionel could have called it quits after introducing the 6417 Porthole Caboose. But 1953 was also the year in which the Erie Railroad introduced an updated bay window caboose. (The first such cabooses had hit the rails in the late 1930s.) Key people at that railroad contacted Joseph Hanson, the advertising manager at Lionel, and suggested an O gauge model.

One more

Top bosses at Lionel might have concluded they had enough different cabooses to fill any outfit, from the lowest to the highest end. Besides, they well knew nobody else in the toy train field was producing a bay window caboose.

But Lionel pressed ahead, and the 6517 made its debut in 1955. In color and decoration, it was a spitting image of the Erie caboose. Yet executives substituted "Lionel Lines" for "Erie" and put "L" inside the diamond herald and not "Erie." A generic model would have more use for Lionel.

The 6517, painted red and rubber-stamped white, dazzled O gauge enthusiasts. It boasted an elongated body with alcoves on each side rather than a cupola on top, plus interior lighting, twin couplers, ladders and handrails at each end, a smokestack, and O-27 passenger trucks. At 10" in length, it stretched beyond the 7" porthole caboose to complement Lionel's near-scale diesels.

As often occurred, this model came decorated, not for an actual railroad, but for "Lionel Lines." Being lettered for that fictitious railroad, whose three-rail tracks spanned North America, enabled the 6517 to blend with any locomotive and rolling stock. No region would feel left out.

Best came later

Through 1959, Lionel kept this impressive, near-scale model of a bay window caboose in its line, both as a component of its best O gauge outfits and as an item that could be purchased separately. Minor changes have been reported in the shade of the red paint used and whether key markings were underscored (early production) or not.

Luckily for collectors, the tale of the bay window caboose didn't end when Lionel removed the 6517 from its line. Seven years later, the Accessory Catalog for 1966 introduced a magnificent replica of the Erie prototype, done with so much intelligence and care it even used the railroad's number "C301."

More information

- $7.95 ($71.62)
- Cataloged from 1955 through 1959
- Measured 10½" long
- Price lowered to $5.95 for 1959

6814 First Aid Medical Car

The history of toy trains charted how well inventors and marketers nurtured the inner visions of consumers while offering them more to do with the sets and accessories they bought. Extraneous pieces, whether dowels representing logs or figures representing railroad laborers, increasingly proved essential to the fulfillment and enjoyment modelers found in their trains, stations, signals, and loaders.

By the middle 1950s, the movers and shakers at Lionel understood the commercial importance of supplying customers with details they could easily remove and play with. Obviously, loads on flatcars fit that criterion. So also did small items sold with a model to augment its overall purpose. From that angle, the notable spot occupied by the no. 6814 First Aid Medical Car became quite plain.

1959

Work cabooses

The roots of the medically oriented piece of rolling stock introduced in 1959 traveled back more than a decade to 1946. For that watershed year, when Lionel cataloged its first full line of O and O-27 trains for postwar America, it heralded a different kind of caboose, one probably unfamiliar to many people.

Along with the conventional caboose epitomized by two replicas of a Pennsylvania RR cabin car, Lionel announced a long model featuring two miniature toolboxes and a little house at the far end. The no. 2419 was, copywriters insisted, reminiscent of the specialized cars railroads built to handle derailments and other types of wrecks. Even better for pretending to handle disasters was the no. 2420, an identical piece equipped with a floodlight.

The heavy die-cast metal twins, painted a solid gray and lettered for the Delaware, Lackawanna & Western, soldiered on through the remainder of the 1940s. With the advent of an improved knuckle coupler, their numbers shifted to 6419 and 6420, respectively. Then, probably due to shortages of materials caused by the Korean Conflict, Lionel dropped both work cabooses from the line in 1951.

An assortment of versions of the simpler model supported different work trains from 1952 through 1958. Some of the 6419s came with only one coupler. Overall, however, they quite ably carried on the lineage established with the 2419.

New dimensions

The second generation of work cabooses made its debut in 1956. Lionel cut costs by using a sheet-metal frame and a plastic cab and tray. Brown, gray, red, and orange versions of the no. 6119 were cataloged during the next three years.

Everything could have stopped there, with the work cabooses getting less detailed and cheaper until Lionel finally pulled the plug on that venerable model.

Not how things were done at Lionel, however. Engineers found a simple way to inject new life and, presumably, to boost sales of the familiar work caboose. They were going to multiply the fun of owning the model by putting on incidental items kids might enjoy removing and arranging to create action scenes.

Every item could have been patterned after what railroads used to handle wrecks. Designers stayed away from the expected and revamped the character of the work caboose. They transformed it into a rescue unit dispatched to emergencies when medical treatment and first aid were critical.

The men in charge of developing what Lionel trumpeted as the First Aid Medical Car doctored up its decoration. Specifically, they had the sheet-metal frame painted light gray with black rubber-stamped lettering. The plastic cab and tray would be painted white and rescue lettering and insignia hot-stamped red.

Elevating the 9"-long 6814 from earlier models were the ancillary pieces. Adjacent to the white control panel on the car, creators requested there be a blue rubberized emergency medical technician, two stretchers, and a two-piece oxygen tank. Now children could reenact every sort of disaster in their three-rail worlds.

More information

- $4.95 (41.07)
- Cataloged from 1959 through 1961
- Price increased to $5.95 in 1960
- Component of no. 2527 Super O Missile Launcher Outfit in 1959 and 1960 and no. 1647 O-27 Freedom Fighter Outfit in 1961

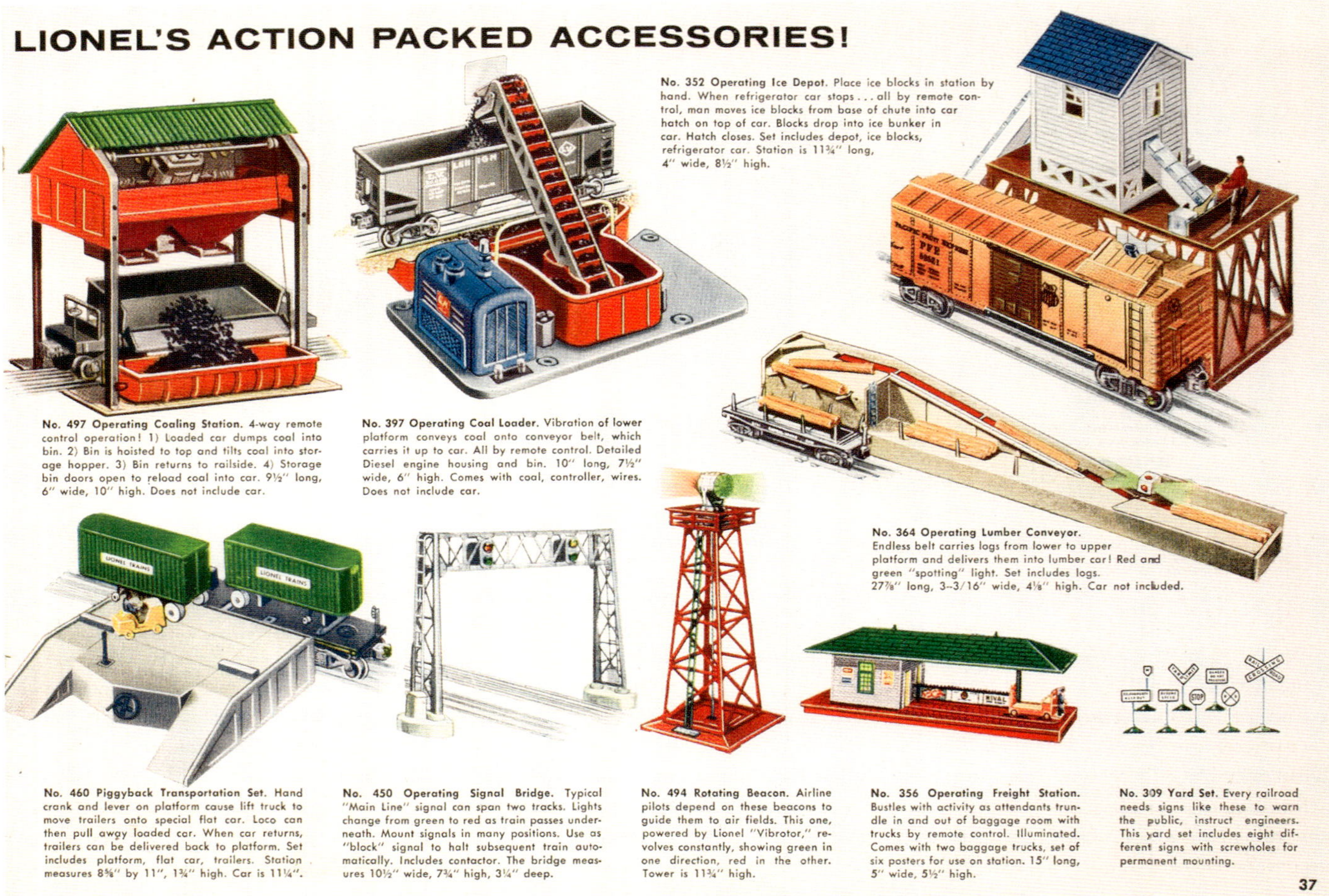

LIONEL'S ACTION PACKED ACCESSORIES!

No. 352 Operating Ice Depot. Place ice blocks in station by hand. When refrigerator car stops . . . all by remote control, man moves ice blocks from base of chute into car hatch on top of car. Blocks drop into ice bunker in car. Hatch closes. Set includes depot, ice blocks, refrigerator car. Station is 11¾″ long, 4″ wide, 8½″ high.

No. 497 Operating Coaling Station. 4-way remote control operation! 1) Loaded car dumps coal into bin. 2) Bin is hoisted to top and tilts coal into storage hopper. 3) Bin returns to railside. 4) Storage bin doors open to reload coal into car. 9½″ long, 6″ wide, 10″ high. Does not include car.

No. 397 Operating Coal Loader. Vibration of lower platform conveys coal onto conveyor belt, which carries it up to car. All by remote control. Detailed Diesel engine housing and bin. 10″ long, 7½″ wide, 6″ high. Comes with coal, controller, wires. Does not include car.

No. 364 Operating Lumber Conveyor. Endless belt carries logs from lower to upper platform and delivers them into lumber car! Red and green "spotting" light. Set includes logs. 27⅞″ long, 3-3/16″ wide, 4⅛″ high. Car not included.

No. 460 Piggyback Transportation Set. Hand crank and lever on platform cause lift truck to move trailers onto special flat car. Loco can then pull away loaded car. When car returns, trailers can be delivered back to platform. Set includes platform, flat car, trailers. Station measures 8⅝″ by 11″, 1¾″ high. Car is 11¼″.

No. 450 Operating Signal Bridge. Typical "Main Line" signal can span two tracks. Lights change from green to red as train passes underneath. Mount signals in many positions. Use as "block" signal to halt subsequent train automatically. Includes contactor. The bridge measures 10½″ wide, 7¾″ high, 3¼″ deep.

No. 494 Rotating Beacon. Airline pilots depend on these beacons to guide them to air fields. This one, powered by Lionel "Vibrotor," revolves constantly, showing green in one direction, red in the other. Tower is 11¾″ high.

No. 356 Operating Freight Station. Bustles with activity as attendants trundle in and out of baggage room with trucks by remote control. Illuminated. Comes with two baggage trucks, set of six posters for use on station. 15″ long, 5″ wide, 5½″ high.

No. 309 Yard Set. Every railroad needs signs like these to warn the public, instruct engineers. This yard set includes eight different signs with screwholes for permanent mounting.

37

Accessories

Bet you the smartest kids—or definitely the ones who already owned a train set—went straight to the back pages when they picked up the latest catalog during the postwar era. Those clever youngsters, and probably lots of older enthusiasts as well, remembered Lionel showcased in the last section the amazing accessories.

Vivid illustrations of signals alerting engineers about what to expect on the tracks ahead shared space with exciting descriptions of sturdy bridges and heavyweight transformers. Riveting consumers to the slick paper must have been breaking news about the annual additions to the line. Every year, Lionel seemed to offer freight loaders and then military or space items unlike anything ever sold.

Gratifying as the locomotive roster was and innovative as the list of rolling stock was, where Lionel really captured enthusiasts and carved out a unique spot for itself was with accessories. Those mind-boggling ancillary items attested to the brilliance of corporate designers and the acumen of marketing executives.

Always central

Frankly, accessories had always elevated Lionel above its competition. Joshua Lionel Cowen had insisted on making them integral to the line almost from the moment he co-founded the firm with Harry Grant at the dawn of the 20th century. He had joked that, without having signals, streetlights, and more to add to their miniature railroads, mischievous youngsters would torment innocent pets, vandalize their homes, and drive their poor parents to the nearest insane asylum.

Joseph Bonanno—the determined, almost imperious man at the helm of the Engineering Department—might have insisted the need to offer additional items to enhance train sets nourished the imagination and creativity of designers and model makers on his staff more than did replicating actual rail equipment.

Arthur Raphael—the far-seeing and urbane national sales manager during much of the pre-World War II era and into the golden years after the war—would have provided a shrewder and more helpful explanation. That savvy marketing executive understood the financial benefits of encouraging consumers to keep expanding their initial purchase. He dreamed of launching lifelong pursuits.

Those illustrious figures and their successors might have been viewing accessories from different perspectives—commercial for some and technical for others. Yet they shared a vision of the range of "extra" items made and marketed. Corporate leaders realized the importance of motivating the consumers purchasing trains to continue adding to their empires.

To put things differently, Lionel needed to provide the materials whereby its customers could progress from dilettantes playing with electrified models to serious hobbyists eager to assemble miniature rail networks. Only by cataloging depots and signals, bridges and tunnels, freight loaders and lights could the firm harness and nurture the passion of individuals and families buying its products.

From that point of view, accessories might be judged as surpassing in importance to Lionel the train sets that typically constituted the initial purchase. With those ancillary items, regardless of their price or complexity, designers and salesmen alike enabled enthusiasts to make a commitment to their railroad. And by cementing the loyalty of consumers, they strengthened their economic destiny.

Expanding heritage

The accessories associated with the postwar era passed through three key phases.

> **By and large, the accessories hitting the market in the first five or so years after the war represented slightly updated versions of the top items introduced late in the prewar era.**

In that regard, they had much in common with the rolling stock cataloged between 1945 and 1969. An overarching view clarified what engineers and their peers at the factory sought to accomplish, always in conjunction with what the men handling advertising and sales in New York City envisioned for Lionel.

By and large, the accessories hitting the market in the first five or so years after the war represented slightly updated versions of the finest signals, warning devices, street lamps, and freight loaders introduced late in the prewar period.

Lionel had shaken the toy field forever when it brought out an automatic gateman in 1935. A large figure dashed out of a shack to warn pedestrians and motorists about an oncoming train and then slipped back inside after the caboose or observation car passed. He performed everything through electric current.

Even better times were coming! Between 1938 and 1940, Lionel heralded a new age in model railroading by bringing out three massive accessories, each of which handled a type of freight in emulation of what full-size railroads had been doing day after day for decades.

Chunks of imitation coal, stained dowels, and scraps of metal could now be unloaded, stored, and then shifted to waiting rolling stock. The thrilling action took place via remote controllers. Touching the cargo or the freight cars was not necessary. Soon the same technology was applied to raise and lower a replica of a modern bridge for rail traffic crossing waterways. What could be more realistic?

All of those revolutionary, entertaining, and commercially successful items helped fill out the Lionel line through the end of the 1940s. Along the way, designers created supplementary accessories, especially freight loaders, so the line never quit growing, appeared to stagnate, or become entrenched in complacency.

New directions

If reviving great prewar accessories and then allying them with even better loaders, bridges, and signals constituted the first act in the postwar saga, climbing unprecedented heights by replicating more railroad facilities proved to be the second. Designers emulated their best efforts with miniature locomotives and cars by studying what was happening on full-size lines and developing superb models.

Never before had toy train manufacturers developed accessories meant to handle small versions of wood barrels, blocks of ice, steel culverts, and piggyback trailers. Yet reliable and fascinating loaders of those products made their debut in the Lionel line throughout the middle 1950s. Better still, the operation of many of those incredible accessories required a specially designed animated freight car.

Bonanno, not to mention top marketing executives, such as Raphael and his successor, Alan Ginsburg, recognized the importance of adding new models on a regular basis. Fortunately for all of them, the fertile mind of Development Engineer Frank Pettit yielded entertaining and popular additions to the line.

Pettit, who more than any of his peers at Lionel had recognized how tiny solenoids and electromagnets could be installed to generate motion, liked best creating accessories. Little wonder he took the lead in devising novel ones to capitalize on the simple yet dependable vibrating mechanism he had perfected.

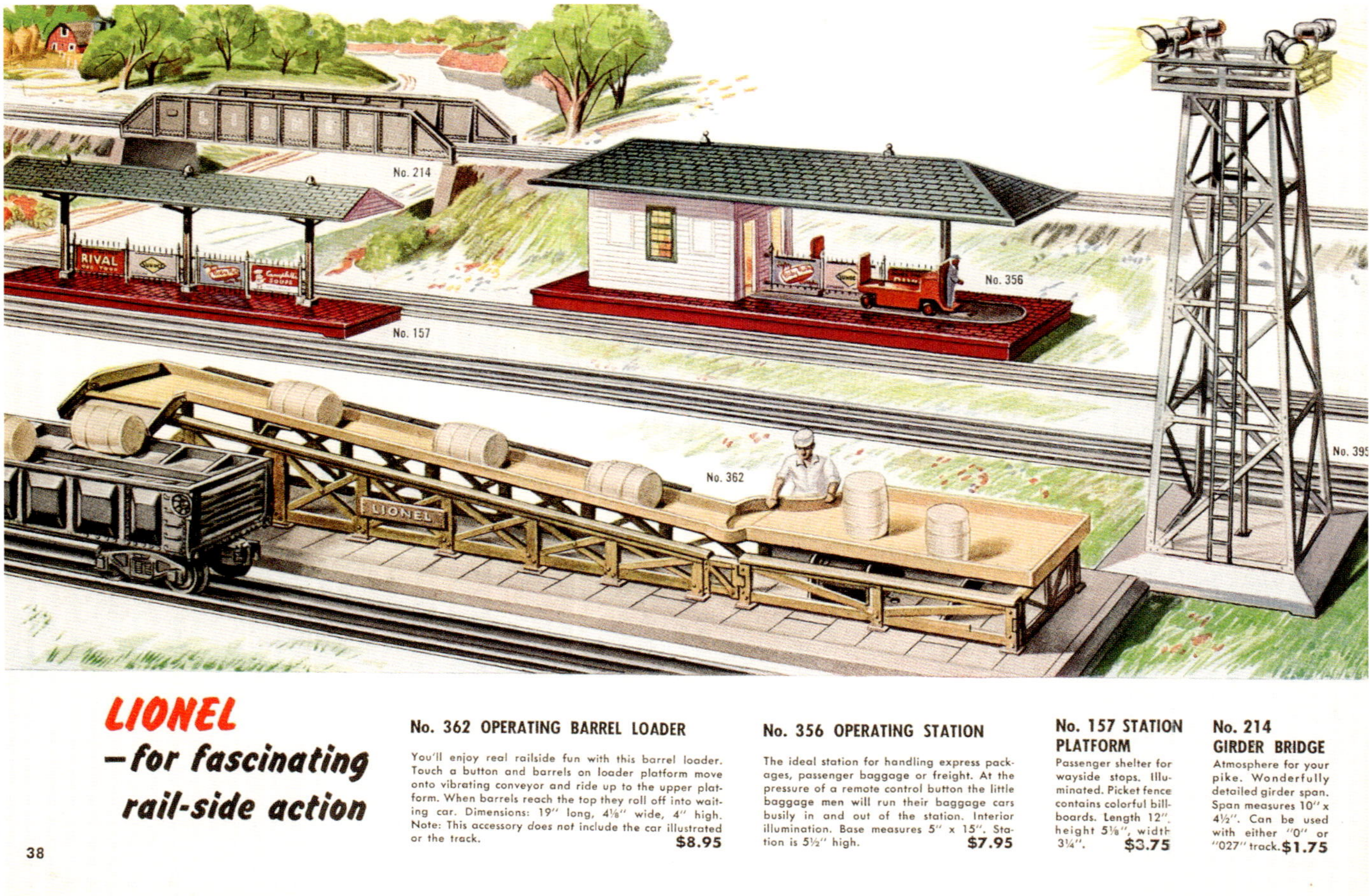

An advantage of the innovative accessories was their demanding more of the modelers, young and old alike, who bought them. Fine motor skills and hand-eye coordination were essential for transferring coal or logs, shifting culverts and lumber, and maneuvering operating cars to pick up loads or dump their contents.

Besides challenging consumers to allot extra space for the array of new accessories, Lionel wanted O gauge enthusiasts to spend more time with their trains. Handling the different kinds of cargo called for greater patience and dexterity. Imagination no longer sufficed with what remote-controlled accessories were supposed to do.

Never before had toy train manufacturers developed accessories meant to handle small versions of wood barrels, blocks of ice, steel culverts, and piggyback trailers.

New frontiers

By 1958, when it seemed Lionel had done about everything possible with accessories, Bonanno's enterprising staff shattered the sound barrier! Everyone was feeling the widespread fascination with the space race and military armament. How, executives wondered, might their firm exploit the growing emphasis on rockets and satellites, on missiles and jet airplanes?

Their answers paved the way for the third phase of the postwar history of accessories. From the late 1950s into the early 1960s, young railroaders were able to halt the trains they were running and launch spacecraft or fire warheads at ammunition dumps and boxcars that exploded into big pieces. They could hoist containers filled with deadly radioactive material. Lionel had entered a new age.

At the same time, sadly, older and familiar accessories were being deleted. Never again—or so it seemed in the 1960s—would logs or coal or ice be essential to the economy of Lionelville. Before long, rockets and missiles disappeared, too.

Gradually during that critical decade, the solid lineup of ancillary items shrank until it was reduced to a few old standbys. Catalogs showed only trusted favorites like the gateman and rotary beacon, plus the signals and crossing gates that in some form or another had occupied spots in the line since prewar days.

Locking the doors of the Engineering Department and then eliminating sales positions hurt Lionel in the second half of the 1960s. Innovation lost out. Instead, corporate heads returned to basic accessories—signals, streetlights, and towers—they hoped would keep bringing in dollars from a declining market.

A rather dismal ending to a once-glorious story. Still, the abbreviated group of accessories cataloged at the close of the postwar era can never rob their superb and groundbreaking predecessors of respect and attention. Everything hobbyists value about the Lionel line from generations ago comes to life with accessories.

97 Electric Coal Elevator

Much as toy train enthusiasts love using their imagination when running their locomotives and accessories, they also appreciate the extent to which a model provides realistic and exciting action. Better to hear a steamer whistle or a loader deliver freight than to pretend it's doing so. That's the magic of electric trains.

Design and marketing executives alike understood that point. It motivated them to keep upgrading Lionel's O gauge models with the goal of making them more realistic. Authenticity, whether expressed through appearance or operation, served as the main criterion for measuring success.

An awareness of that perspective elevates in significance the development of remote-controlled accessories in the late prewar era. Launching that trend and carrying it forward after the war was the revolutionary no. 97 Electric Coal Elevator.

Not quite actual

The 97, which debuted in 1938, capitalized on the idea of a vertical loader with buckets on a chain lifting coal from a receiving bin into an upper storage area. Similar toys used to load sand with a hand crank were popular at that time. They were based on full-size loaders handling soft, granular materials.

In this sense, the Electric Coal Elevator could be described as prototypical—its appearance and operation followed what might be seen at industrial sites and rail yards. All that was necessary to bring a model into the world of toy trains was the proper design of a miniature version by which to dump coal into a car.

The material serving as coal thus took on importance. No parent wanted coal dirtying a floor or carpet. What Lionel described as "coal" must be clean and safe. Bits of a new compression-molded plastic known as Bakelite worked beautifully and wouldn't ruin the mechanism on a 97.

Once the Electric Coal Elevator got to work, its operation was not flawless. Not every chunk of Bakelite ended up going straight from a dump car into the elevated container. Plenty was spewed onto the tracks and rug. So the 97 could be praised as prototypical, even if loading wasn't accurate!

Colorful worker

The Electric Coal Elevator, cataloged through 1942 and from 1946 through 1950, had an unpainted black base (7" x 12⅛") fabricated out of Bakelite, a silver-painted sheet-metal conveyor and tower (gray for 1942), and a yellow-painted metal loft with a removable red roof and red windows.

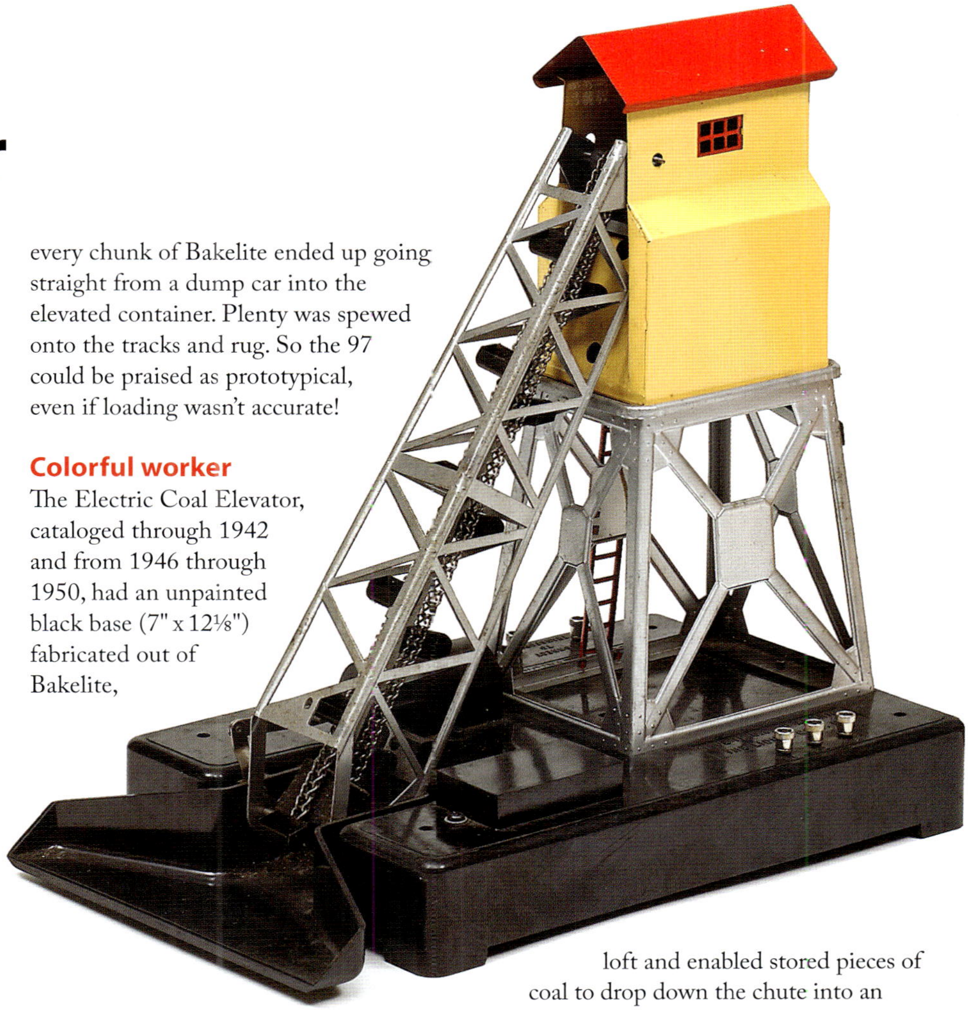

1946

Packed with each Coal Elevator were the "ingredients" needed for it to cook! These were a no. 97C Controller with its 36"-long three-conductor wire, an instruction sheet, and a no. 206 half-pound bag of Lionel's artificial coal.

The instruction sheet outlined how it worked. Key was the controller, connected "by means of three conductors, which are attached in order to the three binding posts on the far side of the elevator base."

A large rotary knob on the 97C switched the motor-driven bucket conveyor on (or off). It activated a solenoid that raised the receiving bin to direct coal toward the buckets on the moving chain. They lifted the chunks until gravity caused them to fall into an open loft. Then a push button on the 97C could activate a second solenoid. That motor opened the gate in the loft and enabled stored pieces of coal to drop down the chute into an empty dump car or hopper.

Cars needed

Of course, the coal had to get to the 97 in the first place. Lionel brought out its first remote-controlled dump cars in 1938 to coincide with the debut of the 97. After World War II, Lionel had a fleet of improved operating dump cars headlined by no. 3459 (silver, black, or green) and its successor, no. 3469. Also on the roster was the diminutive no. 3559.

Lionel brought back the 12"-high accessory in 1946. It stayed in the roster through 1950. Of course, the price kept rising. What had cost $5.75 in 1938 ended up retailing for $15.75 a decade later.

More information

- $13.95 ($172.71)
- Price increased to $15.75 in 1948
- Added to no. 4110WS Electronic Control Set in 1948 and 1949
- Cataloged from 1946 through 1950

156 Illuminated Station Platform

The advantages of selling space on freight cars so manufacturers of consumer goods could promote their wares had influenced the line since the 1930s. Curtiss Candy Co. and Sun Oil Co. paid fees in exchange for Lionel decorating some of its boxcars and tank cars, respectively, with the names and heralds of their products.

What succeeded financially for Lionel with rolling stock should work well with other items. Someone realized O gauge replicas of station platforms could sport miniature billboard-type signs.

1946

Thinking of that nature gave birth to the no. 156 Illuminated Station Platform at the end of the prewar era. Back it roared in 1946, the ideal partner for stations.

New materials

Individuals had been advocating the merits of station platforms since 1930. In that year, the Standard gauge roster gained a vividly painted and decidedly immense accessory, the no. 155 Freight Shed.

No equivalent for the O gauge group of accessories, in spite of the fact that Lionel had depots whose appearance would have improved if owners could have arranged a platform or two alongside those structures.

Then in 1939 the 156 made its debut. Innovative materials helped factory chiefs develop and mass-produce it. Supervisors insisted on manufacturing the rectangular base and ribbed roof for each platform out of Bakelite, a compression-molded plastic.

Laborers painted the base using the shade of light green associated with the no. 45N Automatic Gateman. A pleasing and warm red hue completed the roof. Nickel-plated finials held the 12"-long piece to the painted supports.

Injection-molded plastic, another novelty soon to become common in postwar America, enabled workers to form quantities of the picket fencing secured to three silver uprights in the middle. Die-casting metal enabled crews to make vast numbers of those solid supports.

Back unchanged

Lionel had assembled a smashing array of accessories prior to the holiday season of 1942. Remote-controlled loaders, an operating bridge, colorful stations and signals, and neat warning lights and gates distinguished the line.

Lionel would have been foolish to have deleted key items or ordered engineers to replace them after the war. To the contrary, the finest accessories filled out the line. The 1946 Consumer Catalog featured number of ancillary pieces now viewed as classics.

Included in that parade was the 156 Illuminated Station Platform. The copywriter lauded it as "A beautifully designed accessory for intermediate station stops." Before reciting the fundamental dimensions, he pointed out that the item came illuminated by two lamps in sockets attached to the underside of the roof.

Signs make it

The appeal of the Illuminated Station Platform derived from more than its slick size and proportions. Not even the point that layout builders might arrange a few of them end to end to develop a scene with a no. 115 City Station told the whole story.

Emphasis belonged to the enameled billboards folded to hang over the fencing. In every box, Lionel packed an envelope containing four of those sheet-metal items.

Every one featured on both sides the name of a popular consumer good and a related graphic. As was true with freight cars, Baby Ruth candy and Sunoco gasoline and oil products stood out. Joining those familiar brands were often Rival dog food and Remington portable typewriters.

Perhaps the most desirable of the Illuminated Station Platforms were the ones cataloged in 1948. They alone came with a colorful billboard promoting Lionel's brand-new construction sets with different words and pictures filling each side.

More information

- $3.95 ($48.90)
- Price increased to $4.50 in 1948
- Cataloged from 1946 through 1949
- Included additional no. 156-6 Fence Section to connect adjacent station platforms

182 Remote Control Magnetic Crane

Find a small object to move and snag an end with a dangling hook. Then pull it up and forward. Decide on the best place to drop the load and finish the process. If satisfied with the results, take a breath and start all over.

Those four sentences summarize the pleasures of using a miniature crane. Hard to imagine any child who doesn't enjoy the challenges of operating one manually or via remote control. A boy or girl's fine motor skills and hand-eye coordination come into play and make the activity fun.

Designers at Lionel, really beginning with co-founder Joshua Lionel Cowen, grasped the delight a crane might generate. Derrick cars launched a trend, one advanced when engineers created a novel stationary accessory. After World War II, they felt compelled to update and modernize their specialized operating crane, an effort culminating in 1946 with the no. 182 Remote Control Magnetic Crane.

Magnets away

Only one domestic firm brought out a hand-powered crane during the prewar period—and it wasn't Lionel. Its leaders knew what Dorfan was doing in the early 1930s, yet doubted the benefits of a crane.

Until 1940, when Lionel heralded an innovative item that vaulted over what Dorfan offered. Using technology refined by its engineers, Lionel brought out a loader that used, not a hook grabbing odd items, but an electromagnet able to pick up scraps of metal as full-size cranes did.

1946

The no. 165 Triple-Action Magnet Crane, another classic developed by Henry Ferri, enabled modelers to energize the magnet hanging from the hook at the end of the boom and rotate the derrick until it could be lowered to seize bits of scrap. Next, they raised the boom and turned it so dumping the pile of metal into a waiting gondola or empty unloading tray could be done flawlessly.

"Enough thrills, excitement, and action there alone to keep any model railroader on the tip of his toes—loading and unloading cars by magnetic action," promised the text in the Consumer Catalog for 1940.

Better still

Leaders had expressed their intention to catalog again the impressive remote-controlled accessories that had garnered acclaim in the years before Lionel had to curtail production during the war. Therefore, the Consumer Catalog for 1946 highlighted nos. 97 Coal Elevator, 164 Log Loader, and 313 Operating Bascule Bridge. At best, minor changes were made.

Matters turned out to be mixed in 1946 with the 165 Triple-Action Magnet Crane. The Advance Catalog showed the prewar accessory virtually unchanged, suggesting it would return from four years of inaction. A picture in the opening of the Consumer Catalog left the same impression.

Readers noticed something curious elsewhere in that catalog. The artist rendering of the Triple-Action Magnet Crane hearkened back to the prewar accessory. So did the description with that illustration.

Sharp eyes caught a slight yet significant modification: the item was listed as 182. A Price List issued later in 1946 also specified the Magnet Crane as 182.

Proof of how much had been altered surfaced the next year, as the picture in the Consumer Catalog for 1947 showed. Designers took the contemporary cab they had fabricated for the no. 2460 Crane Car and installed it on the magnet crane.

Other cosmetic changes included painting the 6" x 6½" Bakelite base black rather than light green. The die-cast metal cab platform was new, and a injection-molded plastic boom took the place of the Bakelite one on the 165.

The 182 operated in the same manner as the 165 had, thanks to the motor originally used in the OO gauge Hudson steamer in 1938. The reliable no. 165C Controller still handled the animation, raising or lowering the hook and rotating the cab and attached boom 360 degrees clockwise or counterclockwise.

More information

- $22.50 ($278.57)
- Cataloged from 1946 through 1949
- Priced lowered to $19.95 in 1948
- Came with nos. 160 Receiving Bin, 165C Controller, and 182-22 Bag of Steel Scrap

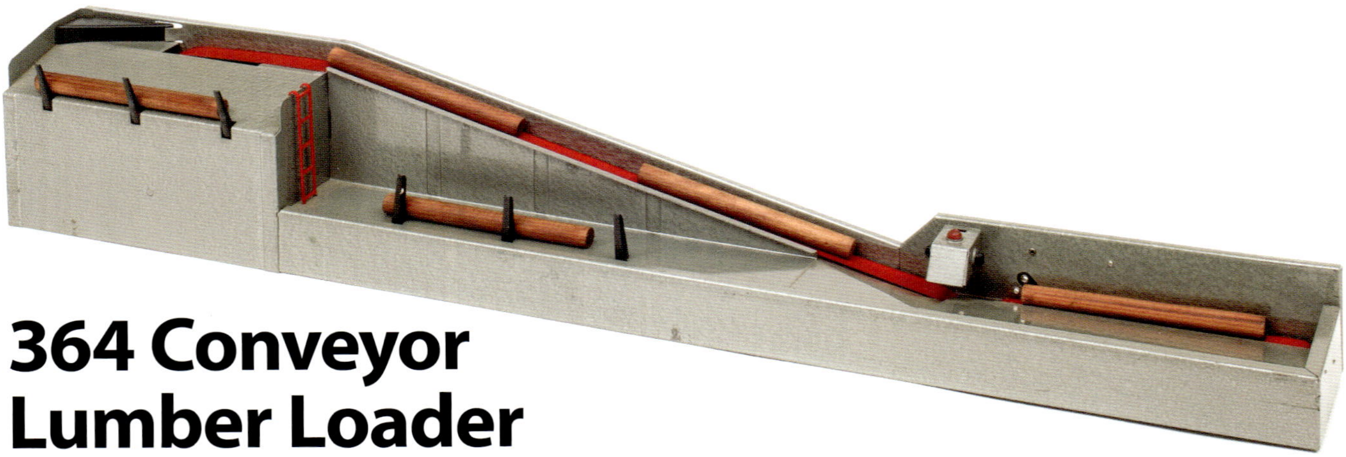

364 Conveyor Lumber Loader

Lumber—the long planks and boards used to frame residential and business structures, to serve as floors and ceilings, and to be shaped into tables and cabinets—became the first load Lionel created for its flatcars. Standard and O gauge models came packed with flat pieces of wood by the middle years of the 1920s.

The boards riding on Lionel flatcars needed to be rectangular so they wouldn't slip off. Not until the no. 3651 Operating Log Car joined the line in 1939 were dowels necessary. A car designed to dump modeled examples of lumber through remote control required they be cylindrical.

A log-loading and -unloading accessory needed smooth, rounded wood. No other way for the no. 164 Lumber Loader to perform its magic. Thanks to having dowels, an operator could empty a dump car and watch as the logs rolled off to be picked up by the motorized chain conveyor and lifted to the upper unloading platform. To improve the handling of wood and boost sales, engineers devised the no. 364 Conveyor Lumber Loader.

1948

Going vertical

The strategy when World War II ended and production of toy trains was given a green light boiled down to bringing back as many of the finest prewar items as the market was likely to appreciate. That approach characterized the thinking at Lionel with regard to accessories.

Not a reluctance to innovate. Merely an understanding that consumers had not lost their appetite for the biggest and most innovative operating models that had broken new ground right before the war.

Three remote-controlled accessories had shattered barriers in 1940. They joined the no. 97 Coal Elevator, which Lionel had announced two years previously. Nos. 164 Lumber Loader, 165 Triple-Action Magnetic Crane, and 313 Operating Bascule Bridge thrilled O gaugers.

Kids pretending to be lumber magnates begged for a 164. That accessory, another of the inventions credited to Henry Ferri in the Engineering Department, stood between parallel lines of track. Logs dumped into the base on one side were carried up to the storage platform under the roof of the 9"-high loader. When modelers were ready, they released the lumber into a car on the other side.

So good was the 164 Lumber Loader that Lionel revived it in 1946. Responses must have been positive because the vertically oriented accessory remained a solid member of the product line through 1950.

Getting horizontal

Was there a temptation to stick with only the 164? Somebody probably argued for doing so, yet the individuals overseeing marketing knew better. They wanted to surpass what had been done before and trusted designers to go further.

They did—yet in an unconventional way. The 364 Conveyor Lumber Loader, debuting in 1948, aimed not to update its companion or speed up the process of vertically moving and unloading dowels.

Instead, the steel accessory represented a reimagining of how miniature lumber might be shifted. The 364 simplified the process by depending on only one main line or industrial siding for its action. All an operator needed on his or her layout was a section with three straight pieces.

As the instruction sheet for the 364 explained, "A remote control section should be placed in the track layout in front of the loader receiving platform and the Lumber Loader positioned so that its receiving platform is in the center of the remote control section." Unload the logs, let them travel up the conveyor belt, and wait to release them one by one into the now-empty no. 3451 Lumber Dump Car.

Hardly changing

The 364 challenged layout builders as it measured almost 28" in length. Creating a siding long enough to handle it might not be easy. But dependable and straightforward operation made it a pleasure to own.

Everyone must have been happy with the look and operation of the Conveyor Lumber Loader. After all, the accessory underwent no genuine modification after its first year in the line.

The dark gray crackle finish yielded to one described as silver-gray and smooth hammer-tone. In addition, engineers added a metal guide tab at the uppermost end of the loader to facilitate movement of the logs into a waiting railcar.

More information

- $12.50 ($125.22)
- Cataloged from 1948 through 1957
- Packed with five no. 164-64 logs
- Price increased to $13.95
- Green and red lenses for lightbulb

397 Operating Diesel-Type Coal Loader

Accept what is available while striving to make improvements. That nugget of advice neatly characterized the approach executives adopted toward accessories after the war. They eagerly revived the freight loaders, stations, lights, and signals cataloged through 1942. Yet they also prodded designers to create better ones.

1948

Coal- and log-handling loaders exemplified the dual paths corporate leaders took. They brought back nos. 97 Coal Elevator and 164 Log Loader. In the meantime, they hoped the Engineering Department would develop accessories for those two commodities because both prewar carryovers had an inherent shortcoming. Namely, operation of the 97 and the 164 required two tracks, one for unloading materials and a second for piling them back in a car.

Designers declared victory in 1948 with the introduction of accessories meant to fulfill their functions on a single main line or industrial siding. The nos. 364 Conveyor Lumber Loader and 397 Operating Diesel-Type Coal Loader met those major goals.

Endless activity

The 397 brought instant gratification to its users. Unlike the 97, which permitted an operator to pause the action by storing the coal in an upper bin, the 397 featured endless activity, all generated by remote control.

Modelers launched the process by moving a dump car into position next to the accessory. Next, they tossed its imitation coal into what the instruction sheet called a "coal receiving scoop" (located at the front of the die-cast metal base).

Two cams mounted on an extension of the motor shaft then "give the scoop a snapping reciprocating motion." That caused the chunks to shift from the front up an incline to a "storage well" at the rear of the enclosed holding area.

Once there, "an ingenious vibrating mechanism" (to quote the Consumer Catalog for 1948) shook the coal toward the bottom of a steel beam assembly. The rubber conveyor belt secured to it picked up the coal and lifted bits to the top.

Gravity then took over. The black pieces cascaded into the same dump car, either waiting to head off on another journey or ready to be emptied into the scoop once more. Kids who enjoyed the show likely wanted to get it going again.

Little improvements

Unfortunately for the kids setting up a 397, they soon learned the hard way how uncooperative it could be. The obstinate diesel-type loader had a tendency to jam, as the itty-bitty pieces of coal became lodged in the conveyor mechanism and prevented it from moving. Or they bounced off the clear plastic screen at the apex of the belt, scattering in every direction and all over the track.

Complaints about the performance of the Operating Diesel-Type Coal Loader must have reached the company from disgruntled modelers and frustrated service technicians. Chief Engineer Joseph Bonanno heard orders to resolve the problems, and he set his team of designers to work. Before long, they had upgraded the 397 in subtle ways so it broke down less and sprayed far fewer chunks of artificial coal.

Ironically, while operators currently hunt for later versions of the Diesel-Type Coal Loader because they operate more smoothly, collectors prefer the first rendition of the 7½" x 10" accessory, which stood 6" high. On arrival in 1948, the 397 boasted a metal floodlight (what Lionel cataloged as the no. 70 Yard Light in 1949 and 1950) mounted to its gray-painted metal base as well as a yellow-painted plastic motor housing with a General Motors decal on one side. Both elements enhanced the realism of the 397.

Within a year, however, Lionel had chosen to substitute a blue-painted motor cover for the yellow one. In addition, the receiving scoop assembly, which was originally painted red, went to being molded out of red plastic in 1949.

Finally, designers removed the yard light, probably to save on production expenses. They intended to fill in the two holes in the base needed to accommodate parts securing the lamp stand; nevertheless, indentations still could be detected.

More information

- $10.95 ($109.69)
- Cataloged from 1948 through 1957 (motor cover typically blue)
- Included a bag of no. 206 or 207 Artificial Coal
- Price increased to $14.50 in 1950 and eventually hit $17.95 in 1957

ZW-Type Transformer

Including a transformer among the accessories recommended for assembling a deep and meaningful collection of Lionel trains from the postwar era may seem surprising. What good is a power source unless you intend to build a layout?

To be honest, that objection applies to every transformer cataloged by Lionel between 1945 and 1969—with a single exception. Small or large, slight or meaty, not any of those trusted power sources deserves a home with enthusiasts planning to let their locomotives, motorized units, and so forth sit idle—save one.

Anybody who appreciates what Lionel achieved during the postwar era simply must acquire and show off a ZW-Type Transformer. Few other items more perfectly symbolize the greatness of Lionel.

So impressive

Everyone who loves toy trains has seen a ZW. Or can envision it. The oblong body and sturdy handles represent the power and the glory of Lionel trains from postwar days.

Why, even American Flyer and Marx operators know and respect this dynamic stable of electric current. No wonder Lionel introduced as the latest incarnation of what it proudly labeled the Trainmaster Transformer with such fanfare in 1948. Planners of the line made the ZW a staple through 1966.

1950

The ZW (rated as 250 watts in 1948 and 1949 and boosted up to 275 watts thereafter) empowered children by handing over to their trembling hands more electricity than they imagined possible. Thanks to the four independent voltage control circuits added to each ZW, they could run as many as four trains at once.

Power boost

Lionel had offered large and impressive transformers in the past, so power was no stranger. The behemoth in that group of warhorses had been the 250-watt Type Z. Cataloged from 1938 through 1942, that veteran returned after the war.

But with the ZW, designers, led by Chief Engineer Joseph Bonanno who earned a patent for the transformer in 1953, magnificently combined function with form. They created a transformer looking like something Dr. Frankenstein might have used to harness lightning so the current surged into his monster.

Bonanno, assisted by his top electrical engineer John Salles, wanted a multiple-control transformer that, as the Consumer Catalog for 1948 stated, had "two built-in, finger touch Reversing Buttons and dual Whistle Control Buttons."

Engineers added four independently controlled output circuits and a built-in automatic circuit breaker. Designers then packed the electronics and wiring inside a case made of high-impact Bakelite.

The controls on each side enabled an operator to start, stop, or reverse each train and to increase or decrease its speed. There were also buttons intended for blasting a whistle or bell, depending on how an engine was equipped.

The ZW let boys realize their grand dream of being able to run several trains simultaneously, just as full-size systems did. One kid could do it all, or he could invite a buddy to share the controls. Imagine the sense of power offered to a child with a ZW Transformer!

Futuristic look

Good as were all the different functions, what amplified the appeal of the ZW Transformer and made it a legend in its own time was the model's unique appearance. The massive Bakelite case came with a red pilot light that indicated current overload and a green one, which was illuminated when the power was on.

On each side of the center section was an oblong black piece—like half of a football—that was rotated to change the speed of a train. There was something about those that won over a generation addicted to electrical power and speed.

From the time Lionel first cataloged the ZW through the 1950s and well in the 1960s, it was the sine qua non of power supplies. Even kids running American Flyer trains wanted a ZW. Acquiring one of those monsters made a statement that a youngster's commitment to his trains was total and full and therefore his layout should be taken seriously.

More information

- $25.00 ($250.44)
- Rated at 275 watts and 115 volts AC (1950 to 1966)
- Price increased to $40.00 by 1965
- Featured four voltage controls (two for trains and two more for trains or accessories)
- Included with Super O outfit no. 13150 (cataloged 1964 to 1966)

145 Automatic Gateman

The greatest accessories usually feature animation. They entertain with movement generated magically by electricity. Illumination enhances the fun. They may also please because once activated they do not require additional attention. They rely on the weight or motion of a train to go into action.

Signals launched the revolution in electrically controlled accessories. Their bulbs glowed or flashed, and their warning pieces shifted position, thanks to switches, contactor, solenoids, and electromagnets.

The next phase witnessed more innovative uses of those devices. Like producers of motion pictures, inventors aimed to impress viewers by replicating activities associated with railroading. The landmark stage in the rise of postwar accessories was the no. 145 Automatic Gateman.

Prewar parent

More than anything else in the legendary postwar roster, the Automatic Gateman had a long heritage. Nothing else offered after 1945 could trace its roots as far back.

By the time Lionel released the 145 in its golden anniversary year of 1950, 15 years had passed since it first announced an item modeling the activity regularly occurring at grade crossings guarded by watchmen. Other than the basic materials used to make the 145 in vast quantities, nothing about it was new.

1950

The no. 045 Automatic Gateman and its Standard gauge twin had made their debut in 1935. Their novel animation—the simple yet hands-free movement back and forth of a miniature railroad laborer—proved to have enduring appeal.

General Foreman Romualdo Camuso had brought the concept to the Engineering Department. At home, this longtime employee relaxed by tinkering with models, letting his imagination suggest what he might fabricate next. It would in time open the possibility of replicating an activity often seen in neighborhoods like his.

Imagining a model of such a common structure hardly stretched Camuso's brain. The challenge lay in devising a method by which the little flagman might pop out of his shed at the right moment, handle his duties, and return inside. He had to repeat the sequence of actions time after time.

Chief Engineer Joseph Bonanno, who later earned a patent for refining the concept of a gateman, adapted a mechanism able to generate linear movement so it could animate a figure. He trusted the solenoid because it had revolutionized accessories since first being used on the no. 77 Automatic Crossing Gate in 1923.

Designers depended on a solenoid linked to a pivoting crank mounted inside the base of the proposed gateman. That mechanism, when activated by the metal wheels of a train passing over a nearby insulated section of track, caused the figure to rush out of the door of his shack.

Returning veteran

A thrilling new age in toy trains was dawning with the Automatic Gateman in 1935. Good as Lionel's flashing signals or dipping crossing gates were, they had never promised full duplication of what happened daily on full-size railroads.

Meanwhile, designers kept fiddling with the signpost, the figure, and other details. Lionel made similarly minor changes between 1945 and 1949 with the returning Automatic Gateman. The item produced out of sheets of pressed steel painted in bright hues remained a favorite.

Widespread acceptance of toys molded out of thermoplastics, which were simpler to manufacture and cost less, led Lionel to redesign some models. There seemed no excuse for continuing to make the Automatic Gateman out of metal. Plastic parts could be substituted, so long as the animation and the mechanics stayed dependable.

New guy

Lionelville became home to the plastic 145 in 1950. The gateman occupied a newly designed and more realistic house, with a plastic warning sign nearby. The rectangular base, still metal painted green, was new. The galvanized plate secured to its underside changed over the ensuing 15 years.

So much changed at Lionel between 1950 and 1966, yet the 145 never left the line. The unpainted red plastic roof evolved into maroon, and the blue figure, originally with cream face and hands, eventually was left entirely unpainted. His lantern, previously illuminated with its own bulb, gave way to a light in the shack.

More information

- $5.95 ($59.61)
- Price had risen to $8.00 by 1966
- Crossing sign developed for no. 309 Yard Sign Set introduced in 1950
- Component of four promotional outfits between 1963 and 1965

455 Operating Oil Derrick and Pump

The no. 455 Oil Derrick and Pump made its debut in 1950. No other toy train manufacturer had ever developed an operating item to accompany its fleet of petroleum cars. Lionel, in its golden anniversary year, had one that delighted with two forms of animation.

None of Lionel's rivals during the first half of the 20th century—not Ives or American Flyer before World War II or Marx or Gilbert after the war—had devised an ancillary item, even a static one, to enhance the play value of their oil tank cars. For 1950, Lionel's ingenious staff of engineers had come up with an animated derrick and pumper that looked realistic.

More complicated story

Lionel evidently acknowledged the deficiency in its line because its brilliant development engineer, Frank Pettit, wracked his brain in the 1940s to invent a companion to the single- and double-dome Sunoco tank cars being cataloged. According to Pettit's memoirs, he built mock-ups of an oil storage facility and a gasoline delivery truck, but neither was put into production.

Finally, in early 1950, came news of an operating oil derrick, one its manufacturer called the "Oklahoma" Oil Gusher. That title belonged to an accessory heralded by a newcomer to the field as realistic in every detail, right down to the simulated crude oil bubbling up a clear vertical tube in the center of the plastic derrick.

The Colber Corp. sought to carve out a niche for itself in the booming market. The no. 109 Oil Derrick, available assembled or as an easy-to-build kit, made excellent use of the bubbling mechanism added to colored Christmas tree lights. Colber sold its "Oklahoma" Oil Gusher under its own name while producing the same item for Gilbert's American Flyer line of S gauge trains and accessories.

1950

Yet before Colber's accessory burst on the scene, Lionel's engineers had been refining a rough prototype of an oil derrick built by an outsider. Lou Shur, who owned Madison Hardware Co. in New York City, gave Joshua Cowen that mock-up. Cowen handed it to Pettit to transform it into a workable item.

Twice the animation

The Oil Derrick and Pump looked great next to Lionel oil cars. The dominant feature was the 14½"-high metal tower (inspired by a Mobil Oil design) painted dark green. Inside the derrick, Pettit mounted a glass tube partially filled with lightweight oil that boiled when heated—just as the Colber and Gilbert derricks did.

But the 455 boasted a second type of animation generated when a bimetallic switch activated a solenoid and plunger mechanism. The plastic "walking beam" (based on a Parkersburg Rig & Reel prototype) rocked back and forth to simulate oil being pumped from the ground.

Generator and more

Next to the plunger, designers added an orange plastic diesel generator derived from a General Motors model. They had created it in 1949 for the new no. 6520 Searchlight Car (the generator on that piece of rolling stock might be dark green or maroon, along with orange).

With each Oil Derrick and Pump came four solid aluminum oil drums to be placed on a black plastic rack affixed to the red-painted metal base (5½" x 9¼", stated the catalog). Also included was a no. 455-53 Billboard (a sheet-metal placard painted white) with a Sunoco herald matching the one on Lionel's tank cars.

More information

- $7.95 ($79.64)
- Cataloged from 1950 through 1954
- Price increased to $9.95 in 1951
- Platform assembly generally dark green; red and pale green known
- Scarce variation has tower structure painted light green

456 Operating Coal Ramp and Hopper Car

The biggest challenge any toy train manufacturer faced was getting consumers to make a second purchase. The first one—typically a set with everything needed to start a miniature railroad—was easy. Nudging parents or grandparents to continue adding to that nascent empire was where Lionel and its rivals had to be clever.

Check out the message behind advertisements and catalogs. They aimed to convince a family that the boy at the center of their world deserved his own railroad, complete with main lines plus sidings and spurs where accessories ran.

Operating accessories were critical in capturing a family's loyalty because they offered more to do than run a train in circles. Among those innovative items, few proved as successful as remote-controlled coal loaders. The third in the series of models arrived in 1950: the no. 456 Operating Coal Ramp and Hopper Car.

1950

Improving coordination

Put aside the financial justifications executives had in expanding the list of accessories cataloged. Shift attention from the bottom line and corporate prestige.

Adopt the perspective of kids wishing for the largest and most exciting freight loaders and operating bridges and stations. They dreamed of those accessories because they promised interest and adventure.

Youngsters quickly realized the nos. 97 Coal Elevator and 164 Log Loader and all the similar items that followed demanded a great deal from them.

Children had to study instructions sheets to learn how to install and operate the accessories. Wiring their transformer and testing remote controllers were key.

The next step, of course, involved determining whether kids were capable of maneuvering an operating dump or log car into the right position so it could unload its cargo and get the operation going. Refined hand-eye coordination, like an elementary understanding of electricity, ended up being absolutely essential.

Complex fun

Evaluating accessories from the vantage point of both the manufacturer and the young consumer laid the groundwork for appreciating the 456, one of the largest and most complex items ever developed by an American toy train maker.

Even Lionel knew it had something special for its golden anniversary. The Consumer Catalog for 1950 described the Operating Coal Ramp and Hopper Car as "by far the most unusual, most fascinating of all Lionel rail side accessories."

The ramp, which was initially dark gray and then went to light gray, stretched nearly a yard in length. It stood more than half a foot high at its peak.

Operation of the accessory was simple and straightforward, but it still demanded plenty of patience and care from a child to get everything down pat. Additionally, it required another siding or two, which meant more track sold by Lionel.

The 456 represented the end of a spur. A locomotive would push the special hopper included with the ramp (no. 3456 Norfolk & Western) up the ramp to the end, until its coupler latched onto the coupler attached to the end. Then the switcher or other engine would uncouple and scurry down the ramp.

Pressing a button on the no. 456-100 Controller opened the doors at the bottom of the hopper, which released its load (pellets of Bakelite packed in a bag of no. 206 Artificial Coal with the 456). The coal fell into a removable plastic bin mounted on the base of the ramp. Once the hopper was empty, the locomotive returned to pick it up and head out on the next assignment.

In tandem

If kids were fortunate, they also owned a no. 397 Operating Diesel-Type Coal Loader (cataloged from 1948 to 1957) that had been arranged beneath the coal ramp. Instead of locating the bin under the 456, it was put on top of two special mounting posts (included with each Coal Ramp) and placed on the 397.

Coal in the 3456 Operating Hopper Car dropped into the bin before being lifted by the conveyor belt on the 397. From there, the Bakelite pellets fell into an empty hopper or dump car already parked on an adjacent track. Double the fun!

Modelers could generate plenty of action moving coal from one loader to another, in and out of dump cars. With the right setup, they could spend hours handling the transfer and shipment of black diamonds, as though administering the Chesapeake & Ohio, the Norfolk & Western, or another regional line that specialized in coal.

More information

- $15.95 ($159.78)
- Cataloged from 1950 through 1955
- Price increased to $18.50 in 1951
- 3456 Operating Hopper first offered for separate sale in 1952 at $5.75

356 Operating Freight Station

Envy Lionel operators who, owning an outfit and extra rolling stock, were free to assess the accessory pieces available and consider which ones to add to their world. Often they focused on stations, dreaming of a depot where passengers boarded and departed from trains or the structure where cargo of all kinds was put on or unloaded from freight cars.

1952

Consumers never seemed satisfied. They wanted stations able to perform—models equipped with special effects. Lighting sufficed for a while. Then came demands of animation. Engineers acted boldly. For 1952 they showed the no. 356 Operating Freight Station.

Stop and start

Best to see the 356 as a link in the sequence of innovation touching Lionel's model structures launched in the prewar era with stations given the power to stop and start trains. A simple mechanism installed inside different tinplate depots and then wired to the main line automatically halted an express in front for a few seconds as though people were getting off. Then it magically let the train depart.

A device so trusted and esteemed should not be tossed aside, engineers argued. They then used it with success on nos. 115 City Station and 132 Passenger Station from right after the war through the mid-1950s.

Something missing during those years was a station capable of playing recorded announcements. A.C. Gilbert Co. had been selling so-called talking stations since the late 1930s. Around the middle of the century a battery-powered depot from Noma hit the toy market.

Uninterested in duplicating what rivals were doing, Lionel refused to bite. Not until it could equip a model of a contemporary station with a microphone in 1956 (no. 456 Sound Dispatching Station) would sound become part of Lionelville.

Round and round

The real breakthrough with visual special effects on a structure came in 1952. Designers added animation to the no. 256 Freight Station, a rudimentary accessory the corporation had brought out in 1950.

That illuminated, all-plastic structure traced its roots to two other items. Its maroon base, white house, and green roof called to mind the 132 Passenger Station (new in 1949). Its picket fences and lithographed metal billboard-type signs hearkened to the no. 156 Station Platform (cataloged for the last time in 1949).

The 356 Operating Freight Station featured a metal platform suspended over its rectangular maroon plastic base. In the center of the platform was an electromagnetic coil and housing assembly. Pressing the button of a no. 364C Controller or another single-pole, single-throw switch sent AC voltage to energize the coil. Once activated, the coil caused the metal platform to vibrate vertically.

Objects placed on a vibrating platform naturally shake. They can be directed to move horizontally if they have rubber bases with little "fingers" on the undersides.

Frank Pettit, part of Lionel's engineering staff, had shown the myriad possibilities of a vibrating mechanism with the no. 3656 Operating Cattle Yard (new in 1949). He wanted to apply that idea to the 256 Freight Station. His colleague, John DiGirolamo carried the assignment forward and received a patent for the 356.

Trucks not cows

Instead of cows, the 356 came with two plastic baggage trucks, one typically dark green and the other orange (red and light green versions exist). Each cart had two rubber pads on the bottom and a solid-blue vinylite figure perched at the front.

When the platform was energized, the trucks moved counterclockwise along an oval track in and out of the station. A trip, or latching, mechanism held one cart inside until its mate entered. The incoming cart hit a release trigger, which sent the other cart back on its journey.

More information

- $7.95 ($72.43)
- Cataloged from 1952 through 1957
- Used fence from 256 Freight Station with three metal billboards (Baby Ruth, Rival Dog Food, and Sunoco)
- Earliest versions came with tin lithographed baggage load

445 Operating Switch Tower

Ask Lionelers which accessory elicits the widest smiles, and most will name the Automatic Gateman. Enjoyable as the no. 45N and its successors can be, the animation is limited.

What if you could double the amount of movement? Wouldn't children and adults beam twice as brightly if they had an accessory equipped with two railroaders springing into action? General Foreman Romualdo Camuso had the same idea when he started tinkering after the war.

Sometime in the early 1950s, Camuso developed a preliminary model for what, after being refined by the Engineering Department, became the no. 445 Operating Switch Tower.

Basic operation

The final version of the 445 differed from earlier ones, as proved by catalog artwork. The black-and-white illustration in the Advance Catalog for 1952 depicted only one little figure on the tower.

Probably, the man's movement from the upper balcony into the tower depended on a train running over a no. 145C Contactor (or insulated track section) to activate the accessory. Once the train had passed, he jumped back outside to wait.

Further development led to the addition of a second figure, one that moved down the staircase on the left side of the tower after the Contactor was activated. Color artwork in the Consumer Catalog for 1952 reflected the improvement.

Unexpected delay

Typically, when Lionel depicted an item in its color catalog, it would be available for the next holiday season. Further, the model sold would look like the one pictured.

The Operating Switch Tower departed from those general points. As the *Lionel Service Manual* revealed, the 445 did not hit the market until early in 1953.

The cause of the delay almost surely related to the animated features on the accessory. To be precise, industry buyers who had scanned the Advance Catalog and viewed a preliminary model at the American Toy Fair months before likely criticized the animation as too limited.

1952

Featuring only one figure duplicated the action a customer could obtain with a no. 145 Automatic Gateman. Worse yet, the tower operator on the 445 was much smaller than his counterpart on the 145. Also, he never disappeared behind a shut door, a minor yet definitely entertaining advantage of the time-tested gateman.

Once chastised, Lionel instructed its staff of engineers to move rapidly on upgrading the Operating Switch Tower with a second figure in hopes of boosting its appeal.

Plainer look

What eventually was offered to the public differed noticeably from the brown structure with white trim shown in the Consumer Catalog for 1952 and elsewhere.

As produced, the 445 had an unpainted white plastic tower with a green roof and balcony. Major parts, such as stairway and chimney, were unpainted maroon plastic. The 5½" x 6¼" maroon base was unpainted plastic, too.

The pair of vinylite figures ended up being solid blue. No details—face or hands—were going to be painted to make them appear slightly more like humans.

Dependable fun

Lionel ended up with a mundane structure. About as plain as the many simple commercial and railroad facilities filling the Plasticville U.S.A. line of basic kits being sold by Bachmann Brothers.

Fortunately for O gauge modelers, the Operating Switch Tower managed to deliver on its promise of consistent and dependable animation. Designers installed a solenoid-and-plunger assembly in the plastic structure. They connected the mechanism to a forked lever arm so the motion of the plunger animated the two figures. A nylon string connected to the lever enabled the second figure to slide down and dash up the stairs.

More information

- $7.95 ($72.43)
- Cataloged from 1952 through 1957
- Patent awarded to Lionel President Lawrence Cowen
- Illuminated by 14-volt bayonet-type bulb in base

352 Ice Depot Set with Car

The operating accessories cataloged between 1946 and 1954 did not stray far from the obvious. Lionel made it possible to load and unload barrels, coal, logs, and scrap metal, the same raw materials its earliest group of accessories had handled in the years up to the war.

Methods and mechanisms for handling pellets of Bakelite (coal) and unstained dowels (logs) did change. Engineers created new variations on familiar themes. By 1954, they had come up with four coal-hauling accessories, two log loaders, three magnetic cranes, and a barrel loader.

Then for 1955, designers broke out of that mold and finished a path-breaking item: the no. 352 Ice Depot Set with Car. That fascinating accessory worked with a newly invented type of operating model to load and unload a different kind of freight.

Outside ideas

The challenge of expanding the line never ended at Lionel. Engineers scoured reference books and read industrial journals in their hunt for freight-handling facilities and techniques they could replicate. Also, the public relations departments of railroads, manufacturers, and industrial groups bombarded Lionel with requests to make models of what they owned or made.

1955

In November 1950, the assistant director of advertising and publicity at the National Association of Ice Industries Designers suggested that Lionel add "the one important railroading operation not now included ... refrigerator car icing."

Chief Engineer Joseph Bonanno expressed interest and requested photos of ice-handling equipment in operation. He regretted, however, that the Korean Conflict, which had erupted in June, precluded the development of new models.

Still, Lionel's file on how blocks of ice were put into refrigerator cars to maintain frigid temperatures grew thicker. Bonanno might have contacted Richard G. Smith, an outsider who helped finish the no. 164 Log Loader and developed the no. 3462 Operating Milk Car.

Smith generally brought prototypes to Lionel or Gilbert, who accepted and paid for what could be inexpensively mass-produced. The 18 patents Smith earned testified to his immense creativity and mechanical acumen.

The role played by Smith remained uncertain. He possibly built an operating mock-up of an ice-handling accessory. Whatever his contributions to the 352 Ice Depot Set with Car, they must have been significant because in 1958 Smith was awarded a patent for that accessory.

Easily operated

The 352 debuted in 1955 and remained in the catalog through 1957. The depot had a brown (then red) polystyrene support structure and platform 8½" high with a footprint of 4" x 11¾".

On top of that structure designers installed a shed molded in white plastic with a red roof. On either side of the shed were white plastic chutes used to direct the clear plastic blocks of ice (first eight and then five) that came with the 352.

Once the cakes of ice were placed in the housing to slide down, an operator pressed a remote-controlled button to activate a solenoid-driven unit that extended a metal arm from the platform to push open the hatch on the roof of the no. 6352 Pacific Fruit Express Ice Car packed with the accessory. It also caused the blue-and-orange vinylite figure to move forward, creating the impression he was sweeping blocks one by one into the hatch below.

Obsolete functions

The operation of Lionel's Ice Depot Set with Car consisted of a spellbinding sequence of actions (moving the ice, loading the car, and sending it to market). Youngsters learned how perishables were shipped, never suspecting that ice had become obsolete thanks to the introduction of the mechanical refrigerator car.

Ironically perhaps, Lionel had introduced an O gauge model of that modern reefer (no. 6672 Santa Fe model) in 1954, a year before the 352 made its debut. The two models coexisted quite nicely.

More information

- $12.95 ($116.66)
- Included no. 6352-1 Pacific Fruit Express Operating Ice Car
- Cataloged from 1955 through 1957
- Operating Ice Car sold separately in scarce box printed 6352-25
- Had eight and then five cubes of ice

264 Operating Forklift Platform

The mid-1950s saw Lionel launch a wave of operating accessories that were more sophisticated and realistic and demanded more coordination and patience. Those items demonstrated the ingenuity and industry of the designers working for Chief Engineer Joseph Bonanno.

For 1955, Lionel moved from logs, coal, barrels, and scrap metal to a new cargo. The no. 352 Icing Depot loaded plastic ice into the hatches of special refrigerator cars. Then for 1957, designers announced the no. 264 Operating Forklift Loader.

Almost lost

What was happening behind the scenes in the toy train industry revealed how Lionel almost lost its chance at claiming an accessory with a forklift shifting around cargo.

According to Maury Romer, who developed the annual line of American Flyer S gauge trains for A.C. Gilbert Co., an inventor tinkering on his own had created a prototype for such an accessory. Richard G. Smith evidently brought it first to Lionel, which spurned it.

The negative response from Lionel led Smith to show it to Gilbert. Romer and his associates liked it for the Flyer line. They refined the mock-up and released the no. 779 Oil Drum Loader in 1955.

Fast acting

Once merchants started displaying the Oil Drum Loader, Lionel realized it needed to react. Engineers obtained one or two to dissect. They examined the motor inside the shack and the arrangement of gears and pulleys on the underside of the base. Designers then fine-tuned the concept for something new and as appealing. They ended up with the Operating Forklift Platform, cataloged from 1957 through 1960.

The animation, while mirroring that of the Oil Drum Loader, departed in a notable way, namely, reversing the sequence of actions. With the 264, cargo was shifted from a special car to a designated spot on the base—the opposite of what S gauge modelers did with their 779 accessories.

1957

So different

Arguably, the animation on the Forklift Platform differed from anything ever seen in the Lionel line. The sequence opened with a no. 6264 Lumber Car piled with boards being parked by the plastic platform. An operator activated the lift truck (attached to a drive motor through a series of gears), so it snagged a piece of wood off the flatcar and pivoted across the base until reaching the area where it dropped its load before returning to the edge for another board.

The animation on the 264 was fascinating and foolproof. Also making a winner of the Operating Forklift Platform was its appearance. Folks gave thumbs up to the unpainted brown plastic base (10" x 10½") and the orange plastic lift truck.

Another touch increased the appeal of the 264. Having a small worker perched on the seat of the forklift injected life into the loader. Lionel had learned from Gilbert how important it was to add a figure to suggest human beings were performing the work and not invisible electricity.

Sets, too

Executives expressed confidence in the commercial possibilities of the Operating Forklift Platform. Besides offering it for sale, they made it a component of top-of-the-line freight outfits for three consecutive years. One high-priced Super O set included a 264 in 1957, 1958, and 1959.

Even after Lionel dropped the 264 from the line, it wired one to each D-291 Super O display layout pictured in the Advance Catalog for 1961. Why not let kids enjoy it a bit longer?

More information

- $16.95 ($145.63)
- Priced increased to $17.95 in 1960
- Included in three promotional outfits in 1960
- No. 6264 Lumber Car could be purchased separately for $4.95

175 Rocket Launcher

Sending rockets and manned vehicles into outer space fascinated Americans throughout the 1950s. Motion pictures depicted brave individuals venturing into the solar system to explore the Moon and nearby planets, to deal with unforeseen perils, and to battle alien beings. In the meantime, scientists backed by federal funds struggled to turn the dream of traveling thousands of miles from Earth into a reality.

Youngsters caught the fever as they watched science fiction movies, paged through comic books, and listened to their parents talk about satellites and rockets. Kids wanted miniature versions of spacecraft, whether as simple toys or elaborate models.

An irreversible shift in the nature of accessories was taking place. No longer would the biggest and most action-packed focus be on handling coal and logs. Loading and unloading simulated raw materials seemed obsolete and irrelevant to children. Everything young modelers wanted was shown in the no. 175 Rocket Launcher.

Out to space

The 175 made a splashy debut in 1958, its powerful image dominating the front cover of the annual catalog for consumers. What boy or girl wouldn't covet one of those intricate and thrilling launchers after studying the illustration?

Yet the same cover picture also depicted an accessory accurately described as the first space-oriented model shown in a Lionel catalog: the no. 197 Rotating Radar Antenna (introduced in 1957). Although its design seemed a bit complicated and rather realistic, the operation was simple. The radar antenna at the top of the plastic tower structure rotated ominously.

Interestingly, when Lionel released the 197, copywriters characterized it as an integral part of a miniature airport and the scene surrounding a busy railroad. For 1958, though, the catalog referred to the rotating radar antenna as detecting enemy aircraft or seagoing vessels. Now the model was vital in time of war.

Designers adapted the tower structure created for the 197 when they came up with the 175 Rocket Launcher. The majority of other parts and assemblies were unique to that accessory; exceptions were pieces taken from nos. 345 Operating Culvert Unloader, 3360 Burro Crane motorized unit, and 6660 Boom Car.

Sales executives heavily promoted what the *Lionel Service Manual* lauded as a "pocket Cape Canaveral." They underscored the fact that, despite the size and complex appearance of the 175, "it is relatively simple and trouble-free." Because the rocket launcher sold well, Lionel kept it in the cataloged line through 1960.

Rockets were set off

The combination of remote-controlled and manual animation generated by the 11"-high Rocket Launcher began when an operator pressed a button to start up the gantry, which moved along the Super O rails until next to the launcher. Then the U.S. Navy rocket was attached by hand to the launcher. From there, all action was done by remote control, thus increasing the excitement and fun of the 175.

1958

Packed inside the large accessory box was a countdown control panel. The operator relied on it to finish the requisite countdown and to launch the rocket toward the ceiling of the attic, basement, recreation room, or wherever else a boy might have a three-rail layout. Finally, the same remote controller caused the launcher to quietly return to its original site, ready to begin the process again.

Needless to say, youngsters were entranced by the entire sequence, which seemed to replicate what they imagined happened when rockets were launched. That feeling of realism, along with the size and apparent complexity of the action, boosted sales of the 175, enough to justify raising its price from $17.95 to $19.95.

Railcar, too

To bolster sales of the rocket launcher, Lionel released a companion piece of rolling stock in 1958. The no. 6175 Flatcar with Rocket would have been a great item to have been sold with the 175, as Lionel did with the car necessary for operating the no. 352 Icing Depot Set, for example, or no. 264 Operating Forklift Platform.

Instead, marketing executives were satisfied with offering the 6175 alone. Similarly, they packaged replacement rockets as the no. 175-50, a box coming with six individual items. Today, collectors search for original replacement rockets as well as pristine versions of the flatcar with rocket to match with a rocket launcher.

More information

- $17.95 ($148.92)
- Part of Super O no. 2545WS steam freight outfit in 1959
- In four promotional sets in 1960
- Control panel served as no. 413 Countdown Control Panel in 1962

262 Highway Crossing Gate

A certain kind of genius creates something new by taking novel ideas and mental images and striving to transform them into reality. Another kind of genius creates something brand new by taking what has already been conceived and made and combining it with another finished product. Thus emerges innovation.

These processes apply to what occurred under Chief Engineer Joseph Bonanno. His staff built up the line of accessories often by blending what they had.

Wonderful examples included the mobile missile launchers and operating cars. Another more obviously combined two familiar types of warning devices at grade crossings. Because the elements were plain or it arrived toward the end of the postwar era, hobbyists too often overlook the no. 262 Highway Crossing Gate.

Better than one

Looking at the Highway Crossing Gate for a few seconds—or just letting its name sink in—reveals the nature of the accessory first cataloged in 1962. Designers combined the thin bar intended to lower across a road to block traffic from crossing when a train approached with the crossbuck and red warning lights on a signal to protect drivers and pedestrians.

1962

Combining a crossing gate with a road signal had become common in municipalities across the country after World War II. City planners and highway engineers had done so to enhance the safety of motorists. Citizens supported any device capable of preventing collisions with trains.

The modernized versions of traditional warning signals sprouting up in suburbs and villages caught the attention of men developing new toy electric trains. Somebody at Lionel, or maybe a few guys at the plant, recognized the potential of replicating the blended devices.

Longtime favorites

Confidence in the project motivated engineers to evaluate the operating features of two longtime favorites and consider how to combine them. If no one else remembered, then Bonanno definitely knew how long a crossing gate as well as a flashing highway warning signal had been solid-selling items for Lionel.

The firm had been pushing consumers to add one or both of those low-end accessories since the 1920s. Standard and O gauge modelers had been able to compare different versions before purchasing.

In 1940, Lionel put out oversized renditions of those two kinds of warning devices. The nos. 152 Automatic Crossing Gate and 154 Automatic Highway Signal returned in 1945.

Designers revamped the 152 for 1950, coming up with a more reliable crossing gate consisting of injection-molded plastic parts rather than metal ones. The improved no. 252 Crossing Gate entranced youngsters, who often selected it as the first upgrade for their nascent three-rail empires. It lasted through 1963.

The 154 enjoyed a longer life. Regardless of how inappropriate its height made it for O gauge layouts, Lionel disdained major modifications. To the contrary, planners continued to find a spot for the Automatic Highway Signal through 1966. It ran uninterrupted for more than 20 years.

Simple improvements

Whether sales of the 252 were declining or leaders felt the need to pump new blood into the line, designers upgraded it for 1962. They combined its animation (and many of its parts) with the glowing red lights and easily recognizable crossbuck installed on a highway warning signal.

The 9"-high 262 used its predecessor's slightly altered die-cast metal base. The plastic gate from the 252 also found a home on the Highway Crossing Gate, although without the warning lamps and interior bulb illuminating them. Discarded was the clear plastic bar on the 252.

The plastic crossbuck came as black with white lettering. It resembled yet did not match the part on nos. 140 Automatic Banjo Signal and 155 Ringing Signal.

The enormous crossbuck plus the pair of red lights similar in appearance to the fixtures on the 155 doubled the protection the Highway Crossing Gate provided miniature drivers. Too bad designers did not wire them to flash. Instead, the bulbs burned only when the weight of a passing train activated the no. 145C Contactor, which also lowered the long gate.

More information

- $7.95 ($63.55)
- Cataloged from 1962 through 1966 and 1969
- Price increased to $9 in 1969
- Included with eight promotional outfits between 1963 and 1964